KEM WEBER

MID-CENTURY FURNITURE DESIGNS FOR THE DISNEY STUDIOS

DAVID A. BOSSERT

Designed by Nancy Levey-Bossert
Copy Edited by Diane Hodges
Set in Mouse Deco by Steve Ferrera,
Minion 3 and Kobenhavn used courtesy of Adobe Typekit,
New Press Eroded by Galdino Otten

Printed in Korea.

First Edition, November 2018
Soft Cover Edition, July 2020

Library of Congress Control Number: 2020903909

ISBN: 978-1-7326020-8-3

Jacket photo: Kem Weber and Walt Disney inspecting the furniture during manufacture at the Petersen Show Case & Fixture Company, Inc. in Los Angeles; circa 1939. © UCSB

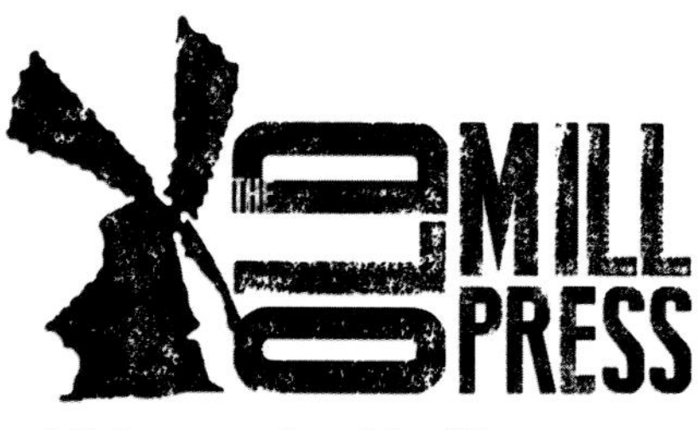

Visit www.theoldmillpress.com

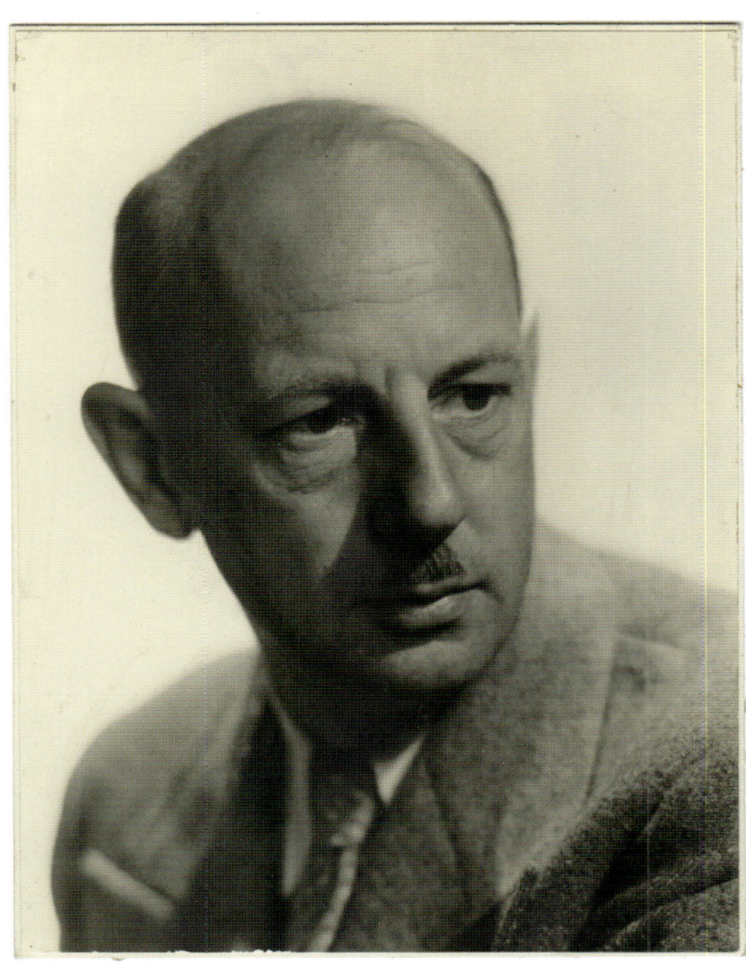

Kem Weber, 1889-1960 ©UCSB

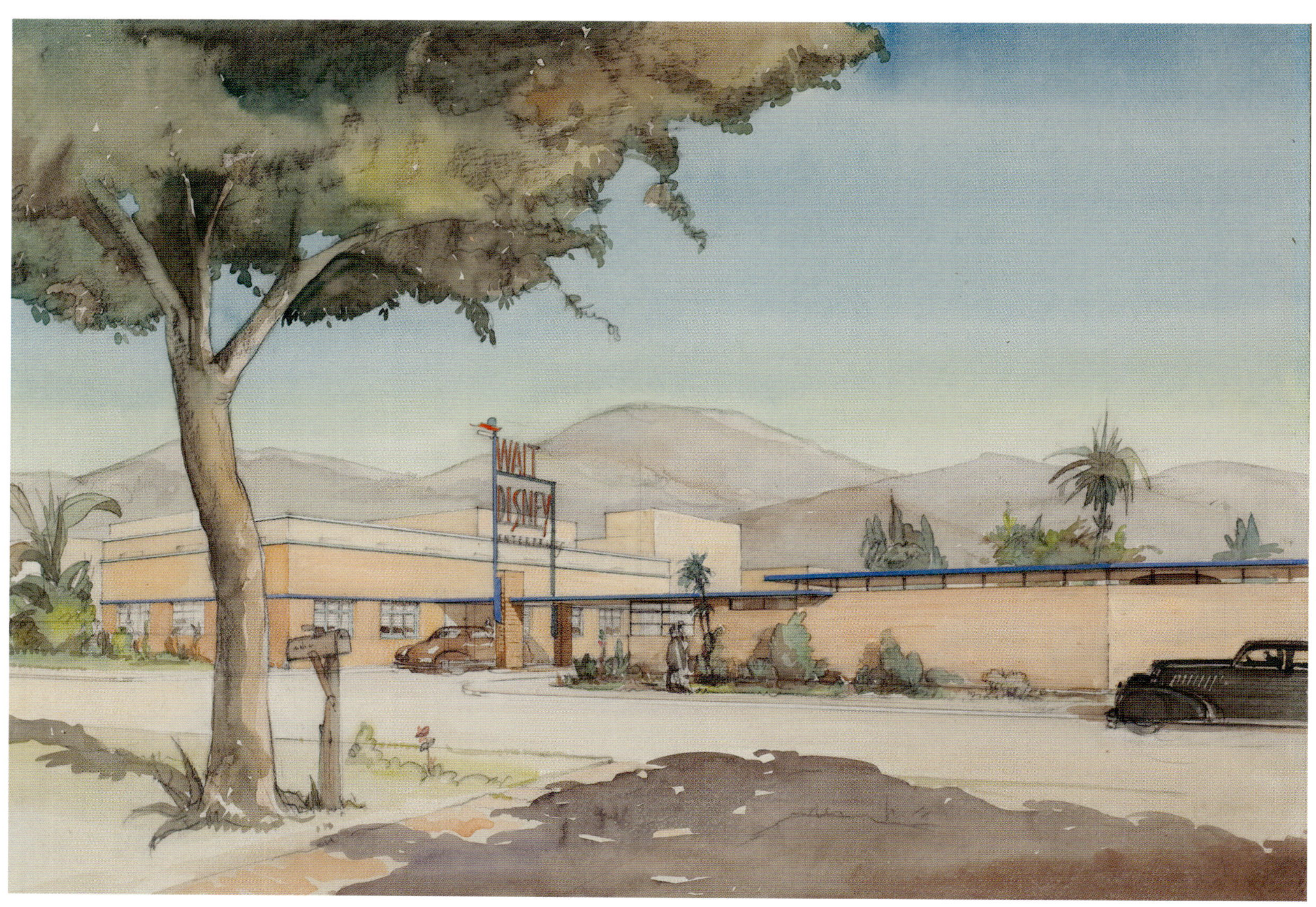

Concept design for The Walt Disney Studios main entrance with casting building on Buena Vista Street, Burbank, 1939; Kem Weber; ©UCSB

Dedicated to the following for their generous support

Keith Williams

Neil Cantor

Benjamin Breitbart

Ken Duncan

Diana Waller

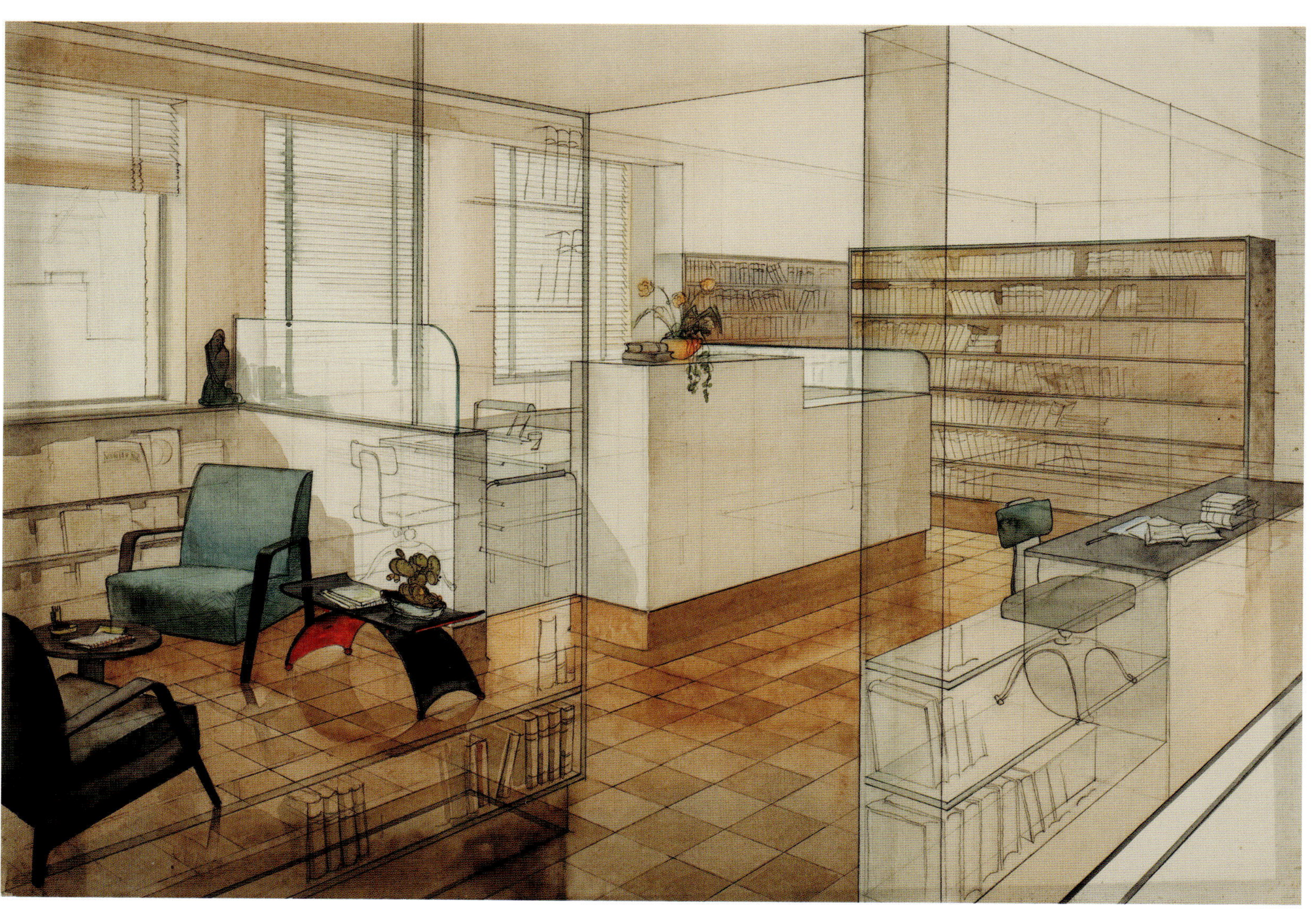

A study of the research library in The Walt Disney Studios Animation Production Building; circa. 1939, Kem Weber. ©UCSB

TABLE OF CONTENTS

Acknowledgements 9

Chapter 1: Introduction 10

Chapter 2: Mid-Century Moderne and the Rise of West Coast Modernism 20

Chapter 3: A New Studio Complex in Burbank 30

Chapter 4: Director's Desk 38

Chapter 5: Story Desk 44

Chapter 6: The Air Line Chair 48

Chapter 7: Layout Desk 58

Chapter 8: The Versatile Animation Desk 64

Chapter 9: The Assistant's and Inbetweener's Desk 78

Chapter 10: The Background/Color Keying Desk 82

Chapter 11: Checker's Desk 86

Chapter 12: Ancillary Furniture 88

Epilogue 94

Construction Notes 96

Quick Reference Guide to the Disney Animation Furniture 98

Gallery 118

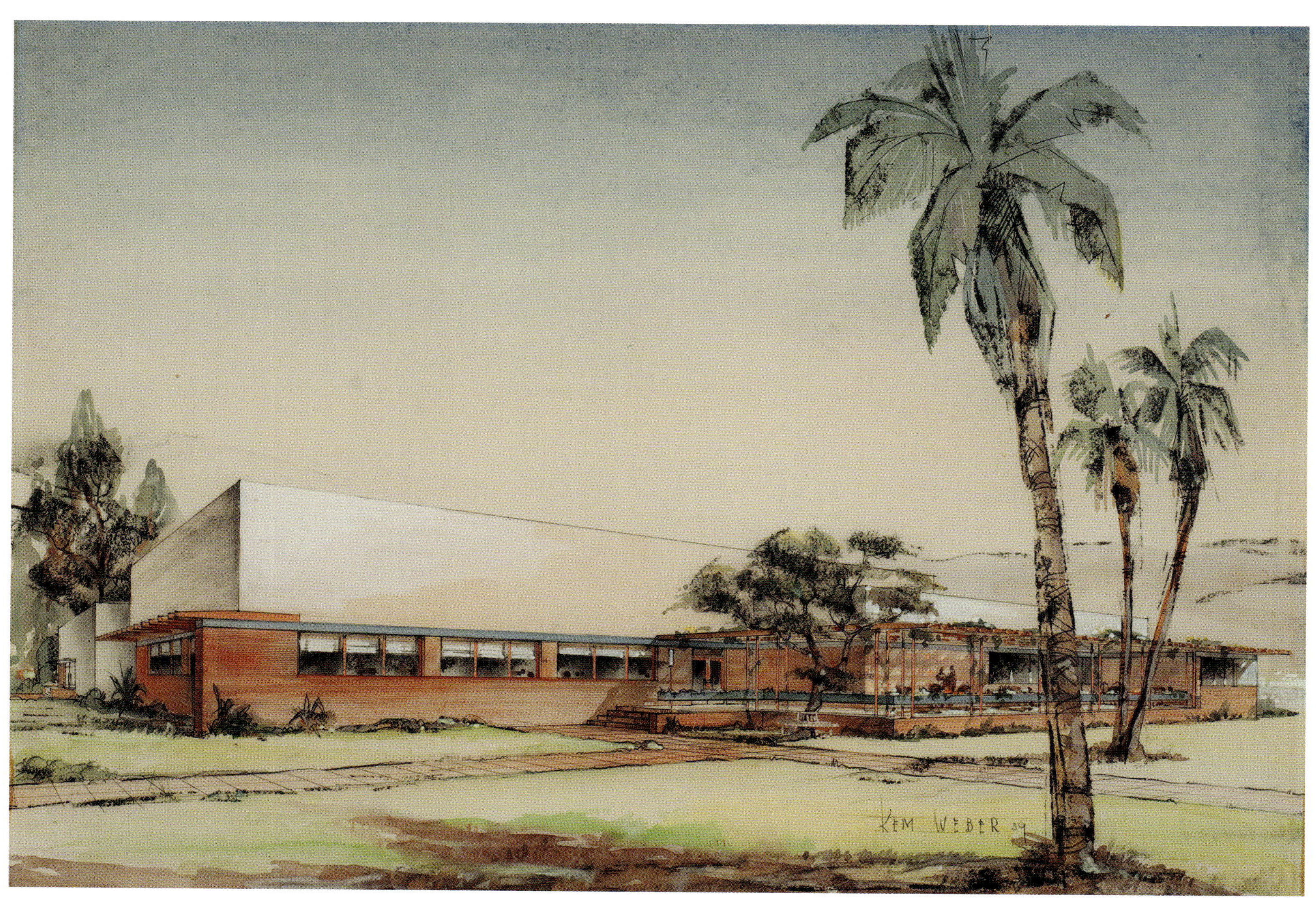

Concept design for The Walt Disney Studios main restaurant (commissary), 1939; Kem Weber; ©UCSB

ACKNOWLEDGEMENTS

I decided to write and publish this book for several reasons. It's not only documenting the historic nature of these pieces but is also a love letter to the furniture that I have worked on for more than thirty years. In doing so, the single biggest expense in creating a book is printing. With that in mind, I decided to use the online crowdfunding platform AIM/Hatchfund to cover the cost of printing as well as to gauge interest in the project. To my pleasant surprise, the level of interest was very high for this topic and the funding goal was achieved quickly by a group of individuals that also saw the value in preserving this piece of history.

One of the first people to make a contribution was Keith Williams, who lives in Chicago and is the CEO of the Underwriters Laboratories (UL). Keith is a patron of the arts and immediately responded at a generous support level. Thank you Keith.

Neil Cantor, a friend and the owner of Magical Memories Galleries in the Forum Shops at Caesars Palace, Las Vegas was also supportive of this endeavor. Neil has been a lifelong fan and leading purveyor of animation related art. He came onboard the campaign right away with a top tier contribution as well as making the commitment to carry this book in his gallery. Thank you Neil.

While I was doing a podcast for LaughingPlace.com, interviewer Benjamin "Benji" Breitbart, made a top tier donation to the project as I was talking about it in the interview. Benji has been a great supporter of everything Disney and has gone out of his way to promote and support authors and their Disney related books. His site is a terrific resource for everything going on in the Disney universe. Thank you Benji.

Ken Duncan is a world-class animator who worked at the Walt Disney Animation Studios before leaving and opening his own studio. He animated on the Weber furniture for many years and didn't hesitate in contributing his support. Aside from being one of the premiere traditional animators in the business, he is knowledgeable on the history of animation and a fan of the Weber animation furniture. Thank you Ken.

I also extend a heartfelt thanks to all the additional contributors, Alison Bossert, Caroline Bossert, Mike Dean, Alex Herrell, John Musella, Donald Kimbal, Sydney Bossert, Rick Ryan, Meghan Davis, Angelo Shake, Lenora Hume, Elizabeth Spatz, Marty Alchin, Elichi Ogawa, Scott Eaton, Ross Anderson, Matthew Feige, Diana Waller, Richard & Michele Golden, Didier Ghez, Mark Gorog, Jeremy Patrich, Paula Sigman-Lowery, Lynn Bodell, Todd Pierce, Giovanna Bourassa, Christopher Hagerty and the Hyperion Historical Alliance. I appreciate their interest and support of this monograph.

I have the very good fortune of being married to a talented graphic designer and ceramicist who is experienced in print production. Nancy Levey-Bossert was a joy to work with on this, our first book collaboration. It was easy since our respective offices are steps apart. She has done a wonderful job designing this book.

Special thanks to Harry Youtt for his edits and Diane Hodges for her copy editing.

Also, I want to thank artist Christy Maltese for her beautiful illustrations of all the Kem Weber designed animation furniture. She is an incredible talent who I've had the pleasure to work with on and off throughout my career. Christy puts heart into every project regardless of how big or small which is evident by her work in this book.

I would also like to express my gratitude to all the artists and filmmakers I interviewed for this book including Don Hahn, John Musker, James Coleman, Tony Anselmo, Jorgen Klubien, Andreas Deja, Brenda Chapman, Tom Sito, Chris Hibler, and Karen Keller. Also, thanks to Peter Loughrey of Los Angeles Modern Auctions and a repeat appraiser on PBS's *Antiques Roadshow,* for his invaluable insights and knowledge of the Kem Weber furniture and the Mid-Century Modern design movement. Thank you to Julia Larson, ADC Reference Archivist at the Architecture and Design Collection, Art, Design & Architecture Museum, University of California, Santa Barbara for all her help with the Kem Weber archives. And Mindy Johnson for her help with some rare photos.

It is also important to express my gratitude to the Hyperion Historical Alliance (HHA), which is an independent group dedicated to the research, documentation, and preservation of Disney history. I had this manuscript vetted and received valuable feedback from animation historian Paula Sigman-Lowery and HHA president Didier Ghez. I am proud to be a member of this esteemed group of committed authors and historians.

Finally, last but not least, a heartfelt thanks to my family, Nancy, Sydney, and Marlee, as well as my mother, Virginia, sisters Caroline and Alison. And to Anita, Andrew, and Stephanie for all their love and support. I know that my father, Philip, my brother, Phil Jr., and my mother-in-law, Eleanor, are with us in spirit and looking down with eternal smiles.

—Dave Bossert

Los Angeles, California 2018

CHAPTER 1
INTRODUCTION

> "The more you know about the past,
> the better prepared you are for the future."
>
> -Theodore Roosevelt

Over the course of a life, each of us becomes connected to *stuff*—those *things* that we accumulate. That connection could be because of its intrinsic value or its aesthetic nature or both. We all have items that adorn our homes and offices which hold a significant place in our lives and often we don't know that much about those things. Maybe you have a piece of furniture that belonged to a grandparent that you have fond memories of from your childhood yet you don't really know the actual history of that piece. Where it was made? What kind of wood was used? What was the significance of that design period? I can completely relate because I had worked on a Kem Weber designed animation desk from 1939 for nearly three decades and knew little about it.

In 2016, after more than thirty-two years at Walt Disney Animation Studios, I was packing up my office readying to leave the company. As you can imagine, after such a long tenure, I had a lot of "stuff" that accumulated over the years. There were books, artwork, papers, reference files, notes, documentation, and all kinds of knick-knacks, lanyards, statues, and whatnots. Just think for a moment of all the things we are given over decades. In my case, there were caricatures of me by John Musker, director of *The Little Mermaid* (1989), *Aladdin* (1992), and *Moana* (2016), funny drawings from any number of projects that I worked on, one-off art prints, signed limited editions by James Coleman, Walt Peregoy and others, animation cels,—and the list goes on. Some of the items were special gifts for the completion of a project or a gift bag from a premiere, crew gifts and department gifts from one film or another. There were trinkets, stuffed characters, music CDs, boxes of note cards, and my scrapbooks and photo albums— it was an endless stream of memories, a partial record of Disney animation history. And so much of it was on and in my Weber animation desk.

Sorting through all of this stuff was tedious and truly difficult to thin down for the simple reason that each item had its own story. These items were, in some cases, historical artifacts that had significant meaning to me and just couldn't be thrown away. There were even some items such as original animation art from any number of Disney animated films that belonged to the company. That material was boxed up and sent to the Animation Research Library (ARL) or other relevant departments that might want to archive them, whether they wanted to or not. Sometimes there are individuals that lack the knowledge or experience to see the value, figurative or intrinsic, of certain items that are part of a definitive historic timeline.

Years ago, when we received our weekly paychecks, the envelopes that they came in also were advertisements of whatever new movie the studio was releasing or new attraction opening at the parks that the Studio wanted to promote that week. Collectors used to pay to buy those empty envelopes, as well as the Studios' internal newsletter for employees. If it was Disney-related in some way, it had some value to fans and collectors— the same is still true today. If I was looking at something and waffling on whether or not it was worth keeping—I kept it. If it was pertinent to any one of the films that I worked on over the decades—I kept it. Into a box it went, and I have no doubt that years from now I'll find some of it and wonder why I kept it in the first place, or I will be elated because I had the forethought to hold on to it. I did my best to sort out what had real historical significance from what didn't as I boxed up all my personal belongings.

As I was standing in a half-packed office strewn with boxes and packing material, the head of operations came by to see how things were going. I had known her for years. She could see there were stacks of books and papers covering most flat surfaces in my office waiting to be placed into the official brown moving boxes that were ubiquitous at the animation facility. Artists are constantly moved around the various buildings. It was obvious that I had a ways to go even though there was a hefty number of boxes already filled and sealed. As we chatted, she asked me a simple question.

"Do you want your animation desk?"

Looking deadpan at her for a moment, I looked at my Weber animation desk still cluttered with stuff and thought to myself; *"Oh my God, are you kidding me? You want to give me my original Kem Weber 1939, Disney animation desk that I have been dragging around with*

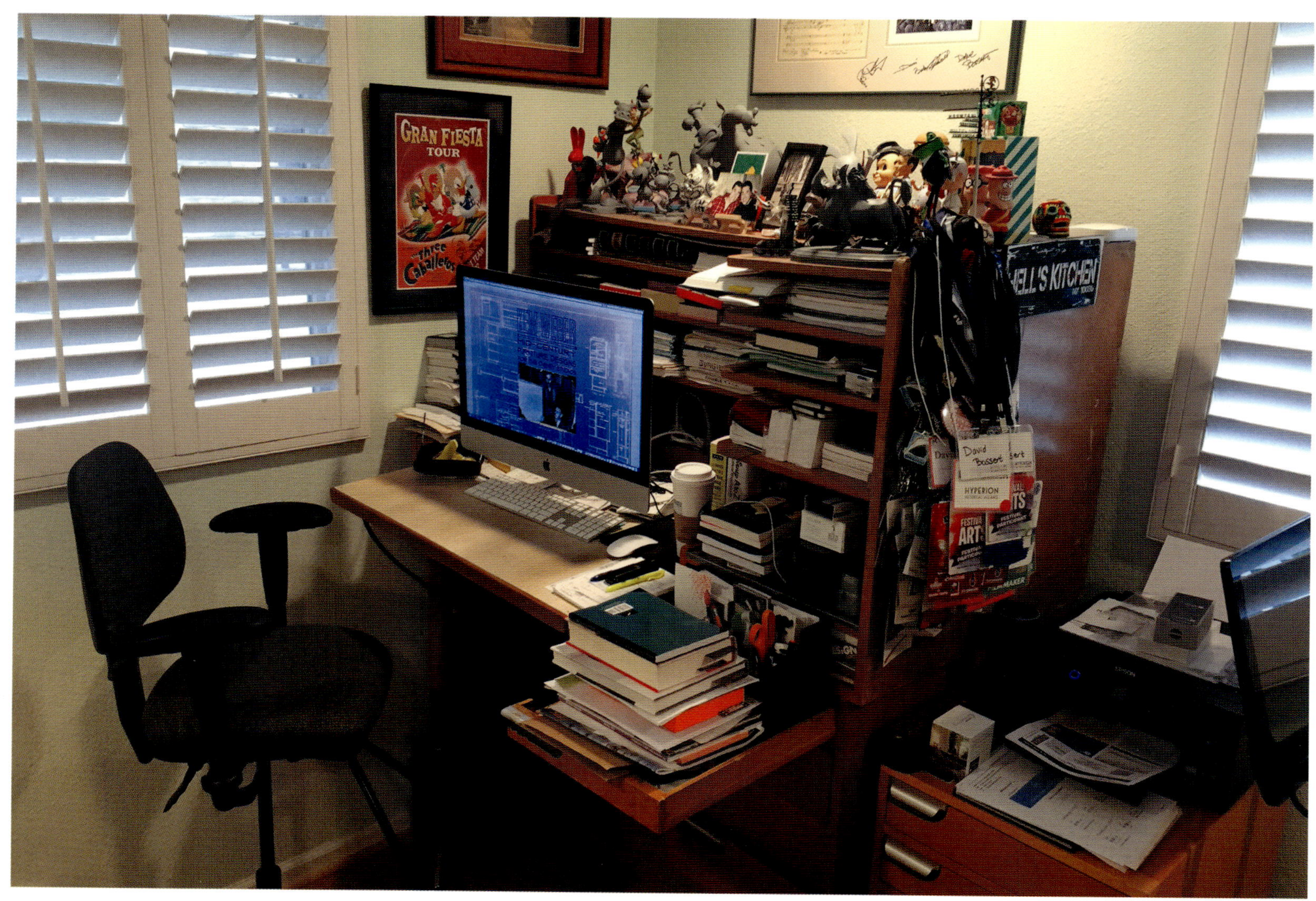

The author's Kem Weber designed Compact Animator's Desk, UNIT No. 19. Photo ©Dave Bossert

me for decades? This animation desk that was designed specifically for Disney under the watchful eye of Walt himself and with input from some of the legendary Nine Old Men? The desk that a former operations manager said was valued at an obscene amount of money? This incredible piece of mid-century furniture design, mine for the taking? My desk, which is a rare example of what was known as the compact or modified animator's desk and is smaller and taller than the regular animator's desk and of which there are very few examples in existence? And it's mine, all mine for the taking?!"

"Okay, sure... if you don't want it." I said. "But how will I get it home?"

"We'll have the studio movers take it and all your stuff up to your house."

Thinking to myself, "*No way! You're giving me this original Kem Weber 1939 Disney animation desk AND you're going to deliver it to my home. I've hit the jackpot!*"

"Okay, that's great," I said rather nonchalantly.

In all of a few minutes, I acquired my Kem Weber animation desk complete with the drawing board, the animation disc and attached under lighting. The desk was a fixture in my offices for decades. It included the blocks that were made for me at the Studio mill years ago that allowed the desk to be raised twelve-inches higher so that I could sit or stand throughout the day as I animated. It also had all of the original patina that included a five-inch round nicotine stain on the bottom-side of the second shelf. The previous animator kept his ashtray underneath while smoking as he worked. (Yes, it was common for people to smoke in offices decades ago. Thank goodness it's no longer allowed.) This was the desk that I worked on doing effects animation for *The Little Mermaid* (1989), *Beauty and the Beast* (1991), *Aladdin* (1992), *Pocahontas* (1995), *Hercules* (1997), *Fantasia/2000* (1999), and so many other films. The desk that I spent so many hours at working overtime to get films done and ate lunch and dinners at over the years.

It is the desk that I continued to use as I was promoted into artistic supervisory and eventually management roles as the years slipped away. Even in those new roles, I still would jump back on the drawing board and do animation or help assist on animation that needed to get done to meet a tough deadline. So, having the desk in my office enabled me to still draw, animate, and design—still be an artist, which I am at my core. For me, it was a necessity so that I could use it to quickly sketch up an idea during a meeting that would instantly convey how

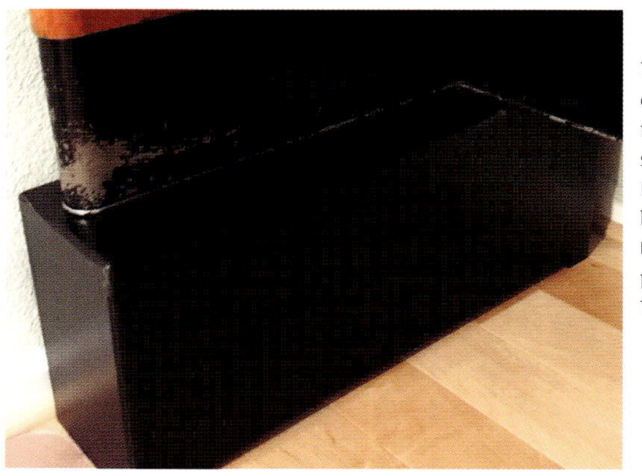

Detail of desk base on riser blocks made at the studio mill shop. Note the grey linoleum showing through the chipped paint on the desk base. Photo ©Dave Bossert

we might do something or solve a creative issue. The desk held everything I needed to get my job done. As we transitioned into the digital age, I used it with my various computers mounting the CRT monitors on the top shelf of the Weber designed worktable that was a close companion piece.

The desk, my boxes of stuff, all fifty-two of them, and other items were all taken by the Disney Studio movers up to my house. Once there, the desk was set up in my new office. I've had the habit of setting up my offices nearly identically as I moved around through the animation facilities from picture to picture. So, it was only natural that this final move was not that much different. I liken it to a comfortable old shoe that you don't want to get rid of because it fits well and feels good.

As I unpacked, I added all the statuettes, bobbleheads, pictures, toys and other trinkets to my desk, setting it up just like it has been for years. I had plenty of reference books and other reading material within arm's length. It's like a security blanket—a comfortable surrounding that is inspiring and conducive to creating, which is now all about writing. I took the drawing board and laid it down flat, removed the animation disc and put a thin, quarter-inch piece of birch plywood over the top to cover the hole where the disc used to be. On that new surface I placed my computer. Instead of animation, I now write books, articles, program notes, or whatever at this desk.

I spent the spring and summer of 2017 researching and then writing a book on the making of *Tim Burton's The Nightmare Before Christmas* (1993) on my vintage Kem Weber desk. Coming to work every morning in my own office and sitting at this desk, with a hot cup of tea, to create like I had been doing for decades. Instead of creating animation art for a new Disney feature film or short, I was now cobbling words together—wordsmithing. Telling stories of some of those animation projects for which I was fortunate enough to be a part of, and writing about some of the history that I've been researching for years for the sheer love of the art form.

Already a published author, I was always on the hunt for a new topic to explore, one that hadn't been written about in any length or ever. Believe it or not, there are still plenty of Disney related topics to write about that have not been covered in any depth already. I know that may sound hard to believe with the hundreds of books on Disney that have been published over the years, but there still are plenty of stories to tell. These are the stories behind the stories, which sometimes are the most interesting and fascinating.

It was on one of those summer mornings, working at my Kem Weber desk, that I leaned back in my chair and put my clasped hands behind my head to rest for a minute. Sitting at my desk, I started looking at this gorgeous piece of handcrafted furniture. The solid birch plywood, the joinery work, the way the drawers were built, the ingenious pencil tray and the stark linear shelves, which held so many memories. There is a rigidness and weight to the furniture that conveys a permanence and sturdiness.

This is often counter to the very kludged-together animation desks that were used at other studios, those sometimes flimsy desks that had a slight wobble to them, which were indicative of the many boutique animation studios that came and went over the years. Those desks lacked the shelf space or accoutrements of the Kem Weber designs. The Weber desks are solid. It is an undertaking to move them, and when in place in an office they are a solid foundation for the creation of animation for what likely would become a Disney classic. There is an unmatched level of quality to the furniture similar to that of the Disney house style. These desks were as important a tool for creating that animation and art just like the pencils, paper, brushes, straightedges, pan-sticks, computer stylists/keyboards and other implements of the trade used daily by the Disney artists.

As I sat there looking at my Weber desk, I wondered to myself if anyone had documented this specialized furniture. There must have been a book on this furniture—there had to be. The furniture was designed specifically for animation and therefore, I reasoned, there had to be some documentation on it, perhaps complete with interviews of various animation legends creating magic on these desks. After all, with the number of books and articles on Disney related topics that have been published over the years, the furniture must have been covered at some point. Yet, when I spent several hours researching the topic online I found that nothing in fact had been done to fully document the design, construction and use of the animation furniture at The Walt Disney Studios. There was one book and an exhibition catalogue on Kem Weber but these focused mostly on his buildings, the structures for which he is known. There were some notations on the furniture he had designed, including his famed Air Line Chair, which is now part of many museums' furniture collections.

It was a clear oversight, an unintended faux pas that needed to be corrected before it was too late. What was also evident was this subject, the animation furniture, was such a specialized topic that it was doubtful that any large publishing house was going to publish it as a book. It's a struggle to get books published on well-known topics, so forget about the small specialized subjects and behind-the-scenes stories. The Weber furniture certainly fell into that category, and was just too niche a subject matter to be of any interest to established publishers.

So, what then? Do you just forget about it and let the subject vanish into history? Does it fade away over time until some distant day when a researcher is trying to piece together the facts about this furniture and there is little left to be found? That's unpalatable, since at that point in the future there would likely be no one left in this world who actually worked on the furniture. Then there would only be speculation and supposition on how it was designed, manufactured and used.

Think about it: Disney is not doing any hand-drawn animated feature films now or in the foreseeable future. What is left of the furniture is collecting dust in a warehouse and that inventory is slowly eroding away through sales or being given to employees moving on or retiring. There had been warehouse sales to dump much of the furniture at fire-sale prices, and even some of it was carted off to the local landfill over the years. Can you imagine that? The furniture could very well be an archeological find in some distant century.

As the animation business at Disney changed from hand-drawn to computer generated, the Kem Weber animation desks were no longer being utilized. This is the furniture that was used to make animated classics from *Fantasia* (1940), *Bambi* (1942), and *Dumbo* (1941) to *Cinderella* (1950), *Peter Pan* (1953), and *Sleeping Beauty* (1959), to *One Hundred and One Dalmatians* (1961) and *The Jungle Book* (1967). Those films and so many others were handcrafted on these well designed and functional desks.

The more recent generation of animation artists that worked on films like *The Rescuers* (1977), *The Fox and the Hound* (1981), *The Black Cauldron* (1985), *The Little Mermaid* (1989), *Beauty and the Beast* (1991), *Aladdin* (1992), *Pocahontas* (1995), *Hercules* (1997), *Fantasia/2000* (1999) and others in the latter part of the twentieth century, known as the "Renaissance of Disney Animation," used this furniture as well. Those Disney artists are dissipating—scattering to the wind—an entire generation retiring or leaving as their careers evolved and changed. Those are the last artists who used the Weber animation furniture, who prized it for its design of form and function. It was praised for being standardized for a specific discipline, yet allowed for the individual customization of workflow and use by the artist. For some of the artists, it was a source of pride to have a desk that belonged to a previous Disney legend or even one of Walt's Nine Old Men. The desks had a lineage to them, a traceable history that was documented by many artists who wrote their names on the desks, or others that did it for them as a visual record like hieroglyphics on an ancient tomb or cave wall.

So, I felt that the Kem Weber animation furniture was a niche subject that still deserved to be researched and written about. All the information available should be aggregated into one reference source if possible so that there is a record of its existence, design, use and appreciation. If the established publishers had no interest in the topic, then the only way to do it would be through an independent imprint that was able to handle a niche topic as a monograph, which is a small work of specialized writing on a single subject.

As with every book project that I have worked on, this one could not have been accomplished without the help and support of many individuals. It is an arduous task to dig into a subject that has, for the most part, been neglected for more than seventy years. To no one's fault, it is furniture after all, and at the time it was designed and built for a specific purpose—a means to an end—to make Disney animated films. Like the pencils, brushes, paper, and pens, the furniture is also an instrument for creative expression as part of every Disney artist's toolbox. In fact, the furniture, in a sense, was the toolbox that not only held the tools of the trade but was the workbench on which the art was handcrafted. The animation desks and associated furniture were the workhorses of the Disney Studios plant. Pencils get used up, brushes worn-out, and reams of paper drawn on, yet the one constant was the Weber furniture that gracefully aged through each successive hand-drawn animated film. Yet, no one really knew much about the furniture or gave it a second thought.

The research into this topic was when the real work started. There were several sources that had some information on Kem Weber's design work for The Walt Disney Studios, but there was not a voluminous amount. The real treasure trove of visuals was in the papers that Weber left to the University of California at Santa Barbara (UCSB), which had been lovingly cared for at the Architectural archives on campus. It is a misnomer to say "left his papers" because there was little to no correspondence or other written papers on the Disney Studios project to speak of, other than artwork.

By the late 1930s, the economy was rebounding from the Great Depression and Kem Weber had received numerous commissions for which he either lacked the time to keep proper documentation or inventory any correspondence. If he did, it had not survived. From what is documented, Walt Disney was so actively involved with Weber in every aspect of building the new studio plant and all the furnishings that went into the complex, that there didn't appear to be a need for much in the way of formal letters or correspondence.

It is a disappointment that there is not more in the way of written material. However, all of Weber's drawings, sketches, photos and paintings of the Disney Studios complex and furnishings have been inventoried, catalogued, and stored in archival boxes at UCSB. Many of the images had notations and descriptions that were not only useful but also informative as to the location within the studio property. Some of the artwork was concept art; other pieces were the final versions or close representations of what was built.

The other aspect of the research was to speak with artists who actually worked on the furniture that was made for the various animation disciplines, as well as to experts on that period of furniture design. There was the well-known animation desk, the scarce compact animator's desk, an assistant's desk, a layout desk, a background painter's desk, a story artist's desk, the small and large director's desks, and a number of side tables and cabinets. The permanent tables and built-ins in the Ink & Paint Department. There were also miscellaneous office pieces such as freestanding closets, chairs, coat racks and wall and table clocks. It was all part of what was known as holistic design where the architecture of a new building included the interiors and all the furnishings so that there was a common design thread. Everything in the building was designed to go with that building. It was important to speak to those artists who worked on and used all the specialized pieces created for Disney to more fully understand why the furniture was designed the way it was. To document it fully for posterity.

Fortunately, many of the artists that I interviewed had Weber animation furniture that was either given to them when they left the company, purchased from the Studios during the periodic warehouse sales, or acquired through private purchases from previous Disney artists or their families. Some artists that I spoke to had contemporary knockoffs inspired by the original Weber designs, which Walt Disney Animation Studios made when they opened satellite animation studio facilities in Orlando and Paris. Some of those artists are still using the furniture to create animation and animation related art. So, it was with a sense of ease that they could talk about the attributes of the desks in relation to the process of creating that artwork.

There was also some reference that pointed to early Disney animators who commented on the furniture origins. Some had their own opinions on what Walt Disney was trying to accomplish when he built the new studio complex in Burbank, California in 1939. Aggregating all of these interviews and research into one text will hopefully give you, the reader, a much more thorough viewpoint as to why the Disney furniture is so revered in the animation world, amongst experts and with collectors of mid-century furniture.

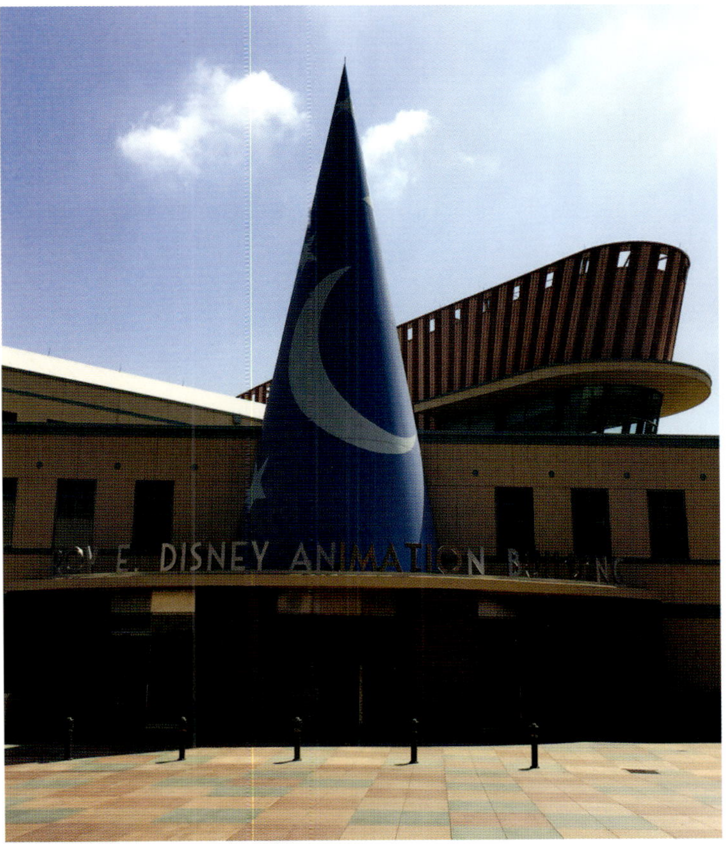

The Walt Disney Animation Studios' Roy E. Disney Animation Building in Burbank, 2018. Photo ©Dave Bossert

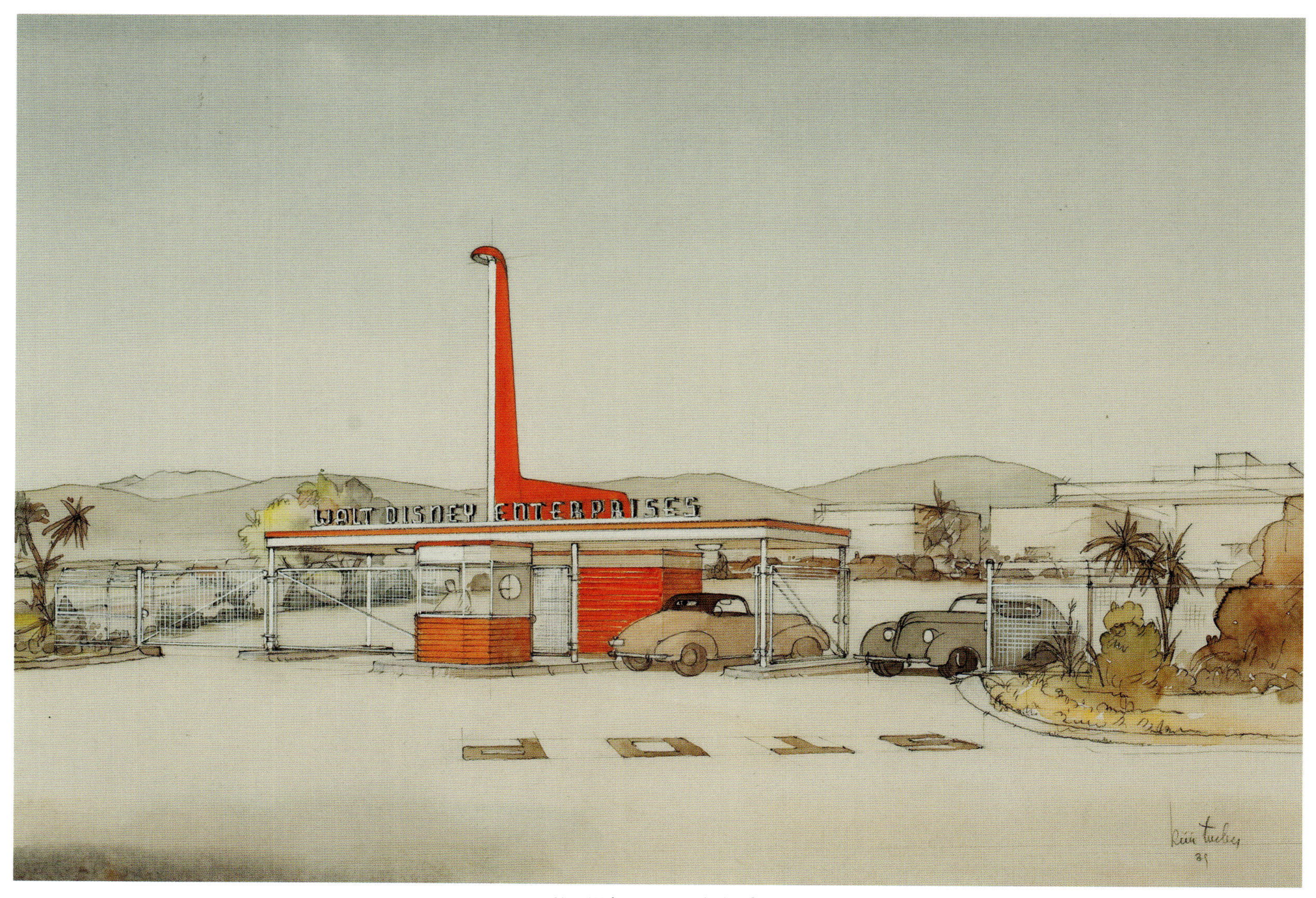

Kem Weber concept design for The Walt Disney Studios main entrance on Buena Vista Street, 1939; ©UCSB

CHAPTER 2
MID-CENTURY MODERNE AND THE RISE OF WEST COAST MODERNISM

"We want to design furniture that is suitable to the modern mass machine production."

-Kem Weber (circa. 1929-30)

To understand why the Disney animation furniture is so revered, one has to first have some understanding of the design period from which it came. This is easier said than done since the Kem Weber furniture falls into the sometimes difficult term to define—"mid-century moderne," which is the period roughly from 1933 to 1965, though some would argue the period is specifically limited to 1947 to 1957. For the purposes of this book, the term mid-century moderne incorporates the design styles of Streamline Moderne and West Coast Moderne from the period of 1933 through 1957 and will be differentiated as needed.[1]

Weber occupied a pivotal role in introducing modernism to Southern California. He was instrumental not only in helping to define the special look of American modernism, but also in shaping its distinctive West Coast variant now known as West Coast Moderne, which includes architectural examples stretching from Los Angeles up the West Coast to Vancouver, British Columbia, Canada. In extolling the virtues and imagery of a new, more relaxed lifestyle, freed of the stiffness and pretensions of traditional interiors, he laid the groundwork for the casual California modernism of the 1950s and 1960s.[2] California was a frontier for the architectural and design concepts of modernism. "It kind of shoehorns nicely with modernism because modernism needed more than anything else a laboratory consisting of space," said Peter Loughrey, an appraiser for PBS's *Antiques Roadshow* and director of modern design and fine art at Los Angeles Modern Auctions. "Architects and designers and modernists found a wide-open blank canvas in California."[3] It was a laboratory for design experimentation and Weber was on the leading edge. It is worth looking at Weber's eclectic background first to see how his early experiences helped to shape him as an architect and industrial designer.

Karl Emanuel Martin Weber was born in Berlin, Germany, on November 14, 1889. By his early adulthood he had taken the first letter of each of his three given names and come up with that distinctive first name, Kem. At the age of fifteen, he was asked to leave school for being too disruptive and was placed in an apprenticeship with Eduard Schultz, the Royal Cabinetmaker in Potsdam in 1904. Later Weber recalled, "I loved tools and was always engaged making all kinds of practical appliances...toy [sic], boats, wagons and such."[4] By 1907, he became a journeyman of the Cabinetmakers Guild of Potsdam, before moving on to study at the Academy of Applied Arts in Berlin. Weber took master classes with leading furniture designer Bruno Paul, a great modernist thinker of the day in Germany and Austria. Weber went on to become an apprentice at Bruno Paul's studio and under his supervision designed the German section at the International Exposition in Brussels in 1910.[5] Pleased with Weber's work, Paul recommended that he design the German section of the 1915 Panama-Pacific Exposition in San Francisco. In May 1914, Weber then left Germany for San Francisco to supervise the construction of the German section of the exposition. But in August, with the start of World War I, the construction drawings were confiscated, and Weber was stranded in the Bay Area.[6]

Weber wrote later about trying to return to Germany during that period, "...was advised by the German consul in San Francisco to stay there; and it wasn't until years later that he realized it was his good fortune that circumstances kept him out of the world struggle." [7] Unable to return home, Weber took on a series of jobs, including decorating flowerpots, designing ads for an outdoor advertising company, working as a lumberjack, and even operating a chicken farm until the war ended in 1918. He briefly opened a design studio in Berkeley, California, but that didn't last because of "prejudice against anything that might be laid out to be of German influence."[8] But California "...allowed him to take what he had learned and what he had been trained in of these early proto-modernist ideas of reductionism and following along with industrialized ideas rejecting classicism, rejecting historical precedent. In that regard, California was kind of the perfect place to practice this kind of philosophy," said Loughrey.[9]

After the armistice was signed, Weber moved to Santa Barbara, where he designed interiors for homes and produced furniture, wood carvings, draperies, and paintings. His work was predominately for homes in

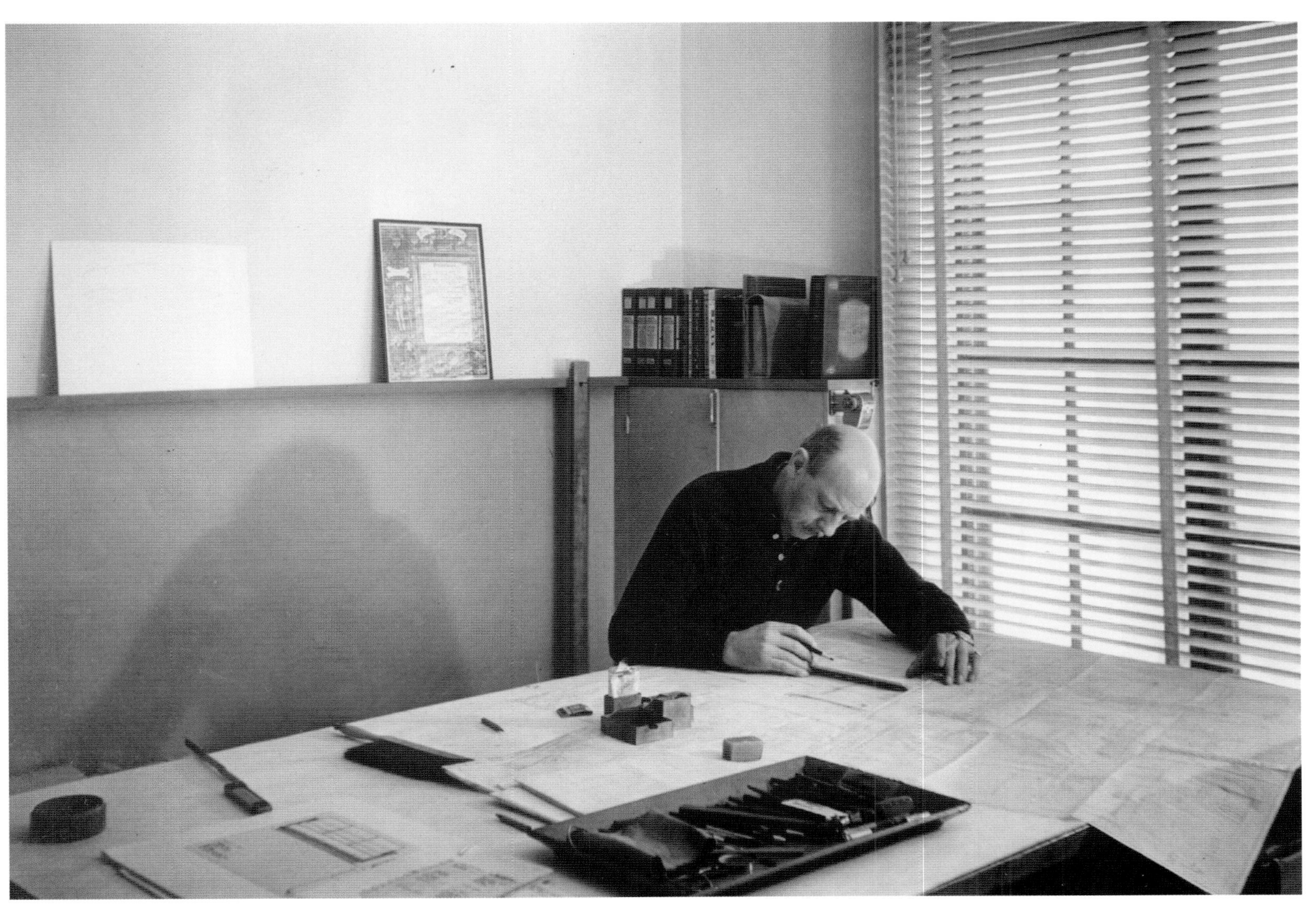

Kem Weber, the designer working at his desk, circa 1935;©UCSB

Santa Barbara and Montecito that were mostly in the Spanish Colonial Revival style. From there, he moved to Los Angeles in 1921 and went to work as a draftsman in the design studio at Barker Bros. Furniture. Within a year, he was promoted to art director. Weber became a U.S. citizen in 1924.

By this time, the Art Deco movement was in full swing. Short for Arts Décoratifs, Art Deco originated in France during the mid-1910s and combined the modernist styles that were emerging in Western Europe with influences from Art Nouveau, the Bauhaus movement, and Cubism. The term Art Deco was coined at the Exposition Internationale des Arts Décoratifs et Industriels Modernes (International Exposition of Modern Decorative and Industrial Arts), held in Paris in 1925, which Weber attended. Art Deco had several variants to it, most notably Zigzag Moderne and Streamline Moderne, both of which were made less formal by American designers as they blended elements of the Arts and Crafts movement from the turn of the twentieth century.

The Zigzag Moderne was a highly decorative form with zigzag designed buildings adorned with geometric ornamentation on the facades. It was inspired by design elements from ancient Egypt, Rome, Asia, and Greece, with aspects of industrialization—the Machine Age. This style was more distinctive to urban areas such as New York with skyscrapers like the Empire State Building, the Chrysler Building, and Radio City Music Hall. In urban centers there was a verticality to design. "People like [designer] Paul Frankel in New York, who had a built-in community of people who were supporting his ideas of the skyscraper mentality, of building big, building tall. Someone like Frankel was obsessed with the technology and industry around him which was building bigger and bigger buildings. So, his furniture and his designs naturally had a tall, thin, elegant structuralism to them. Out here in California it was not necessary to build tall. We had plenty of land, you could build out. And I think that at its core this is the basis of Kem Weber's genius at that time. Almost everything he designed had a sense of

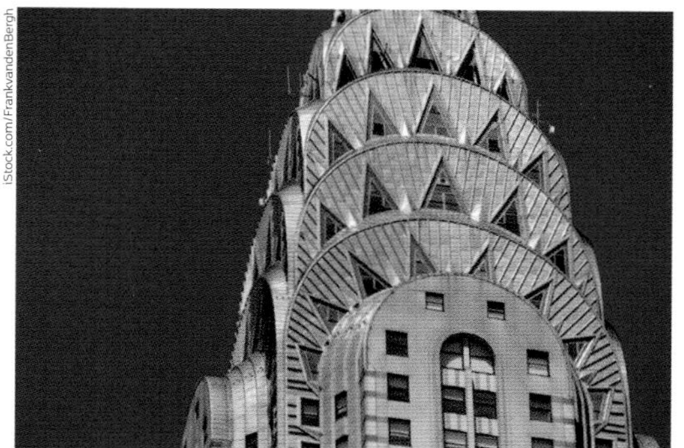

iStock.com/FrankvandenBergh

Left: Ornamental detail on the top of the Chrysler Building in the Zigzag Moderne style.

Right: Sketch of the Empire State building showing the vertical design.

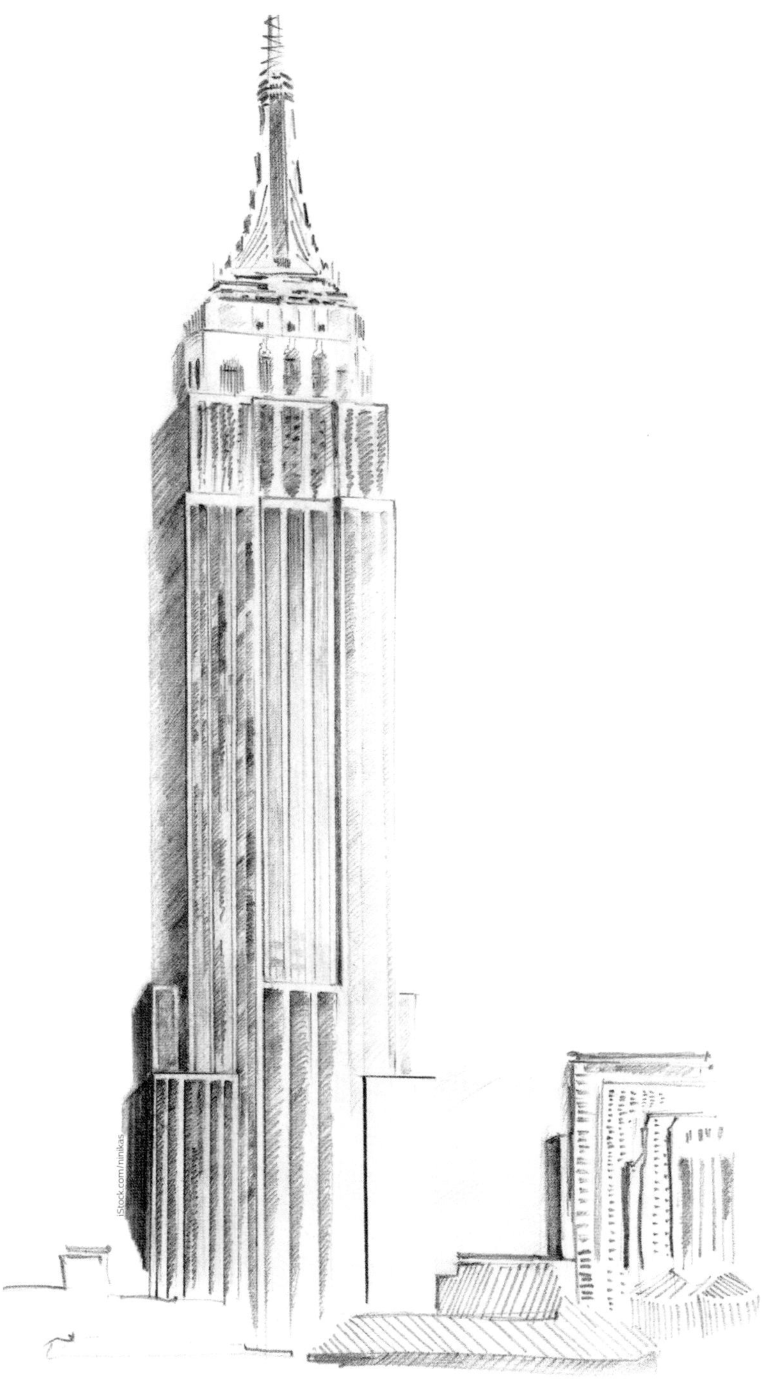

horizontality to it, which was obviously in direct contrast to the verticality of Frankel on the East Coast," said Loughrey.[10]

In 1926, after returning from Europe, Weber created the Modes and Manners shop within furniture retailer Barker Bros. This was one of the first departments in the United States dedicated entirely to modern furniture and accessories, many of which were his designs.[11] The following year he opened his own design studio in Hollywood. He not only designed furniture and products, but also buildings and integrated interiors for hotels, shops, and private homes. Then, in 1928, Weber had the opportunity to design a three-room apartment at Macy's Second International Exposition of Art and Industry that brought him national notoriety, which resulted in commissions from companies across the country.[12] Weber's stature as an architect and forward-thinking designer was rising as he became a leading figure in the Moderne design movement, becoming the chairman of the department of industrial design of the newly organized Art Center School in Los Angeles in 1931. As the aesthetics of art moderne continued to change, Weber was fully immersed in what became known as Streamline Moderne by 1934,[13] the origins of

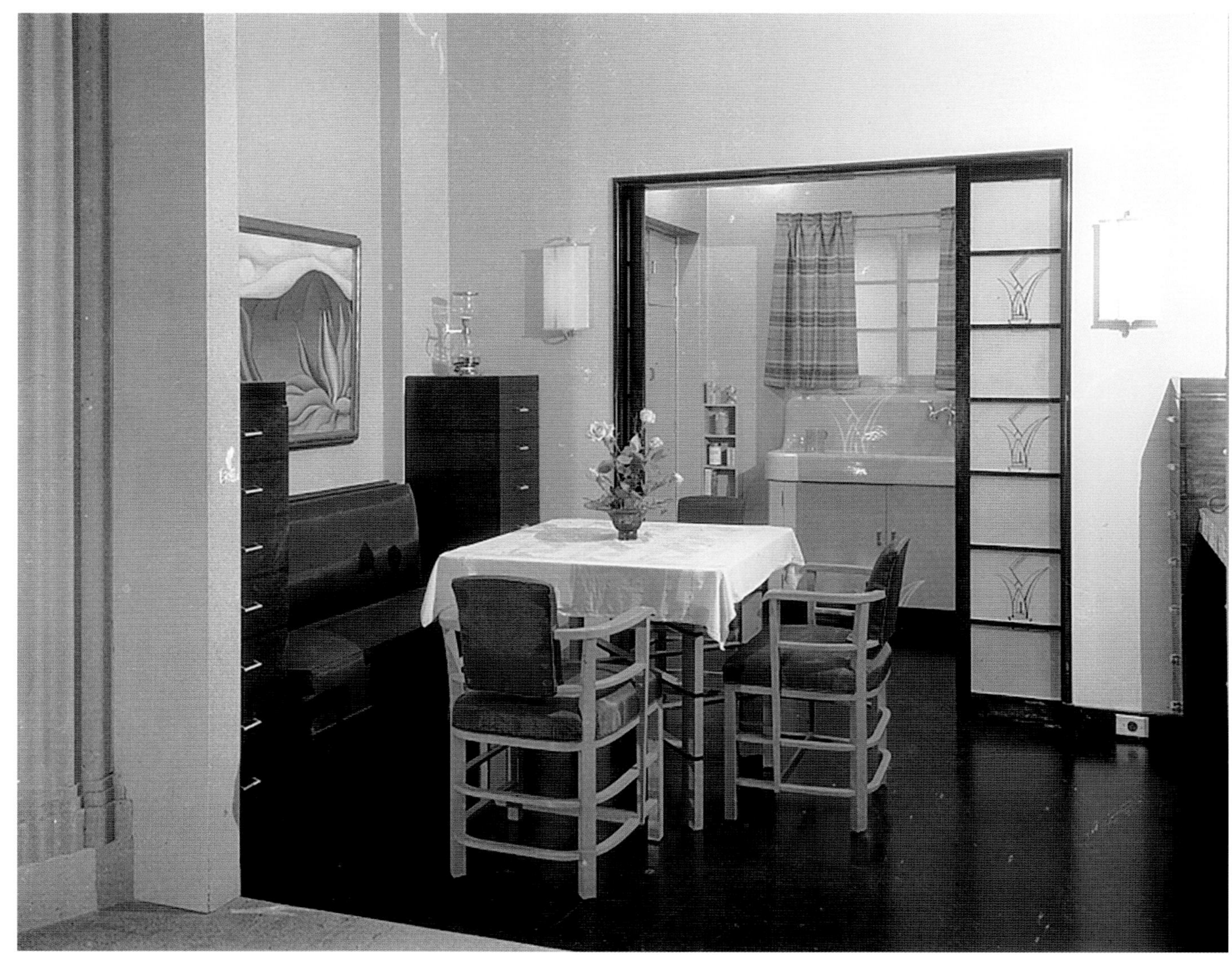

Kem Weber's 1928 Macy's Second International Exposition of Art and Industry apartment dining area; Courtesy of The Library of Congress

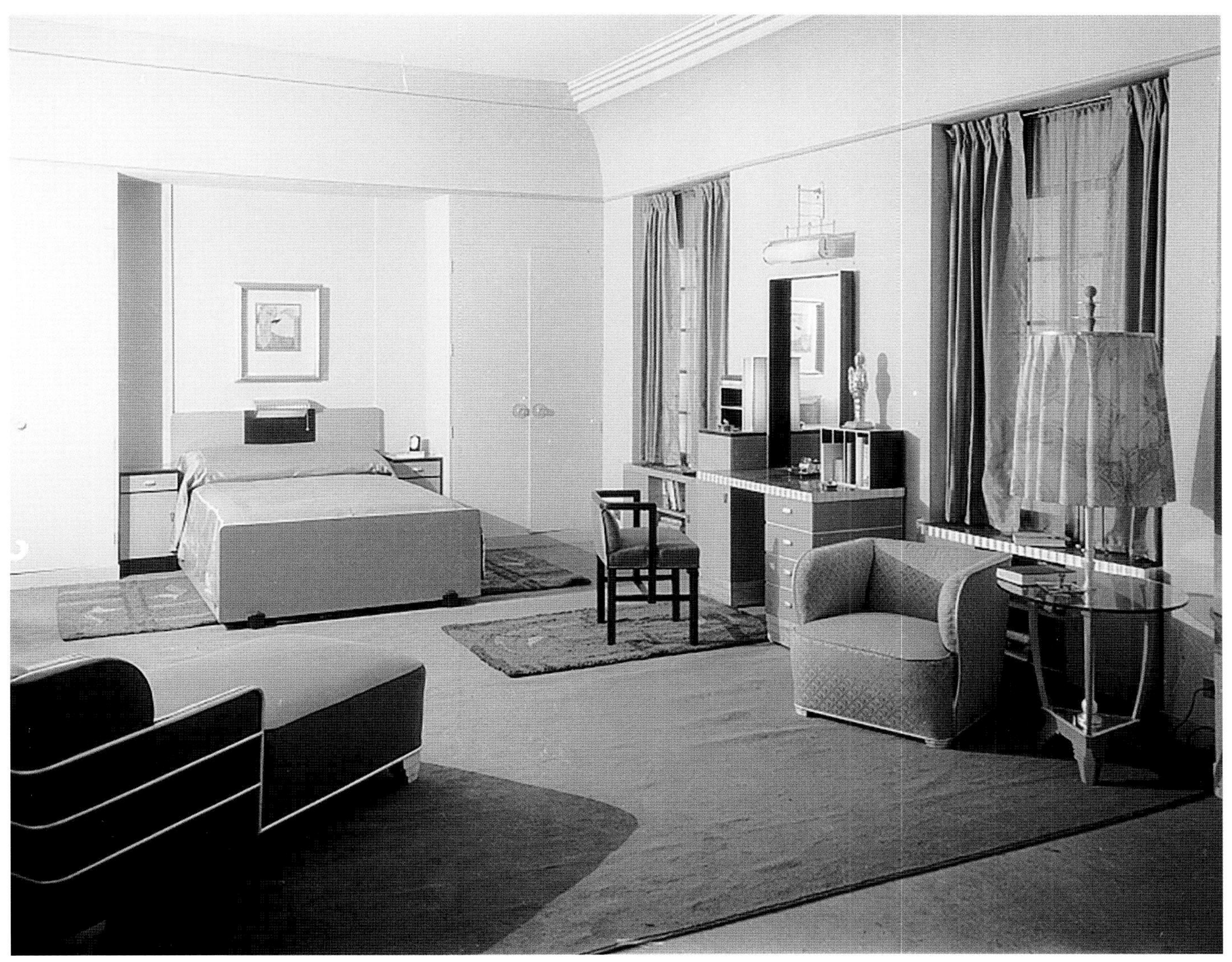

Kem Weber's 1928 Macy's Second International Exposition of Art and Industry award-winning apartment design; Courtesy of The Library of Congress

what is known as West Coast Moderne, a more casual form of the modern movement most associated with the California lifestyle.

The Streamline Moderne style was a continuing evolution of Art Deco that emerged from the Great Depression and focused more on stripping away unnecessary ornamentation and streamlining forms. It focused on smooth curved walls, rounded edges, and long horizontal lines with an emphasis on a clean look. "So, we have these soft rounded edges, which actually come out of the Arts and Crafts movement that preceded it," said Paula Sigman-Lowery, archivist and historian.[14]

There were nautical elements such as circular "porthole" windows, steel railings and "a signature trio of horizontal speed stripes suggesting motion"[15] that acted as a design thread in the holistic thinking of creating the structure, interiors, and furnishing of a single project. The Streamline Moderne style was a direct reflection of the growth of modern transportation during the 1930s—automobiles, planes, trains, and ocean liners—which used aerodynamic design elements to create a clean, sleek appearance. "So, the prevailing industry at that moment was transportation. That was kind of the most modernist industry at the time. Steamship lines were

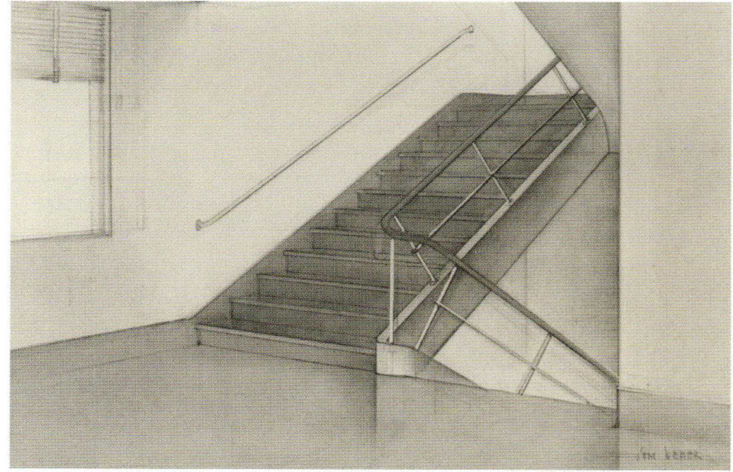

Top: Kem Weber concept sketch for The Walt Disney Studios Animation Production Building stairway. ©UCSB

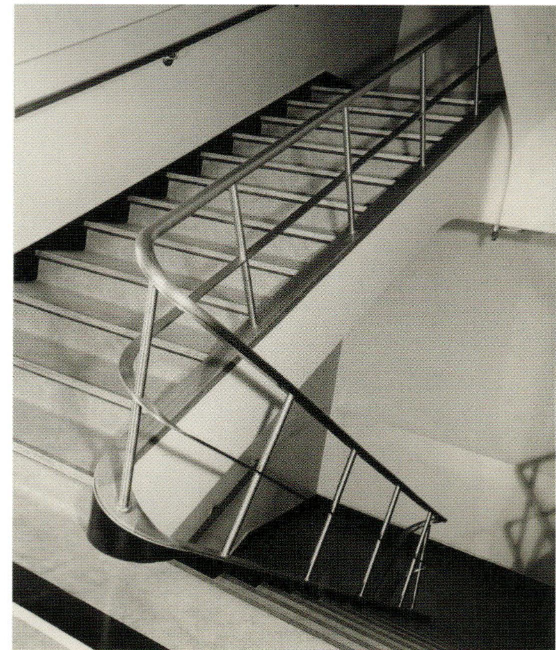

Right: Photo of completed stairwell, which has the feel of a steamship streamline design. Photo by Baskerville. ©UCSB

constantly trying to outdo each other and go faster across the Atlantic. There was this idea of using technology and using manufacturing ideas to constantly create a better ship," said Loughrey. "Airplanes themselves were in their infancy and were becoming a fascination of modernists because here is an object that has no room for decoration. The fuselage of an airplane has got to be functional and for someone like Kem Weber, the fascination with the discipline of that type of object drove his interest in architecture and design."[16] These were design elements that Weber embraced and are evident in his work including the cabin interior he designed for a private airplane. It was those projects and inspirations that influenced the work he did on Walt Disney's new animation studio complex in Burbank later in that decade.

Weber's fortunes were up and down during the Great Depression, and his position at the Art Center School afforded him the ability to have a regular income and to continue his independent design work. He designed sets for Paramount Pictures and established the Tempo shop at Barker Bros., in which he designed the showroom and much of the furniture. He designed clocks, light fixtures, and dozens of chairs and occasional tables for a variety of companies that were in a price range that appealed to a broad middle-class buyer. In describing the furniture in an interview, Weber told a reporter, "It is a matter, as well, of harmonizing lines and low, restful tones, and a sensation of unlimited space even in a small room."[17] Weber also designed high-end pieces for wealthier clients including all the furnishings for the Bixby House in Kansas City, Missouri, for Walter Edwin Bixby Sr., a successful insurance executive who helped establish Kansas City Life as one of the nation's leading insurance firms at the time.

In 1936, Weber wrote a guest column in the *Los Angeles Times* on classicism in design with respect to progress. In the article he writes, "A true modern piece of furniture is designed to incorporate all the advantages of modern materials, production facilities and construction, and if it is good design it will give a beautiful result."[18] The Air Line Chair was a perfect example of that design philosophy. Weber continued, "It will be good to look at, practical in its uses and becoming to ourselves. It will be less expensive and better in quality."[19] That sums up all the furniture that Weber designed for the Disney studio complex—it is good to look at as well as very practical since the designs were arrived at with input from the artists that would be using the furniture.

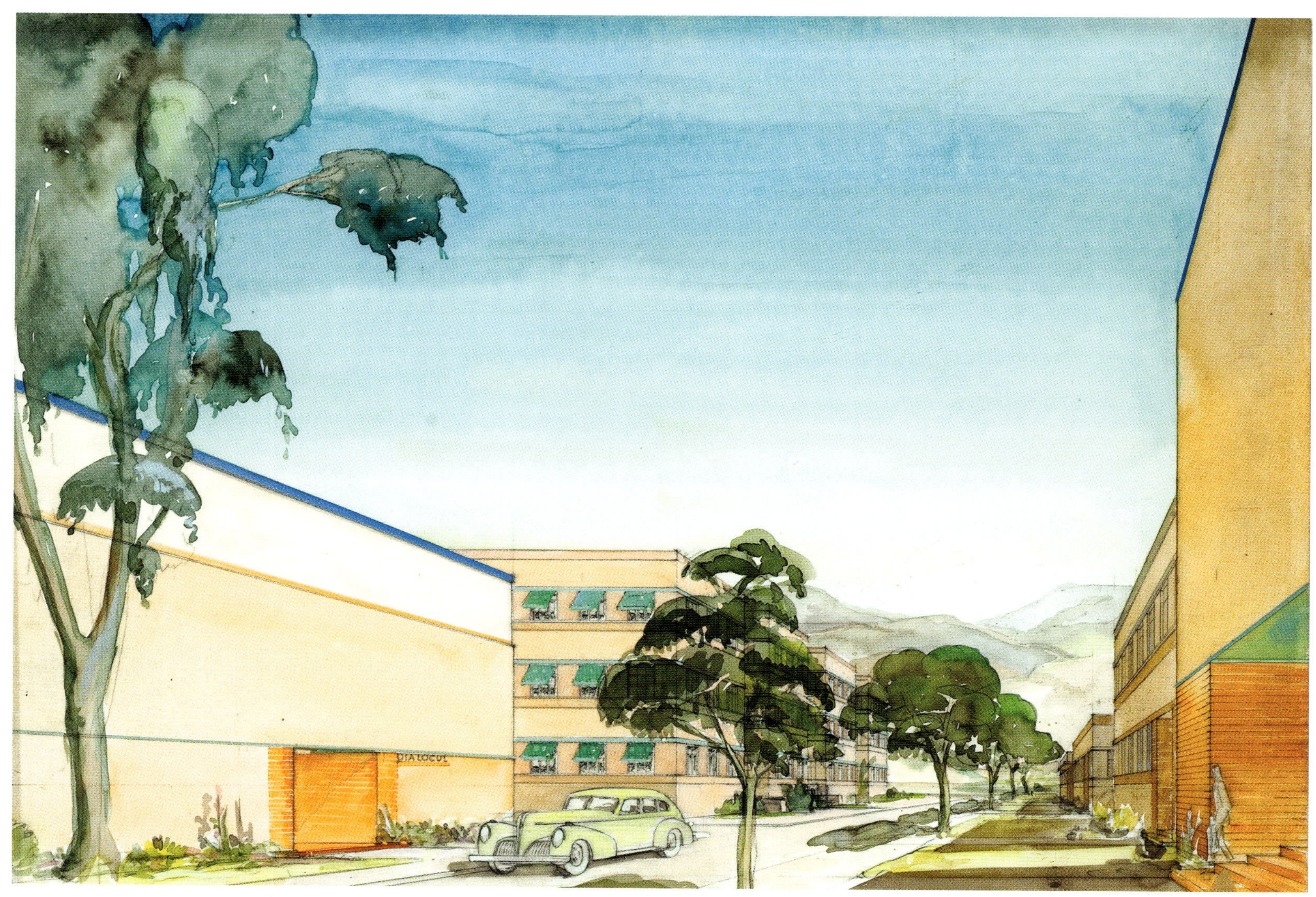

Kem Weber concept design looking north on Minnie Ave. towards the Animation Production Building (with awnings) at The Walt Disney Studios, 1939; ©UCSB

CHAPTER 3
A NEW STUDIO COMPLEX IN BURBANK

"We shape our buildings; thereafter they shape us."
-Winston Churchill

By 1939, Weber was a leader in the Los Angeles arts community. His involvement with the California Art Club along with his role at Art Center gave him local visibility, and his lectures on design in the Midwest and on the East Coast had elevated him nationally as a noted architect and industrial designer. "By the 1930s he had already become a fairly well-known national figure and he had designed for a New York silver company. He had already lectured nationally and published works and had already designed an entire line of furniture for Barker Brothers which was the largest furniture manufacturer in the country at that time," said Loughrey. "By the '30s, he was already part of the modernist establishment. By that time someone like Walt Disney certainly wasn't taking a chance on a young guy. He was saying I want the best and I want somebody whose philosophy I understand and was basically sort of almost picking the Frank Geary of the time sort of thing to do something big."[20]

When Walt and his brother Roy started their studio in their Uncle Robert's garage they quickly outgrew the space and moved down the street to the offices on Kingswell Avenue in the Los Feliz area of Los Angeles. As the studio staff grew, they moved again to a larger facility on Hyperion Avenue, where space kept being added as needed. "So you're making do, and he was constantly modifying the studio as it grew and they'd buy an apartment building here and turn that into offices and so forth," said Paula Sigman-Lowery, archivist and historian. "Walt knew what he wanted to do was create a space that would be the most conducive for doing what he wanted to do—animation."[21]

There is little known as to why Walt Disney hired Weber, but it is likely that Walt was aware of Weber's work in Los Angeles and elsewhere. It is worth pointing out that Walt spent a week crossing the Atlantic Ocean "on the SS *Normandy*, and the *Normandy* was the height of Streamline Moderne style. So he must have been influenced by that, because it was the rage back then. Being on a ship for a week, going from London to New York, surrounded by that style must have been really influential because right after that is when he commissioned his studio," said Don Hahn, producer and director. There is no doubt that we are all influenced by the latest color and style trends just from the mere fact that you get exposed to it daily through advertising and being in new environments. Even today, as I walk around the studio lot I can see strong influences of that Streamline Moderne style in so many aspects of the original buildings designed by Weber with Walt's input, from the simplest stairway banisters to the door pushes and clean design elements.

Early on, Walt realized that he needed an experienced designer to oversee the entire project. Someone who could aggregate all the input from himself and his staff into one cohesive design for the studio facility. A studio complex that could accommodate the growing needs of increased production and one that wasn't a constrained hodgepodge of buildings like the Walt Disney Studios on Hyperion Avenue. The studio had outgrown the Hyperion complex, which was a "cramped, cluttered

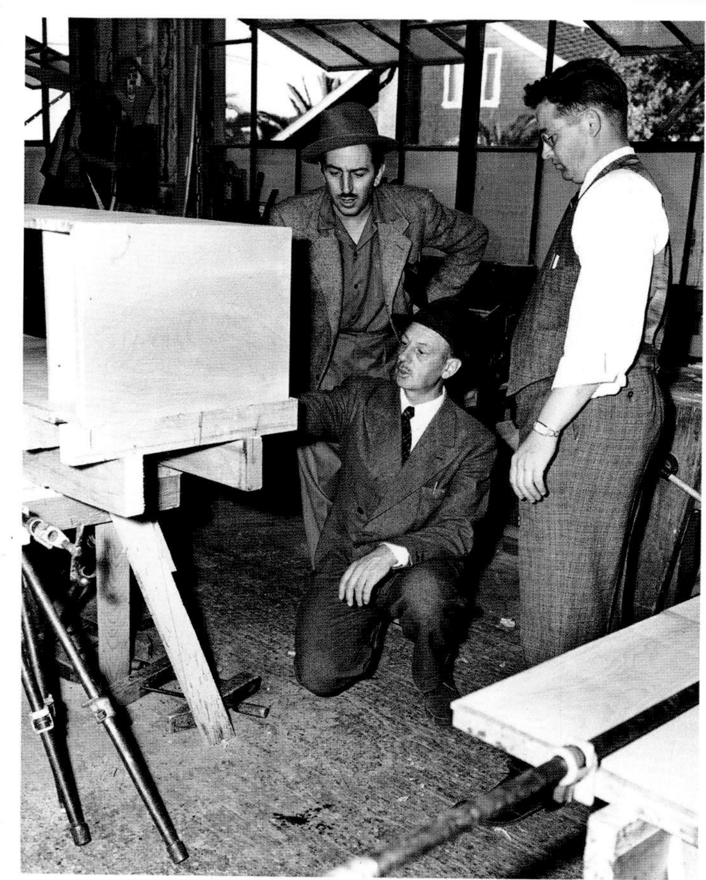

Kem Weber, kneeling while Walt looks on with Howard Petersen at the Petersen Show Case & Fixture Co. in Los Angeles; circa 1939. ©UCSB

space, with poor lighting and climate control"[22] and had spilled into a group of buildings that was constantly short of space.

Although it is often cited that the new studio was built with some of the profits from *Snow White and the Seven Dwarfs* (1937), by the time Walt was able to purchase the fifty-one acres of vacant land in Burbank, the profits from *Snow White* were spent and the new studio required a sizable loan.[23] When Walt began developing the Burbank site for a new animation studio complex, he had already assembled a group of designers and engineers to build the facility, which he wanted designed efficiently around not only the animation process but also for the artists who were creating that animation art. Walt knew that even though he was supervising this group of designers and engineers he needed a chief designer to avoid making the mistakes that were inherent in the existing Hyperion studio.[24] It is believed that Weber joined the process of building the new Burbank facility in appoximately May 1938.

The Disney Studios project was, at that time, Weber's largest commission. He was referred to as the supervising or chief designer because, ultimately, Walt was the visionary and knew what he wanted in creating an artistic campus-like environment. Walt had a firm grip on every aspect of the new facility and was involved in every detail of the new studio. In an interview, Weber recalled Walt's direction being of "comfort of mind and the happiness in the place of your work depends not only upon pure, practical, and functional solutions but also on their appearance." After hiring Weber, Walt commented to a reporter, "I wish I had got Kem earlier in the game. He gets what we want in a flash...." The article went on to note that the interior and industrial design department, which Weber headed at Art Center School in Pasadena, was being enlarged with the addition of "high-ranking architects" and included "Richard Neutra, Frank Lloyd Wright, Gordon B. Kaufman, Harbin Hunter, Joe Fell, R. M. Schindler, J. M. Davidson, and George Sprague. Some ensemble...."[25]

The new studio was to combine art and technology, lifting the animation art form to new heights, and it was appropriate to engage an architect and designer who was noted for a clean and streamlined style that blended form and functionality to perfection. "To me, it's the first creative campus, something we're really used to now like the Google campus or the Apple campus. Part of that was creating environments that were cohesive for the artist,"

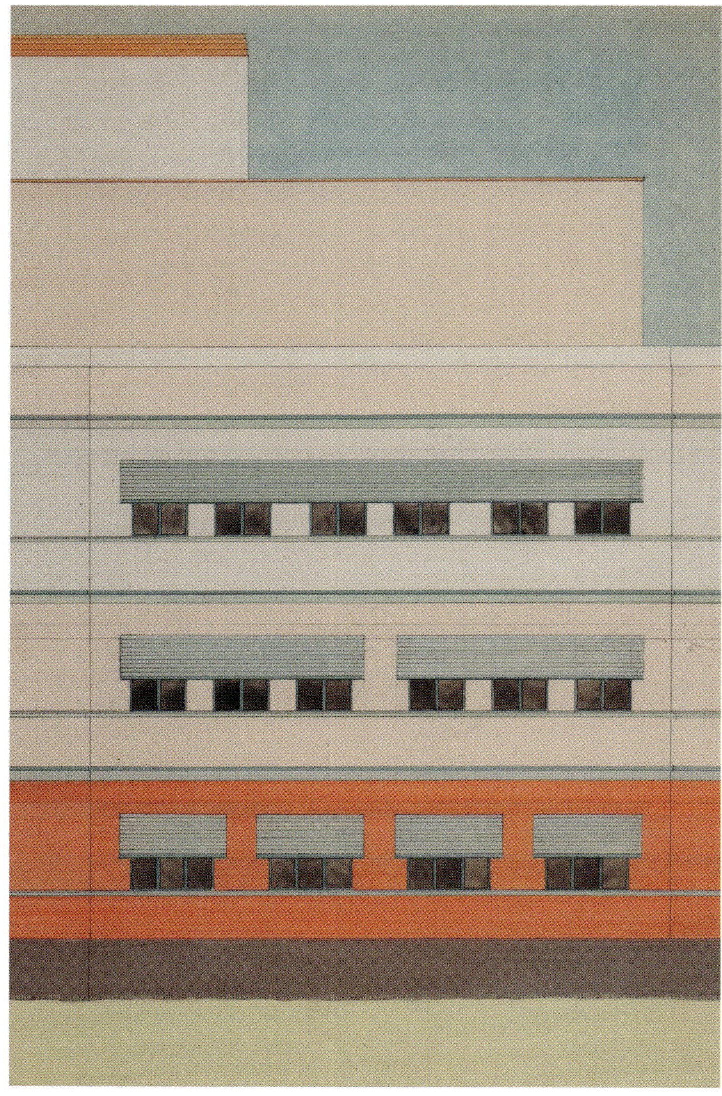

Kem Weber concept painting of desert color scheme elevation for Animation Production Building at The Walt Disney Studios, Burbank, circa. 1939. ©UCSB

said Hahn. "Listening to one old animator tell it, you got a desk, you got a closet, you got a chair, you got a carpet if you were somebody, and that was your space and your setup and happy to have it. It must have been so amazing moving from the Hyperion studio to this place to have all that luxurious furniture to move into."[26] It was amazing decades later for new hires, myself included, fresh out of schools like CalArts to start working at Disney animation on the storied Weber furniture.

Walt for his part left nothing to chance. He discussed every aspect of the new studio and encouraged input from anyone interested in participating in the planning process. He thought through and planned everything. "He went to as much work on that as he did in the creative side of his pictures," recalled producer and director Ben Sharpsteen.[27] Walt used models of the buildings on a site layout to show different possibilities and had night meetings at the studio on Hyperion with staff members. Animator Frank Thomas recalled, "He'd [Walt] say, 'How about if we put the theater here, the Animation Building there, and the restaurant here, the soundstage there, the orchestra stage, the Camera Department, Ink and Paint, Cutting, Process Lab, all those things.' We would move all those models around, then someone would say, 'What do you do in rainy weather?' Then that would spark the discussion of how many rainy days were there typically in Los Angeles, which then led to connecting the Animation and Ink and Paint buildings with an underground tunnel."[28]

I've gone down and walked through that tunnel and it was truly great planning; unfortunately, it was never really used for what it was intended. Instead, it became a storage place and for trysts dubbing it the "tunnel of love." Studio lore has it that Walt himself occasionally went down to the tunnel to flip on the lights and see if he could catch any of his artists during a rendezvous.

The elaborate studio in Burbank was to house some eight hundred employees. It would include new office space for the artists and administration, beauty and barber shops, a coffee shop and restaurant, soundstages, Cutting Building, Processing Laboratory, and workshops.[29] It was billed as a million-dollar home for Mickey Mouse and was Walt's vision of a campus-like utopia for the artists.

Disney legend Ward Kimball, one of Walt's famed Nine Old Men, once joked that Walt Disney's new studio "was the first studio I ever worked in where the furniture all matched, and they took the garbage out every day!" as remembered by Tom Sito, former Disney animator.[30]

Initially many of the employees liked the new campus, but then some felt the "collegiate atmosphere became almost oppressive" and one person thought it looked so nice, "I almost felt like wearing a tie."[31] The new studio complex was clean and ordered in contrast to the "ramshackle" nature of the Hyperion studio, which had a more informal quality that allowed for more impromptu meetings. It was the beginning of an "efficient business"[32] that formalized and refined the animation process melding form and function.

"I think, too, in terms of the idea of form follows function, by thinking about every aspect of the animation process and then deciding to create furniture that supported every single aspect was really important to him," said Sigman-Lowery. Walt could have gone out and bought furniture off the shelf, but that would have been like the Hyperion studio, which he was trying to get away from and improve. "He has the opportunity to create the ideal environment for an animator, for a background artist, for layout and to modify the designs of the desks at which they'd be working so that everything would be within hand's reach," said Sigman-Lowery. "And I think too, by having specific designs for specific functions, it allowed him when he would bring in an artist to work

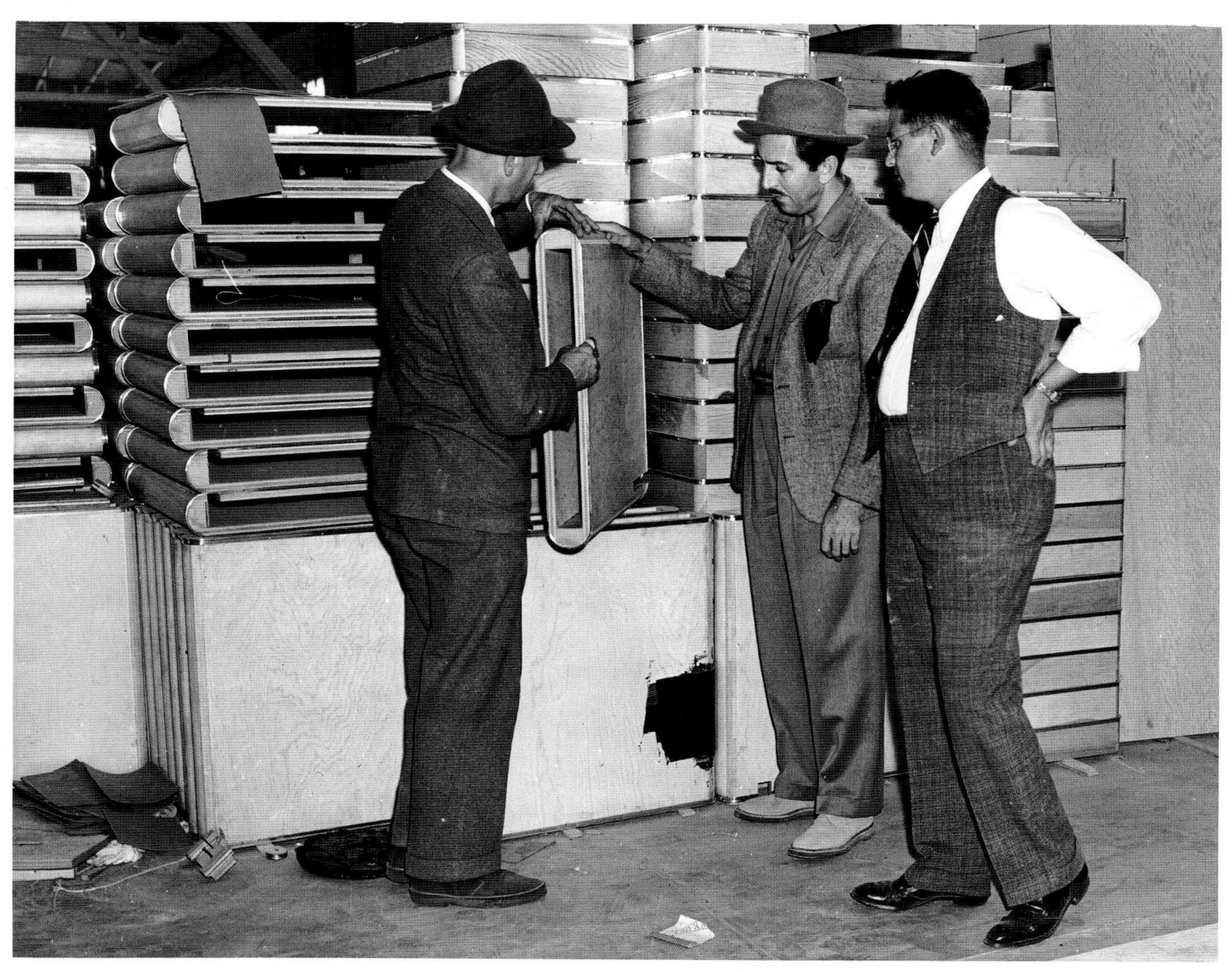

Kem Weber (back to camera) examining furniture support structures with Walt Disney (center) and Howard Petersen (right) at the Petersen Show Case & Fixture Co. in Los Angeles; circa 1939. ©UCSB

at that desk, that artist could actually move into another office and wouldn't have to reinvent his space because it was already there for him."[33]

This was part of the holistic approach to integrating every aspect of the new studio including the furniture design that fit within, and creating the perfect space for an artist to do their particular discipline. The brilliance to this approach was that Weber was able to design custom furniture that was at the same time standardized yet still customizable to the individual artists. Walt asked Frank Thomas, one of his top animators, to help design an animation desk based on his experience. At Walt's request, that design was then refined by Weber, then a prototype desk was fabricated, which was used by Thomas while still working on *Pinocchio* (1940) at the Hyperion studio before moving to the new studio complex in Burbank. Every aspect of the new specialized furniture was reviewed and tinkered with before the final construction drawings were created and the furniture manufactured. Even then, there were visits to the company that was making the desks and further discussions by Weber and Walt.

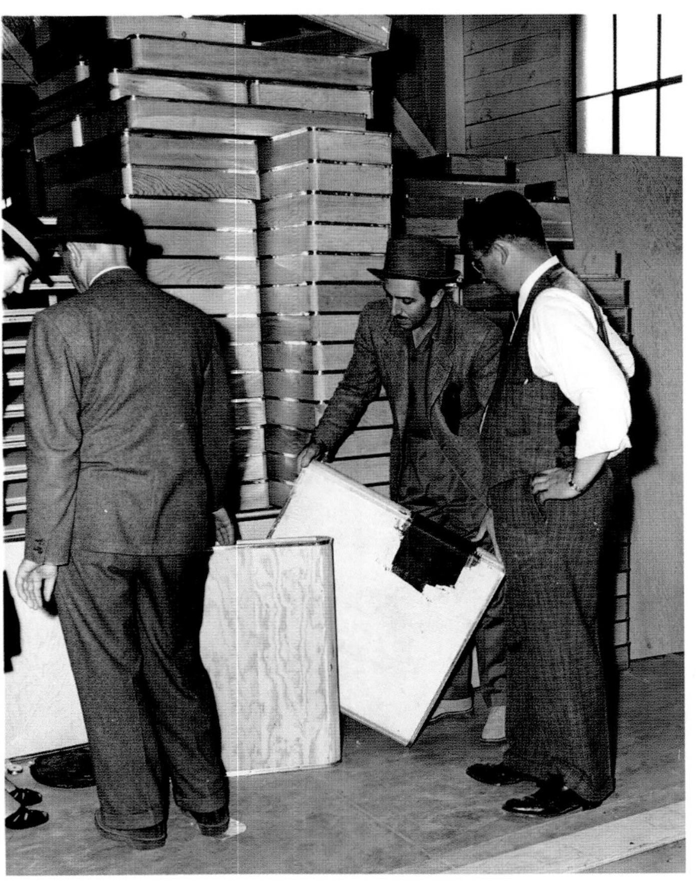

Kem Weber (back to camera) examining furniture under construction with Walt Disney (center) and Howard Petersen (right) at the Petersen Show Case & Fixture Co. in Los Angeles; circa 1939. ©UCSB

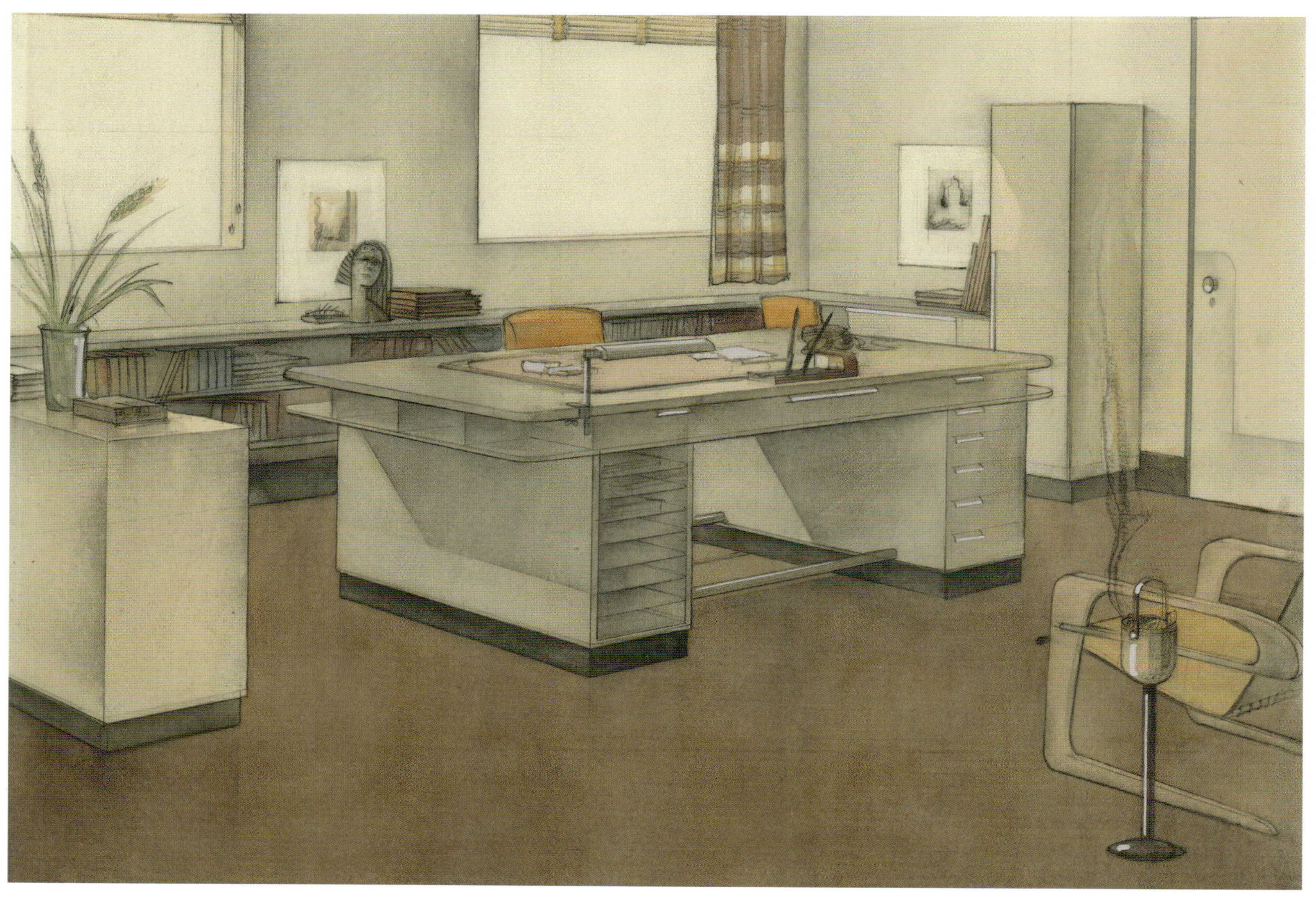

Kem Weber concept design illustration for large director's desk office; circa. 1939. ©UCSB

CHAPTER 4
THE DIRECTOR'S DESK

"If a cluttered desk is a sign of a cluttered mind, of what, then, is an empty desk a sign?"
-Albert Einstein, Theoretical Physicist

The director's desk was a unique piece of furniture and very different from the animation production desk, which is discussed in chapter 8. There were two styles of director desks made, officially named the Large Director's Center Table, UNIT No.15, and a Small Director's Center Table, UNIT No.15-A. Both tables were 48 inches wide with the small table 72 inches long and the large table 92 inches long. In other words, the small director's table had 24 square feet of surface area and the larger version had 32 square feet of surface area. These were big desks, heavy, with plenty of surface space on which to spread out drawings or pan-sized layouts. I often saw these desks just covered with animation scenes and artwork of all kinds.

The major difference between these two director's "desks" were the number of drawers and storage space on the perimeter. The smaller desk had a drawer, slide-out pencil tray and shelves on the left side only, whereas the larger desk had the same drawer, pencil tray and shelves with an additional set of drawers, pencil tray and shelves on the right side. Both desks also had a center drawer and open cubby areas on either side just below the tabletop. These desks were designed so that a director could sit on either side of the desk, or it could be shared by two directors or even story artists. This desk design allowed for the ease of passing drawings across the desk to your colleague as a story idea was being developed.

There was a separate Director's Movable Desk, UNIT No.16, which had an animation disc and two foldout tops that, when closed, hid the disc from view and could be used as an occasional table. The animation disc was a circular metal disc with a rectangular white glass pane in the center. At the top and bottom of the glass were moveable peg bars that had two oblong pegs and one round peg. Those pegs corresponded to holes in the bottom of the animation paper. This was how multiple

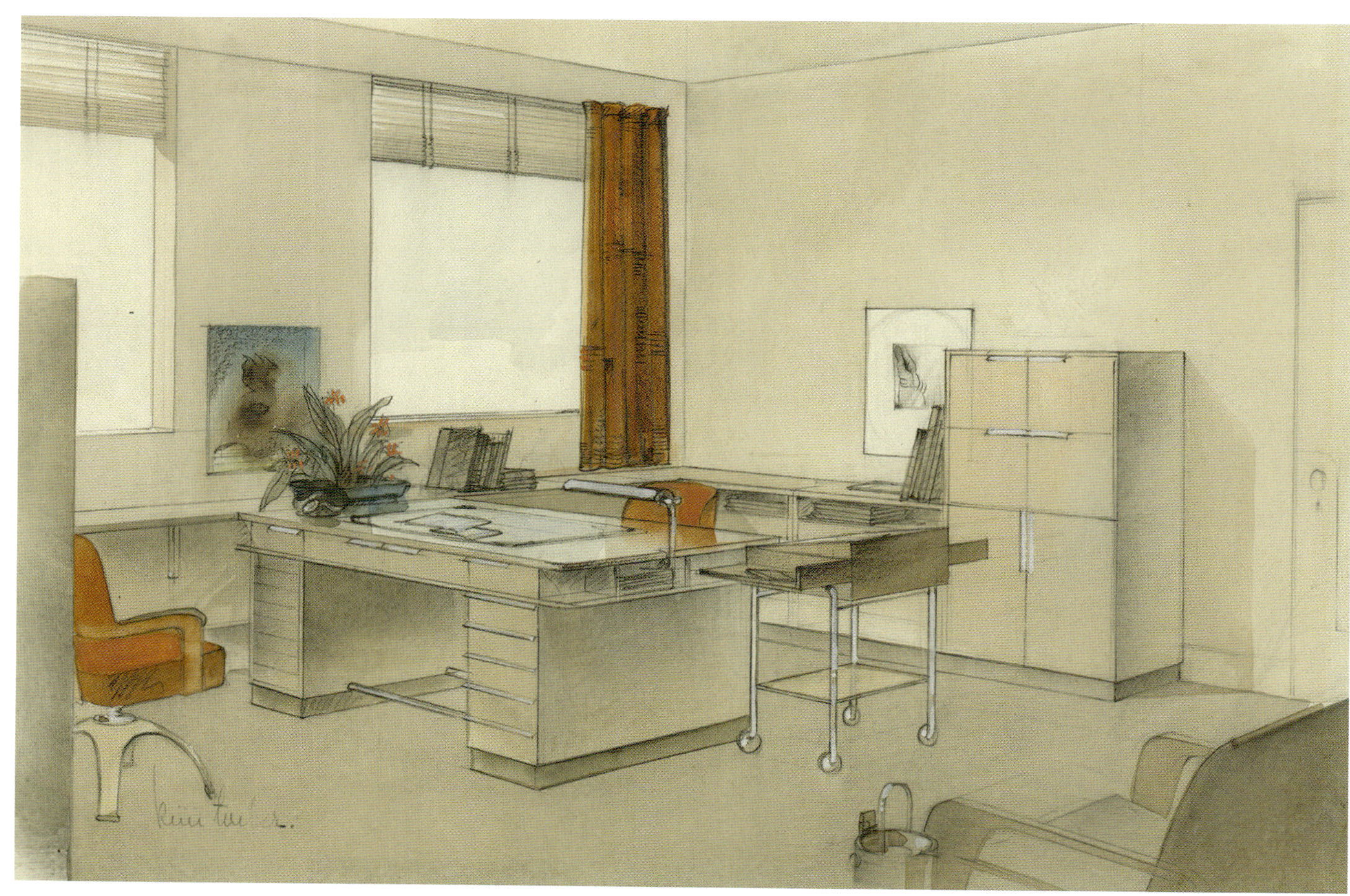

Kem Weber concept illustration for small director's desk office with portable animation disc unit. circa 1939. ©UCSB

drawings stayed registered to one another. The overall unit had a small cubby underneath the disc to hold animation paper and a storage shelf further down below that. The entire unit was on wheels for the director to pull up next to his desk and do drawings or animation poses as needed. It was completely portable and with the top closed measured 26 inches by 26 inches; open, the unit measured 26 inches by 52 inches.

"So I had a director's desk; and of course the director's desk, those were like the 747s. One of the reasons they were so big was for layouts. If you had a layout that was big, a pan, you could actually spread it out, look at the whole thing and it just made sense that way," said John Musker, director of *The Little Mermaid* (1989), *Aladdin* (1992), *Moana* (2016), and many others. Musker's desk was one that was usually piled with drawings, reference books, and so much stuff that it was hard to see the desktop surface.[34]

Aside from layouts, back in the early days of animation, the directors referenced bar sheets, which had the dialogue and music transcribed on horizontal sheets of paper taped together end to end. The bar sheets were used for the overall timing of scenes within a film and could be unfolded on the expansive top of the director's desk. The exposure sheets were more compact and manageable; they were the road map for the animation in a scene and had the dialogue and music beats also indicated on them. The bar sheets became an outdated method as the process evolved and digital technology began to emerge in animation. Eventually, the bar sheets fell out of favor at Disney and the animation industry. The sprawling tabletop of the director's desk was still perfect for oversized artwork or to be able to arrange several large layouts at the same time to discuss continuity. But with any size surface area, it could be easily filled with clutter.

"I'm a pack rat by nature, and because they had so many shelves, both open and closed shelves and cubbyholes on the side, you could put story sketch pads there and drawings. For years, I carried drawings around in the drawers," said Musker.[35] "Sketches I had done, character design ideas, even on *The Black Cauldron* [1985]. I couldn't throw these away and I put those in a drawer and they would move with me for a period of twenty years just staying in that drawer."[36]

These director's desks were not used solely by the directors, either; some story artists worked together with one on either side of the desk. "On *Beauty and the Beast* [1991], I sat across from Roger Allers in a shared office. And he had an old director's desk with its big flat top where two story people could work,"[37] said Brenda Chapman, story artist and director of Disney/Pixar *Brave* (2012). "His desk was covered with all kinds of tchotchkes, and I just loved that desk. It was just beautiful."[38] They worked at a small director's desk, which had one set of drawers on the side and similar cubbies and open spaces around the perimeter of the desk just below the tabletop. Allers "bequeathed"[39] that desk to Chapman when he was named as one of the directors on *The Lion King* (1994) and got the large director's desk. "So that was my desk all through *Lion King* and I just loved it. It was just a beautiful desk and so much fun to work on. I worked on that for a couple of years," said Chapman.[40]

Disney Legend Winston Hibler had a director's desk in his office for many years. "I remember it vividly," said Chris Hibler, his grandson. "My brother Hunt and I used to visit our grandfather at the studio every few weeks because our dad worked there as well."[41] Chris's father, Christopher Hibler, worked at Disney as an assistant director and film director for many years. "I remember that chrome bar underneath his director's desk. I can still see it today. We used to hide under his desk and my brother would hit me with that bar. Yes, I saw that furniture every time we were at the studio," said Hibler. The furniture was so unique and memorable that it made an impression on a young boy visiting his grandfather. "It's the only furniture I ever dealt with that had a soul. It had an energy that came off of it," said Hibler.[42]

The director's desks were so large that when the Animation Department was moved off the Disney studio lot to a warehouse in Glendale, space became a premium and the director's desk took up nearly an entire office with just enough room to walk around it, along with maybe a small sofa. It was like the scene in the film *Sunset Boulevard* (1950), when William Holden's character, Joe Gillis, says, "You used to be big." And Gloria Swanson's character, Norma Desmond, responds, "I *am* big. It's the *pictures* that got small." Well, the office space at Walt Disney Animation Studios began to get small and the director's desk was one of the first to become impractical for its sheer size. The office space got even smaller in the remodeled Roy E. Disney Animation Building.

Opposite page:
Joe Grant (seated in a fabric covered Air Line chair in the foreground) at a large director's desk opposite Dick Huemer (with pipe) with character designer James Bodrero standing and Dunbar "Dun" Roman seated to the left looking at camera during production of Fantasia (1940). Note the drawer details and open cubby on the right side. Also, Grant is resting one foot on the ubiquitous chrome pipe footrest under the center of the desk.; circa 1940. Photo by Baskerville. ©UCSB

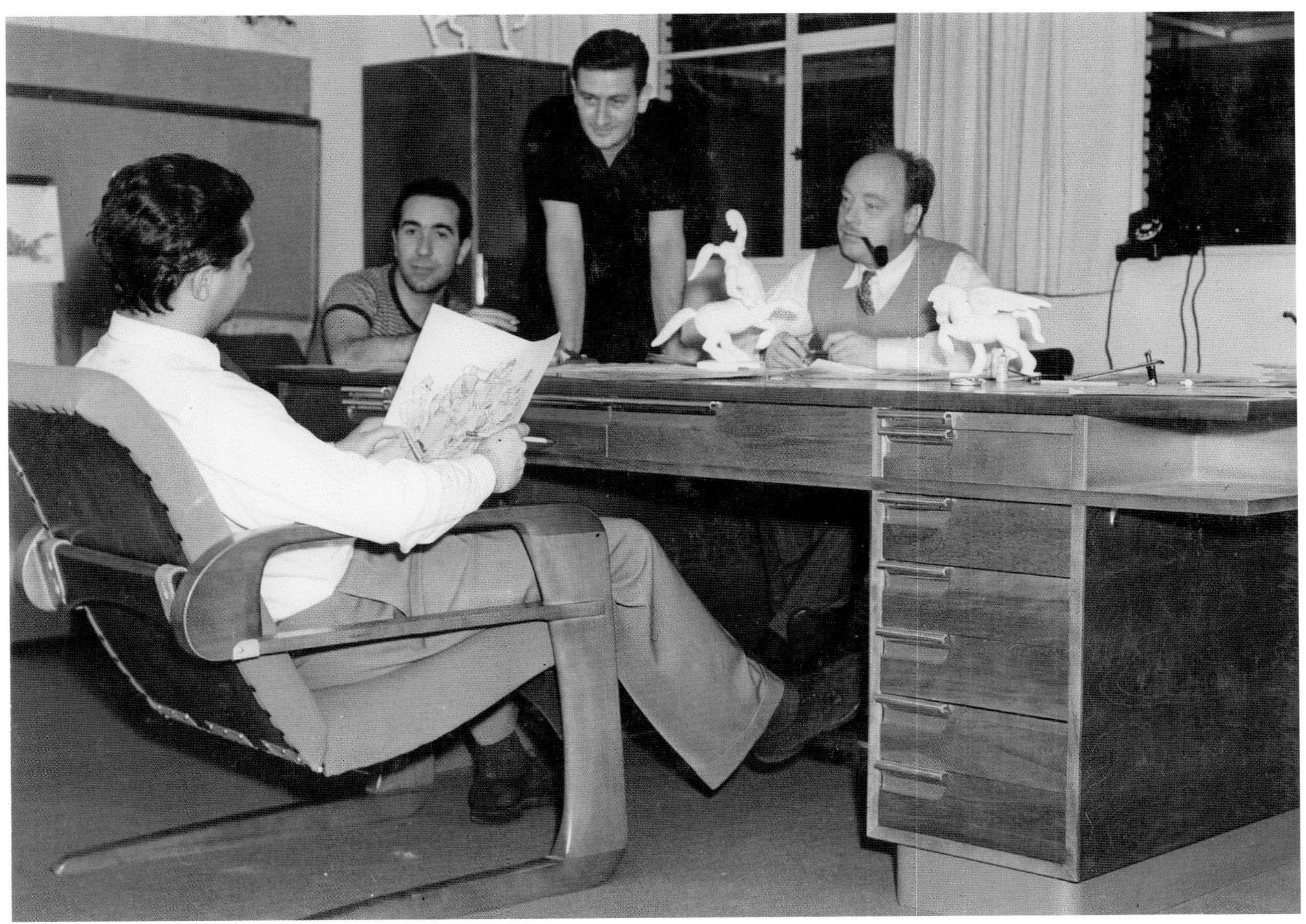

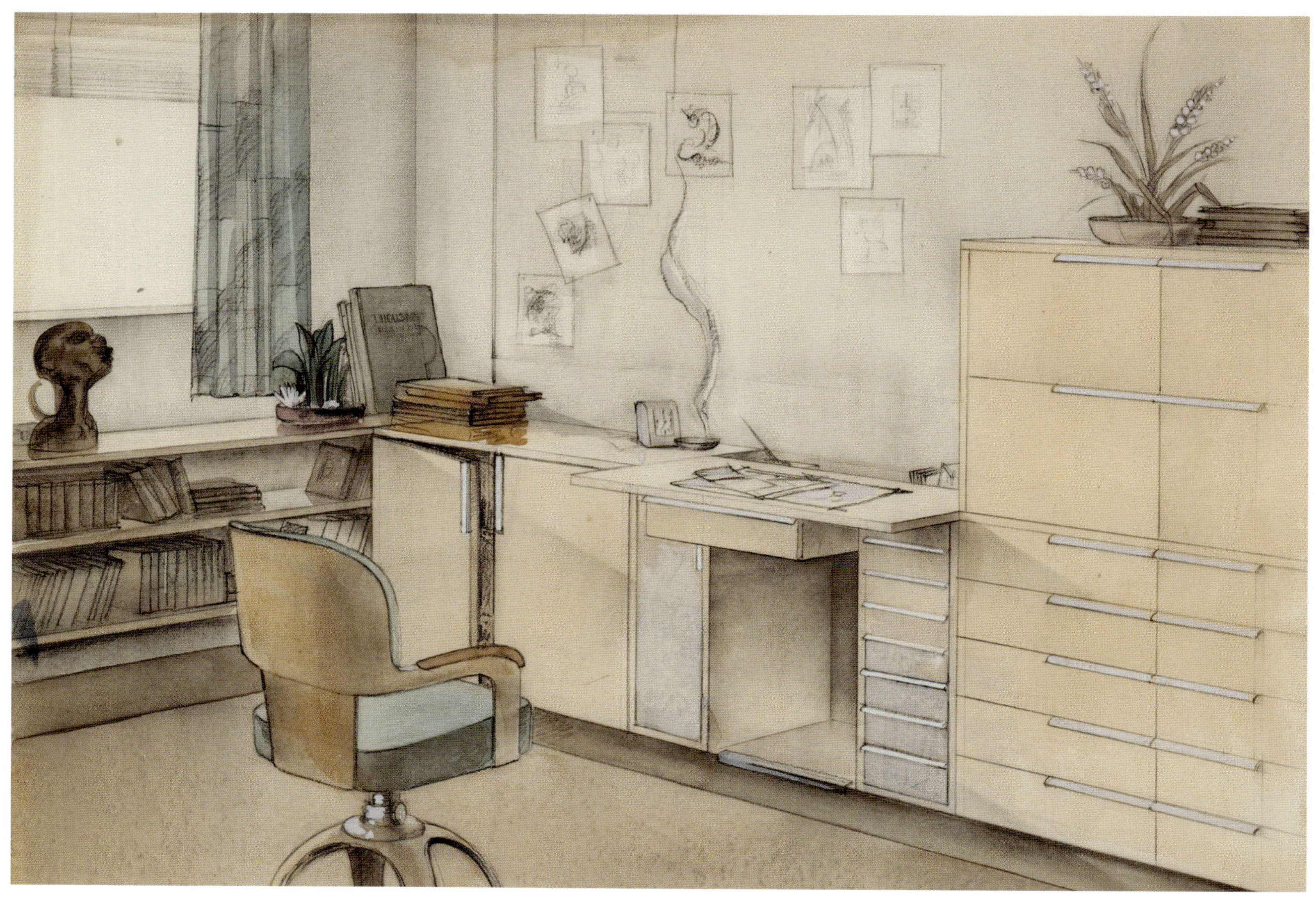

Kem Weber concept design illustration for story artist's desk and office; ©UCSB

CHAPTER 5
THE STORY DESK

> "I stand upon my desk to remind myself that we must constantly look at things in a different way."
>
> -Robin Williams, Actor/Comedian

Officially noted on the blueprints as the Story Men's Sketch Desk, UNIT No.21 looks much like a regular desk in a neutral position of having the tabletop flat. What was unique about this desk was that the top surface of the desk was adjustable, similar to the drawing board on the animator's and assistant's desks. The story sketch desk originally had a circular hole in the drawing board to accommodate a disc, but many artists eventually had a smooth Masonite surface added, which covered the hole, so they could draw and work on the entire surface without the need for a backlight. Masonite is a hard, smooth surface, free of wood grain or roughness, ideal to draw on. The desk also had a drawer with a cabinet below it, both with the standard recessed painted channel and metal drawer pulls on the right side, as well as the adjustable stainless steel bar footrest underneath. The footprint of the desk measured 30 inches by 56 inches. To me, these were simple, clean, and compact desks that were ideal for doing the individual story sketches.

"I always felt how cool it is that Walt Disney with Kem Weber sat down with, I'm sure, some of the artists and figured out what is it you need,"[43] said Jorgen Klubien, a former Disney and Pixar story artist. "You need light, so they designed the building for it. They designed all this furniture. It looked nice and I just thought it was beautiful."[44]

Before the introduction of digital technology in animation, the story artists used 5 by 7 inch pads of paper to storyboard out the films, with each panel or series of panels representing a scene in the film. All the story sketch artist needed was a surface to draw on and having the story sketch desk allowed for them to adjust the tilt of the drawing board to a comfortable angle that suited their needs. The desk provided for a little over 11.5 square feet of surface area, which was plenty of space even if the story artist created an oversized drawing.

As with the animator's desks, there was a sense of pride to having a desk that belonged to one of the early Disney Legends. "I have Ben Sharpsteen's story desk here at my house,"[45] said Klubien. "It has the label on the back still and I checked with Dave Smith [chief archivist emeritus, Walt Disney Archives] as to who it belonged to originally, 'cause he can place it in the different offices, and he said that was from Ben Sharpsteen's office."[46] As with many of the Weber desks for the Disney Studios, there are tables, serial-numbered metal tags, and even names of those who once occupied the desk written inconspicuously in marker on the underside of the drawing board. Sharpsteen, a Disney Legend, was a supervising director on *Pinocchio* (1940), directed on *Dumbo* (1941), and produced many of the True-Life Adventures documentaries at the studio.

Aside from the adjustable Masonite drawing board, the story sketch desk was a basic desk that served its purpose well. Of all the Weber-designed desks, this one in particular could have just as easily been an off-the-shelf solution. But if you are building a utopian campus with that holistic design philosophy of a leading designer like Kem Weber, nothing can be off the shelf. Everything must be designed cohesively to work with other furniture, the interiors, and the overall design of the facility. Although there is anecdotal evidence that some of the artists thought the new furniture was too clean, too sterile, and even as it aged and got banged up—lived in—they preferred the ramshackle, funkiness of the Hyperion furniture. "So I was more like just in awe of it all and never could put together how you could not have loved this furniture, you know?"[47] said Klubien.

There has been at least one example of the Weber Story Men's Sketch Desk, UNIT No.21, that turned up in an auction. The desk, including the original tabletop with white glass disc, sold on May 22, 2016, for $1,250 at the Los Angeles Modern Auctions.[48]

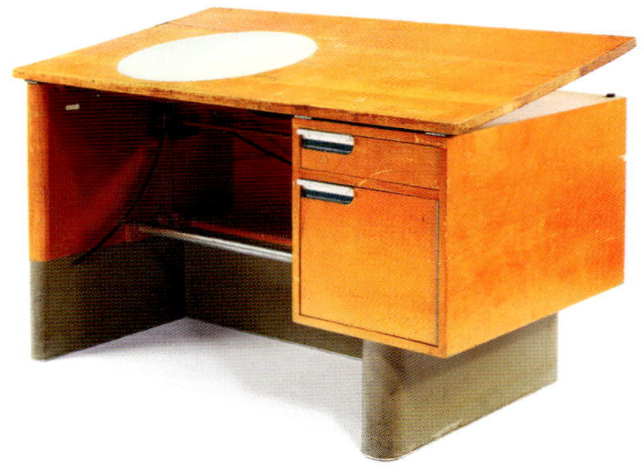

The Kem Weber story desk was designed with a white translucent disc, but some artists covered the surface with quarter inch masonite (see opposite page). This allowed the artist to utilize the entire drawing surface of the desk. Photograph by Los Angeles Modern Auctions

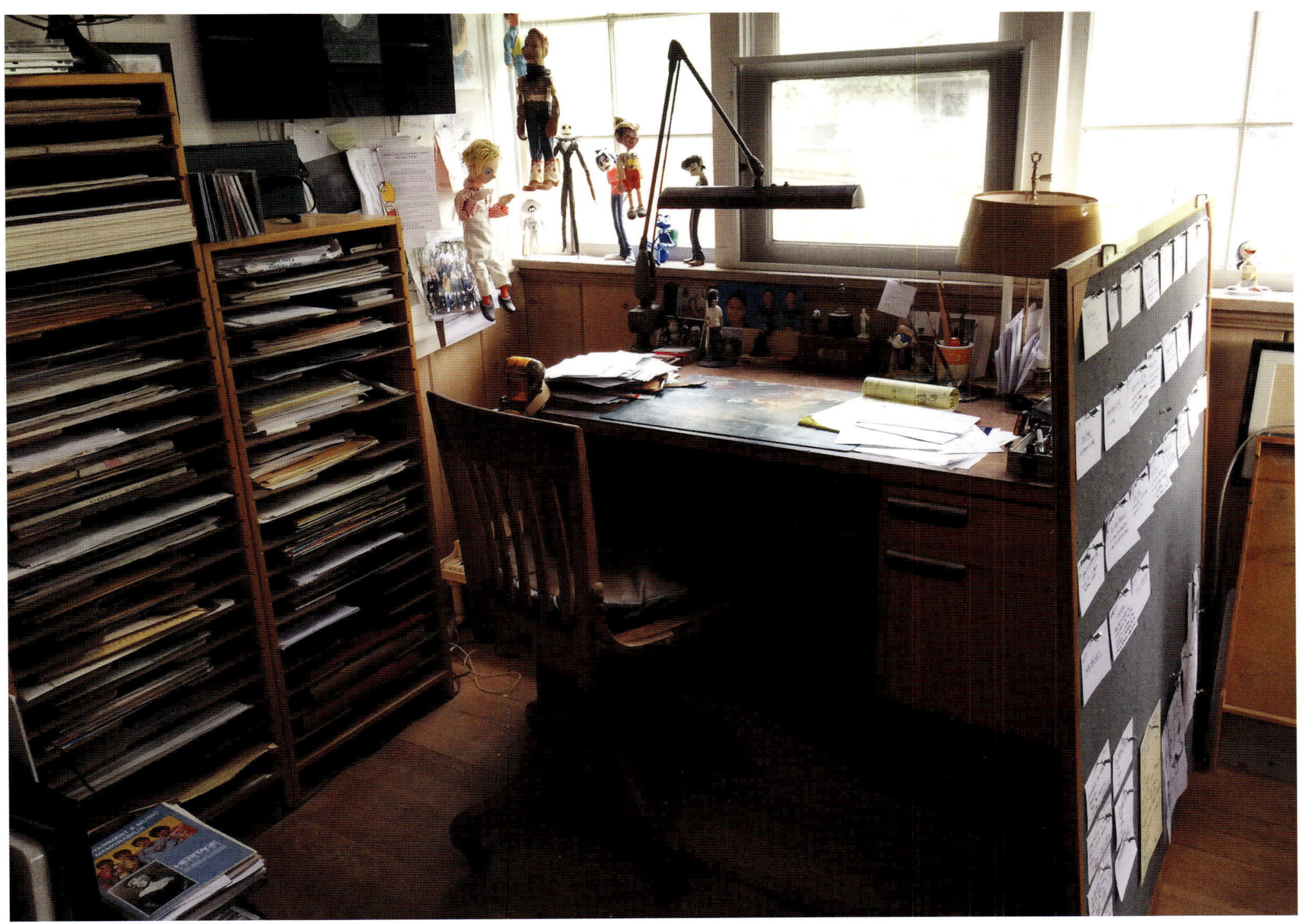

Ben Sharpsteen's Kem Weber-designed story desk; photo courtesy of Jorgen Klubien.

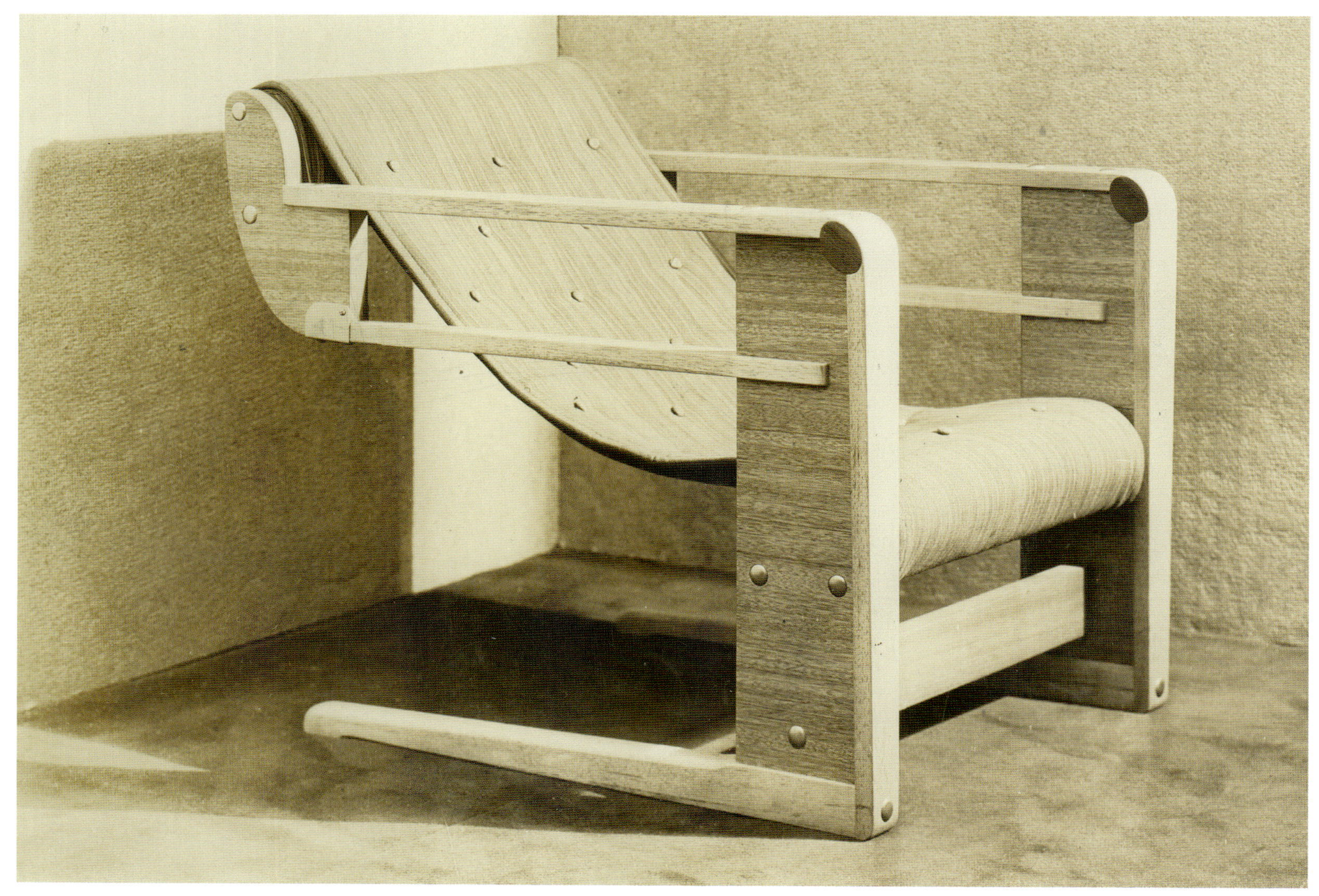

The Kem Weber prototype to his Air Line Chair; 1929. ©UCSB

CHAPTER 6
THE AIR LINE CHAIR

"So-called traditional or period influence in American family life will die and the beauty of modern progress live."

-Kem Weber (ca. 1929-30)

In 1929, Weber developed the first prototype for his now famed Air Line chair and continued to refine the design until he had a viable version by 1935. As Weber described it, "the 'Airline' [sic] chair is a product of a forgotten wood construction. Laminated bows were used by the Egyptians. It is the most powerful method known to combine strength and resiliency." The chair was the product of multiple iterations over a several years experimenting with wood tension for practical use. "In 1929 the first effort in this direction was exhibited in the Brooklyn Museum under the name Bentlock. Since then, many models have been made and discarded and the present result is a practical and, to my judgment, beautiful,"[49] said Weber.

It's probably the first example of a piece of furniture intended to be assembled by the consumer.[50] The later version of this chair was constructed from plywood parts for home assembly. The design featured a raked profile and cantilevered structure that gave it a distinctive look that implied "a visual energy akin to an airplane."[51] On form and function of the Air Line Chair, Peter Loughrey, an expert on mid-century furniture and a frequent contributor to *Antiques Roadshow* on PBS, noted that "it has to be a balance. But always starting with the idea of stripping away and reducing ornament and precedent. A four-legged chair is not necessary. You have to throw out everything you know about chair design when you get to a chair like the Air Line Chair, for example. That only comes from a design philosophy where you're willing to throw out everything that comes before it."[52] This is precisely what Weber was after: a new design that had strength that was "way out of proportion to the lightness of the individual sizes of the parts used."[53] It was about the balance between form and function, with form always following function. Weber stated that "the urge supporting my persistence was the desire to make a comfortable, hygienic, and beautiful chair inexpensively."[54] Having had an Air Line Chair in my office at Disney for decades, I can say without hesitation that it is a comfortable chair. I spent many hours stretched out in mine thinking about a scene of animation or taking a nap.

The Air Line Chair was made up of two sideway U-shaped arm and leg assemblies that were made from laminated hickory. These were connected by two wood stretchers that attached to both sides. A hinged plywood back and seat then attached to the top stretcher while resting on the lower stretcher, which allowed an individual to recline easily by sliding the seat forward while the back remained attached to the upper stretcher with flexible leather straps. The chair had soft curves with strong horizontal lines, and the long, tapered feet of the two main sections that gave it the clean curves and taper of aircraft design. That inspired Weber to name it the Air Line Chair. Although there are references to the chair as one word, Airline or hyphenated as Air-line, it is actually two words, Air Line, based on Weber's original blueprints for the chair. That said, most museums and references indicate it as one—Airline.

Weber saw demand increasing for lower-priced furniture, but his concept of home assembly was ahead of its time. "There are a great number of modernistic arrangements in the various stores, either complicated in construction and expensive, or too cheaply built," wrote Weber. "What we really want are good beds, substantial chairs and tables, and cabinets which we can depend on."[55] He envisioned his Air Line Chair would be available in a flat box that the consumer could purchase at a reasonable price and carry home for easy assembly. It weighed some twenty-seven pounds in a thin box that had a built-in handle for easy carrying.[56]

Weber went so far as to write a detailed description of the functionality and construction of the chair to Lawrence Kocher, managing editor of *Architectural Record* magazine, and said, "The two upper horizontal rails are not constructed as a solid frame, but get their strength through a logical transformation of stresses. The rear block of the upper rail is structurally solid with the rail and moves down with it in action. The distance between the lower end of the block, where the second rail is located, and the front of the chair thus becomes shorter...This principle in connection with the bow construction of the hickory lamination...gives the chair its strength way out of proportion to the lightness of the individual sizes of the parts used. It has withstood the most severe tests, and I am now expecting to get the correct breaking point, which I believe to be over a [sic] 1000 pounds."[57] In the article that eventually appeared in the magazine, Weber writes about the flexible structure of the chair design to move with the sitter: "There is an open space between the lower rail and the block to allow free movement. With a pressure of about 300 pounds the space is closed, transforming the breaking stress into tension on the upper rail and compression on the lower."[58]

Weber set up the Airline Furniture Company to manufacture and distribute the chair. He hired a model and photographed her putting the chair together out of the box. He also produced sales and assembly instructions:

> 1. The chair is sold boxed. As shown above. Box and chair together weigh less than thirty pounds. The box is smart in appearance, durable and has rope handles for carrying. The label on the end of the box is stamped to signify the color scheme of enclosed chair.
> The customer has none of the usual delay in delivery, instead carrys [sic] the chair home with her as she would a suitcase.
> 2. The chair is securely packed and protected in the box, yet is easily unpacked for assembling. Upon removal of chair from the box the buyer

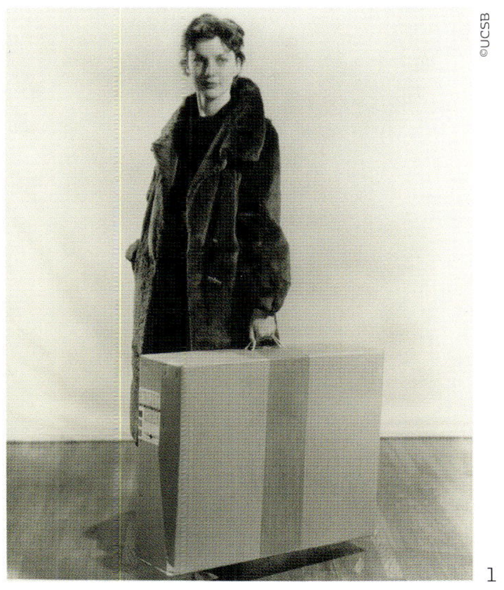

1

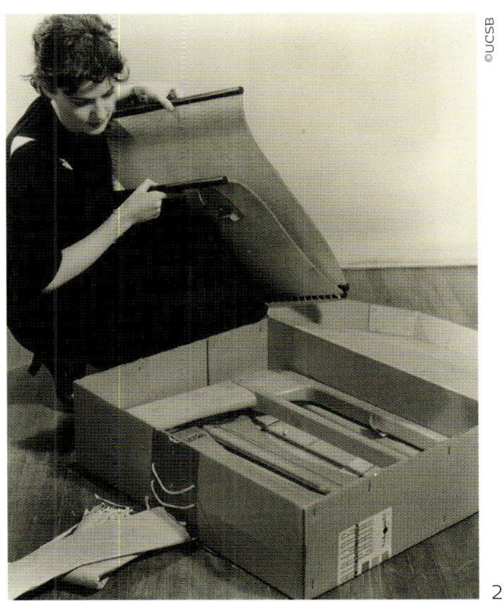

2

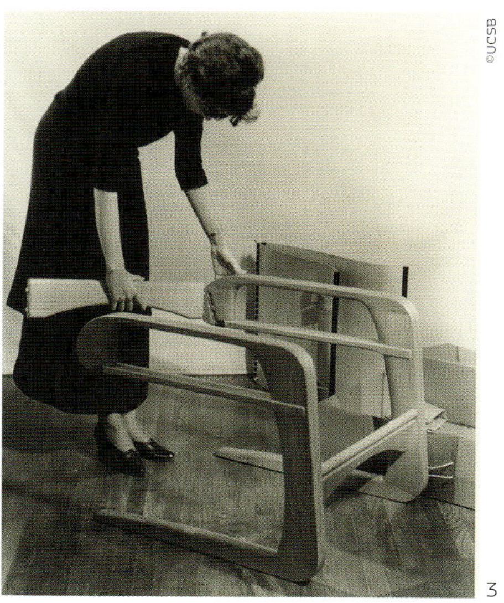
©UCSB
3

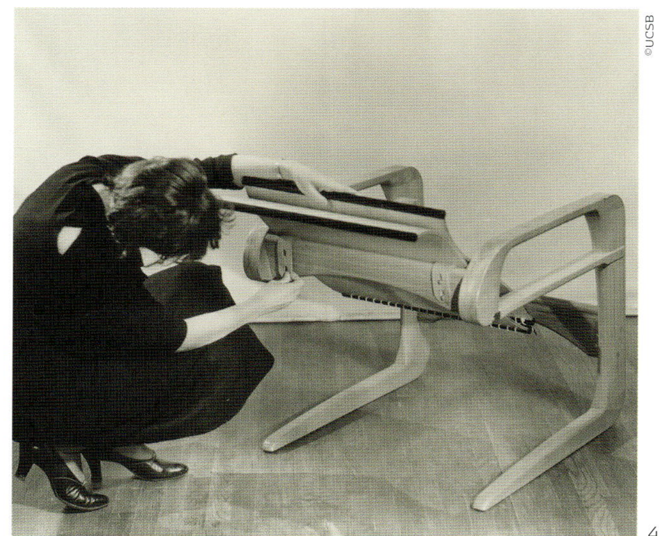
©UCSB
4

has a box suitable for a hundred different uses-storing articles, transporting blankets to the beach, etc.

3. In assembling, the cross members are first slipped into the slots in the sides of the chair. These joints are self-tightening thru use.

4. Next, the back is hooked into place on the back cross member. The seat unfolded over the lower cross member. The cushions are snapped into place and the chair is ready for use. Thus in less than five minutes the customer has been able to assemble her chair in any place she desires.

5. This chair incorporates a new patented construction principle which insures greater strength and flexibility in light construction.

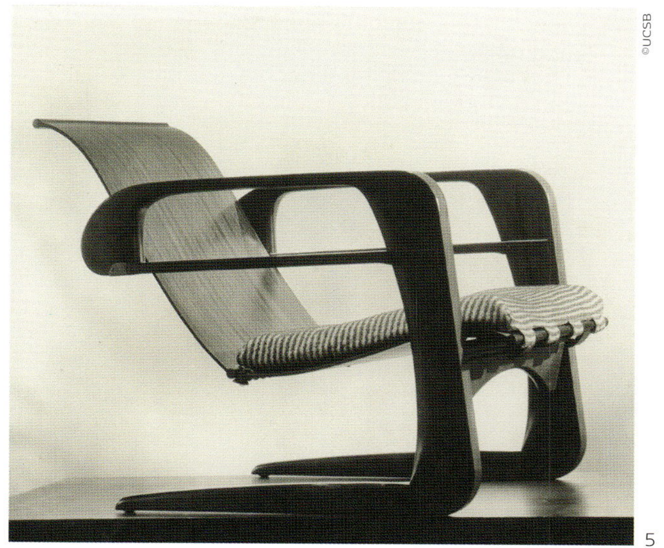
©UCSB
5

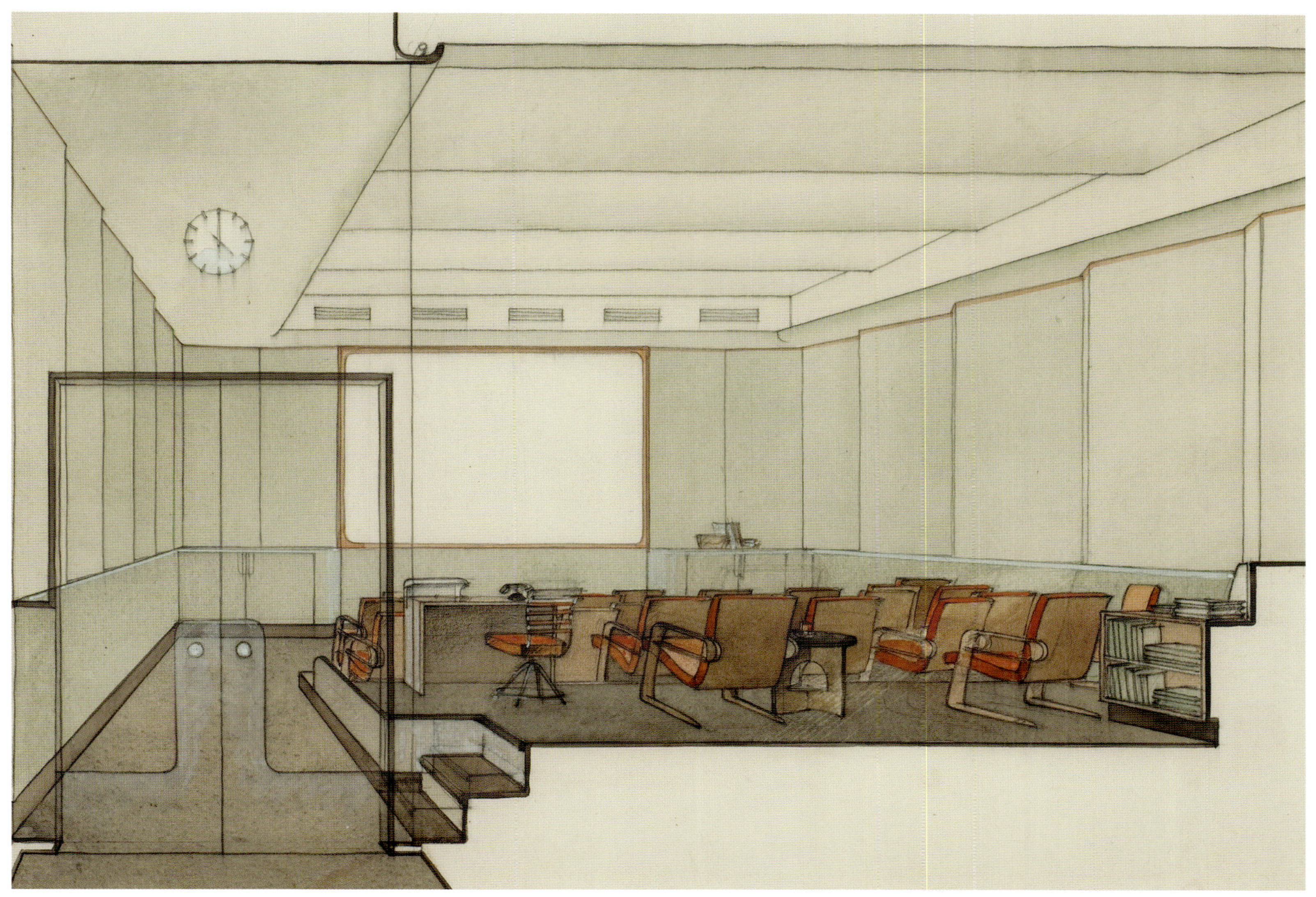

Kem Weber concept illustration of The Walt Disney Studios Animation Production Building projection room featuring his Air Line Chairs for theater seating. ©UCSB

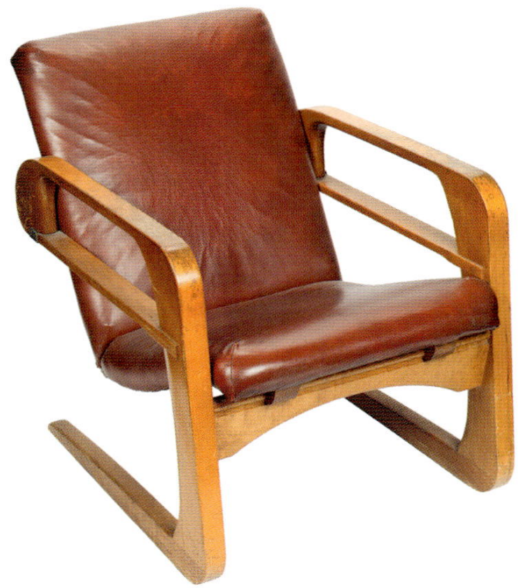

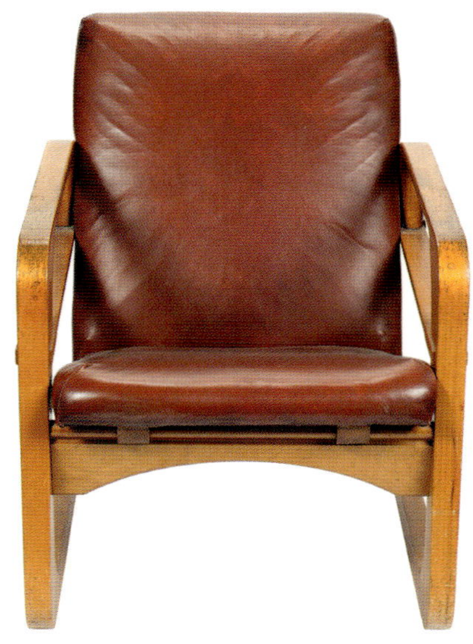

Left and right: The Disney Studio version of the Air Line Chair with seat and back cushions covered in automobile Naugahyde. Photo credit: Heritage Auctions, HA.com

There were even preorders for the chair after it was featured in various design periodicals and newspapers, including *Architectural Record*, the *I, the Chicago Tribune Home Section*, and *Creative Design* in 1935.

Although the Air Line Chair was not created for the Disney Studios complex in 1939, Weber was able to sell two hundred of the chairs to Walt. That was out of approximately three hundred total Air Line Chairs manufactured. Weber shrewdly used the chairs in his concept sketches and paintings for the new studio production building screening rooms. These were chairs that were padded, originally covered with cloth and fully assembled. The cloth covering proved to wear out quickly and the chairs were later recovered in synthetic leather known as Naugahyde, which is a rubber-like composite material over a knit-fabric backing that is used extensively in automobile and furniture upholstery. I can tell you from first-hand experience that the Naugahyde wore very well over the years and had a nice sheen to it as it aged.

By the 1970s, the chairs were considered to be out of fashion and no longer stylish, and were stacked in the basement of the Animation Production Building at the studio lot. The padded seat/back pieces detached from

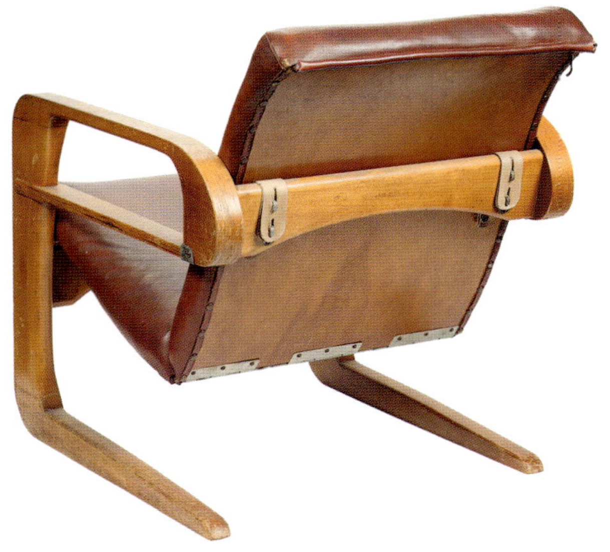

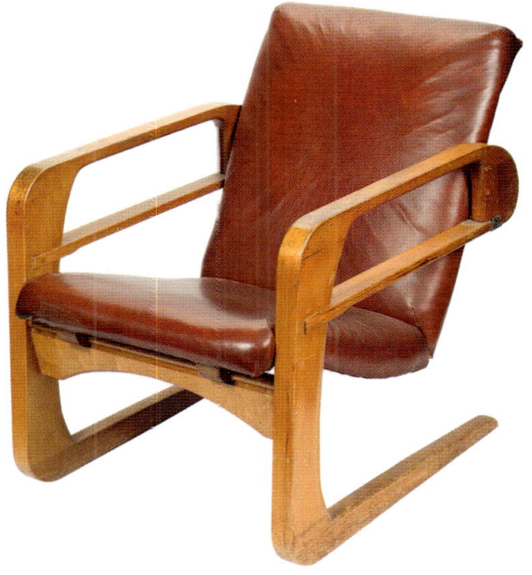

the wood frame of the chairs and piled one on top of another. Eventually those chairs began to come back out of the basement and into animators' offices once they became "cool" again. In the latter part of the twentieth century, the Air Line Chair was one of the most desirable pieces of furniture to have in your office.

One story artist who was in a tiny office that didn't have room for a desk and the four-foot by eight-foot storyboards that she was pinning story sketches to used the Air Line Chair effectively. "All I needed really was one of the Weber chairs and a drawing board," said Brenda Chapman, story artist and Academy Award-winning director of Disney/Pixar *Brave* (2012). "And that's what I used and then I had my storyboards around me 'cause the room was so small that it's, like, well, I don't need a desk. I just need paper and pencils and pushpins. And I loved it, it was the most comfortable chair to sit in and it was just the right angle to just do everything."[59]

The Air Line Chair not only became a prized piece of furniture for the artists but also an important part of their work day. It was a comfortable recliner for a lunchtime catnap or to sit in while thinking about or discussing a scene. A number of the chairs "disappeared" over the years or were given away until one sold at a furniture auction for thousands of dollars. Then the studio tagged all the remaining chairs, and they became even more of a status symbol at the studio. As artists left and the chairs went back to the warehouse, many were redistributed to executives on the studio lot.

The value continued to rise as several more Air Line Chairs sold, one for $9,000[60] in 2003, then breaking through the $10,000 price barrier for a hammer price of $11,250[61] in 2013 and then another sold for $17,500[62] in 2017. The value of these chairs has risen in direct correlation with the resurgence of interest in the mid-century design period.

As of this writing, there are approximately one hundred fifteen Air Line Chairs of the original two hundred still at The Walt Disney Company. Most of the Air Line Chairs are in the Disney Studios inventory with some at Walt Disney Imagineering and elsewhere in the company. Some of those chairs have been refinished and reupholstered for executive offices. When the studio became aware of the increased value and collectability of the Air Line Chairs, each one was branded with a tracking number with an annual inventory conducted as to the location of each chair.[63]

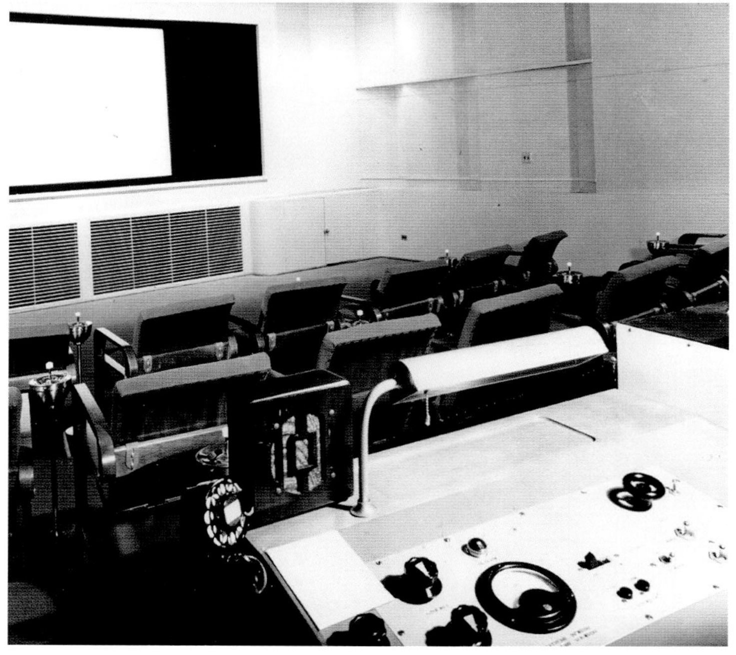

Top left: Projection room featuring Air Line Chairs, circa 1939. Photo by Baskerville. ©UCSB.

Opposite page: Detail of Animation Production Building Projection room featuring the Air Line Chairs for theater seating . Note that chairs are covered in fabric, which wore out quickly and was replaced with automobile upholstery Naugahyde. It is worth pointing out the amount of ashtrays dotted throughout the screening room, which indicates how common tobacco use was during that time period. Fortunately, the facilities are now smoke free. circa 1939. Photo by Baskerville. ©UCSB

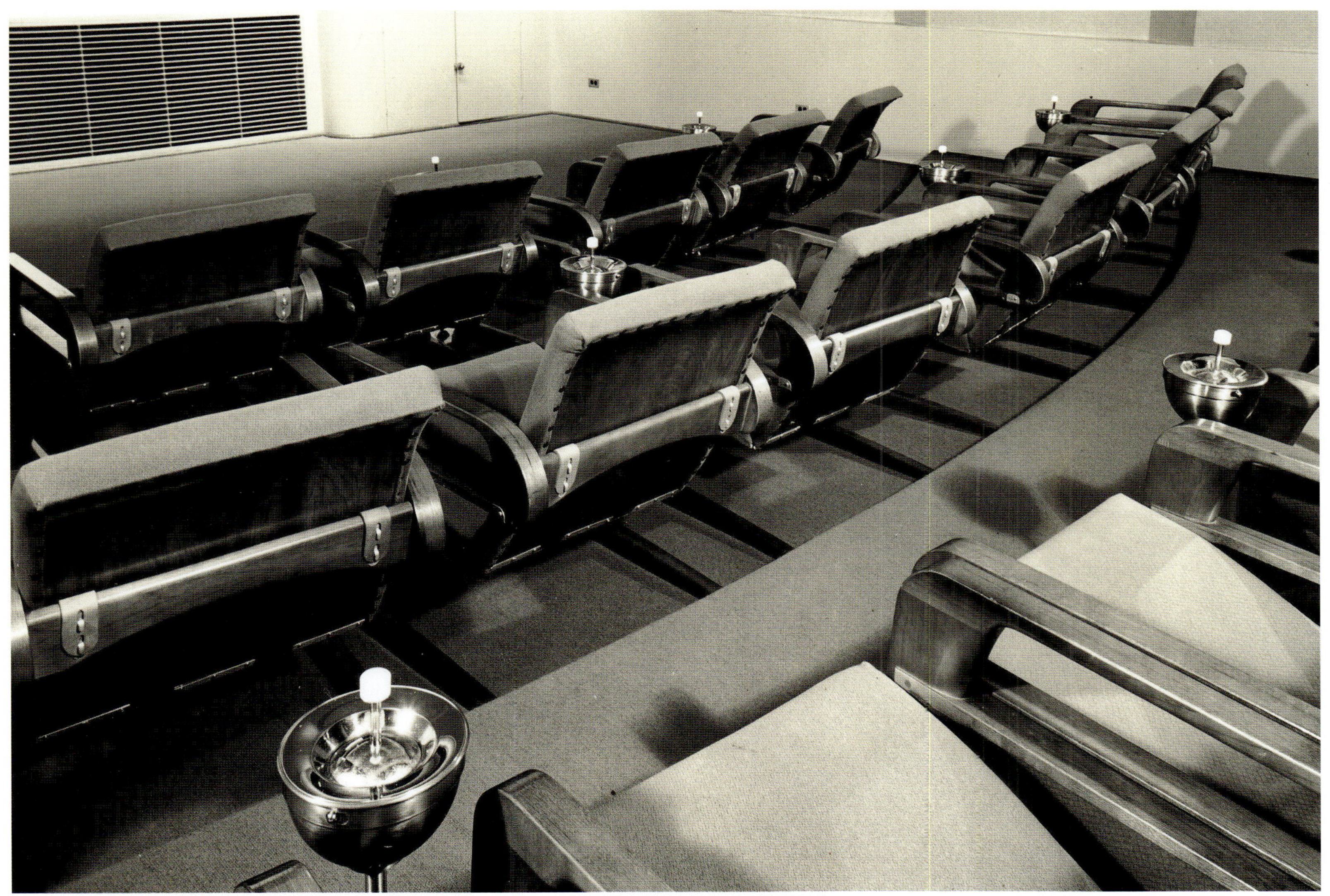

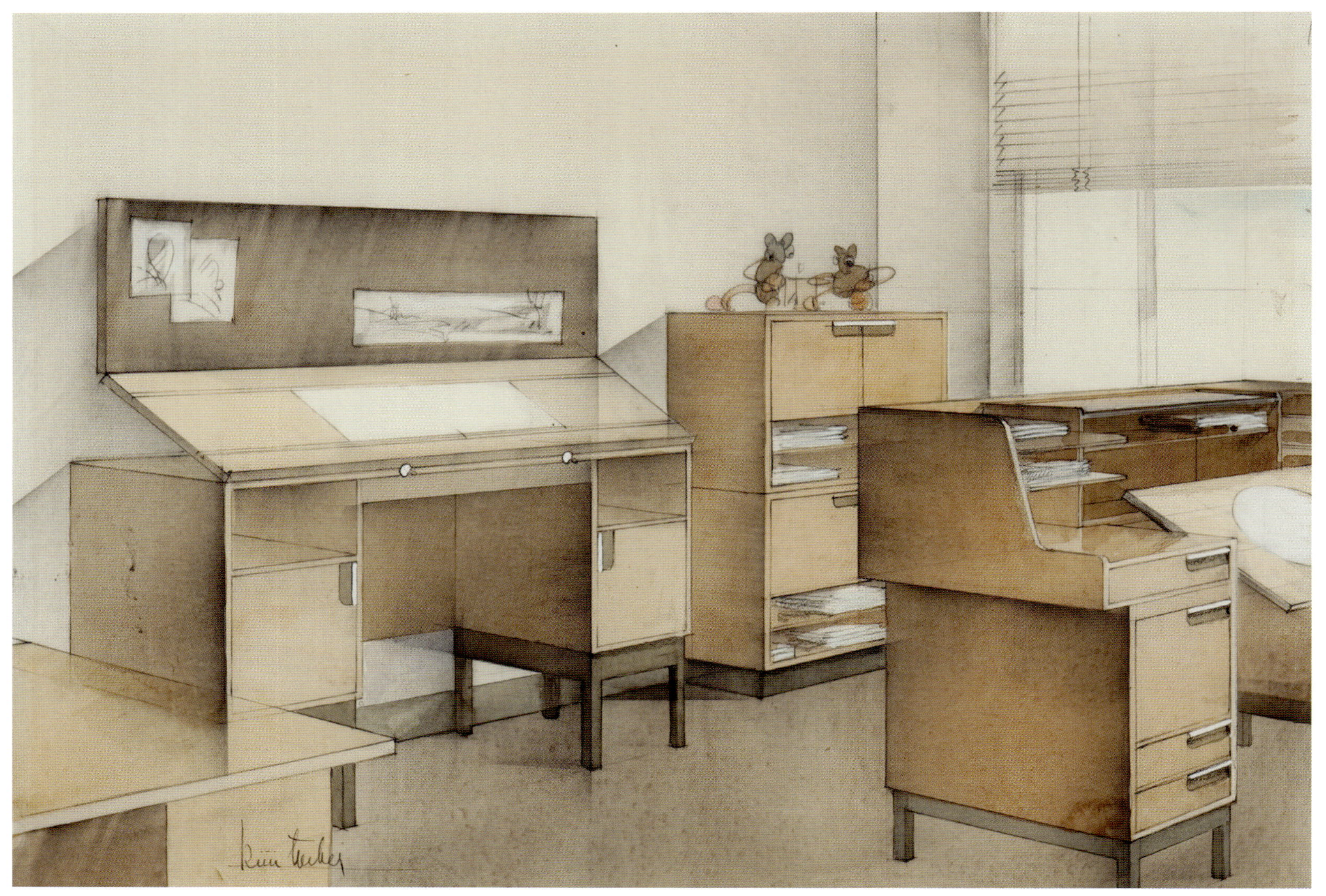

Kem Weber concept illustration of a layout room with layout pan desk; circa. 1939. ©UCSB

CHAPTER 7
THE LAYOUT DESK

"Don't think about making art, just get it done."

-Andy Warhol, Artist

The layout desk, which is made up of lower UNIT No. 1A and upper UNIT No.2A, was also popular with the background artists. The desk's lower unit is a variation of the animator's desk (see chapter 8) lower unit with the difference being the drawer design. The desk measured 30 inches by 72 inches and was indicated on the blueprints as being "HIGH CHAIR HEIGHT." These are hulking desks with their tall backs. Around the studio, I would often see the cork boards completely covered with drawings, layouts and reference material

On lower UNIT No.1A, the large, deep pull out drawer, on the left and right side had a cut out for a water jar and a shallow tray for anything from pencils, pastels, chalk, and erasers, to paints, a palette, and brushes on top of the shelf. Just below the top shelf of the drawer was a slim pull out drawer with several shelves below for rolled-up or folded layouts. These were usually overflowing with drawings and other papers.

Think of a layout artist as a cinematographer setting up and staging each scene in an animated film. They define where the action of the characters will take place and create the environment or background—the setting—for the action including the camera moves. The layout artists are taking the story panels and making the actual scene setup which the animators will animate the characters to in the scene.

The configuration of these large drawers allowed for the layout artists to not only draw the layouts, but also be able to do tonal renderings that help set the mood and lighting for a scene. The layout artist created one line drawing of the layout, the background of a scene and any overlay (foreground) elements, and then did a rendered version that gave a lighting indication to the background painter. That rendering along with loose poses of the characters' action in the scene were used by the background painter to create "vignettes" in the

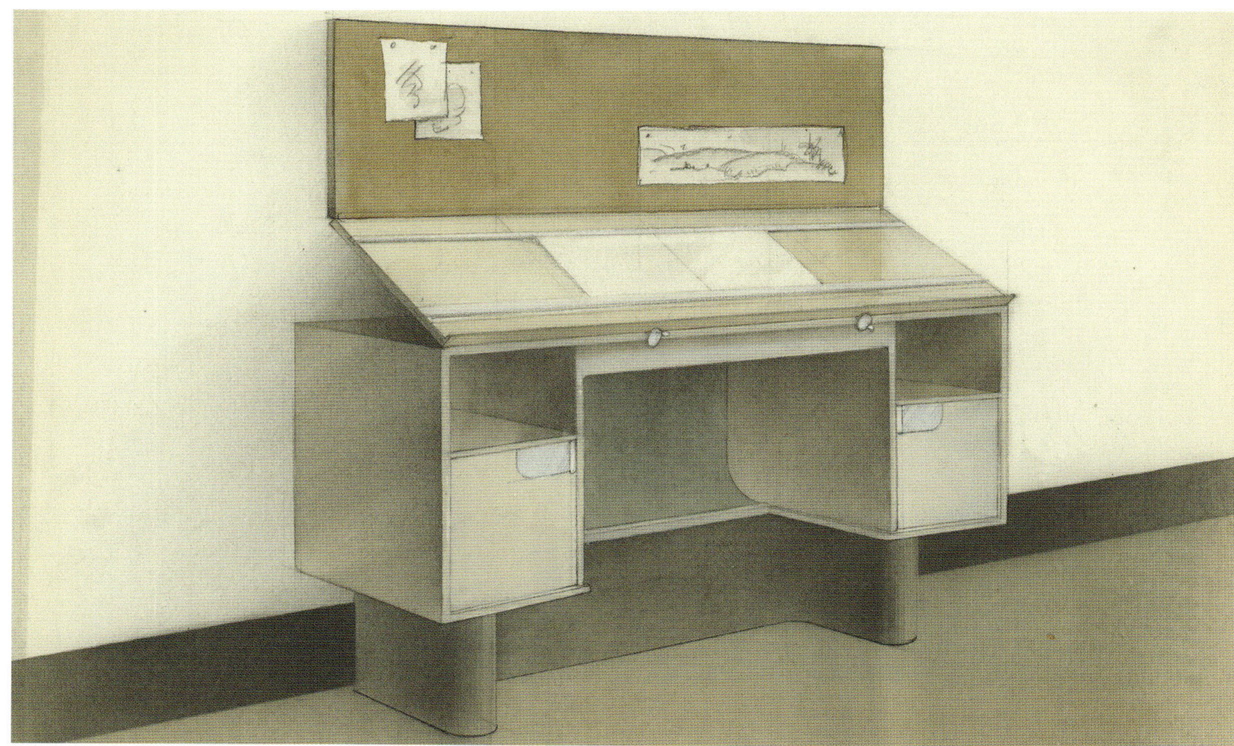

Kem Weber concept illustration of a layout pan table. ©UCSB

paintings to accommodate the animation action.

The upper layout desk unit consisted of a large drawing board that could handle oversized or pan layouts. Think of a pan as a long sheet of paper. If the standard animation paper was roughly 13.5-inches by 17-inches, a pan drawing could be 13.5-inches by 36-inches or more. A long drawing like this was used for camera moves that gave the illusion of traveling with a character say as they walked along a street.

The vertical back of the upper desk that was lined with cork board material for pinning up reference images, this is similar to the background desk discussed in chapter 10. Reference images could be anything from artwork to photographs or anything that provides visual reference and inspiration for the artist.

There was also a long narrow shelf that ran the length

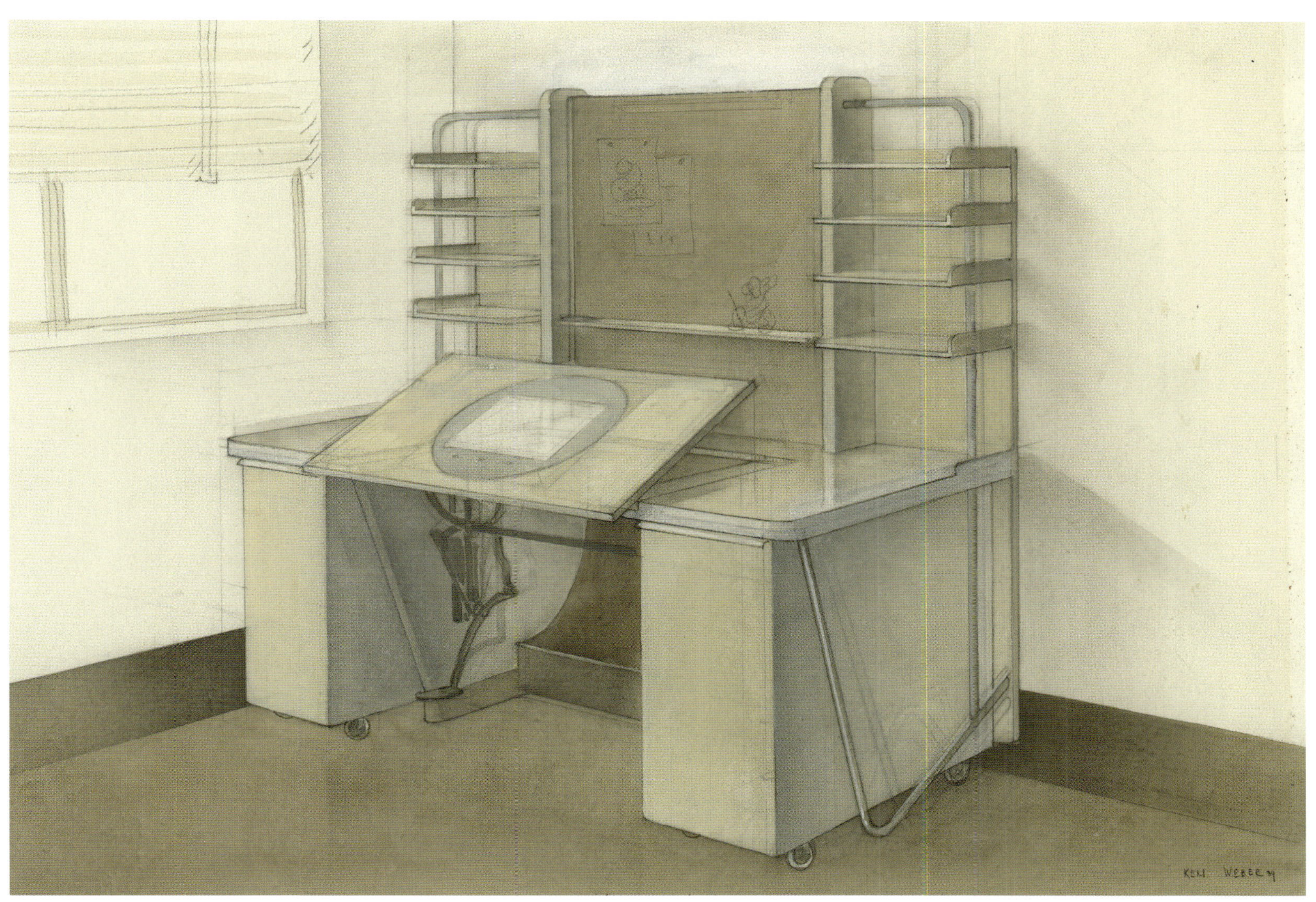

An early Kem Weber concept illustration of a layout desk. Note the foot pedal mechanism for adjusting the angle of the drawing board, circa 1939. ©UCSB

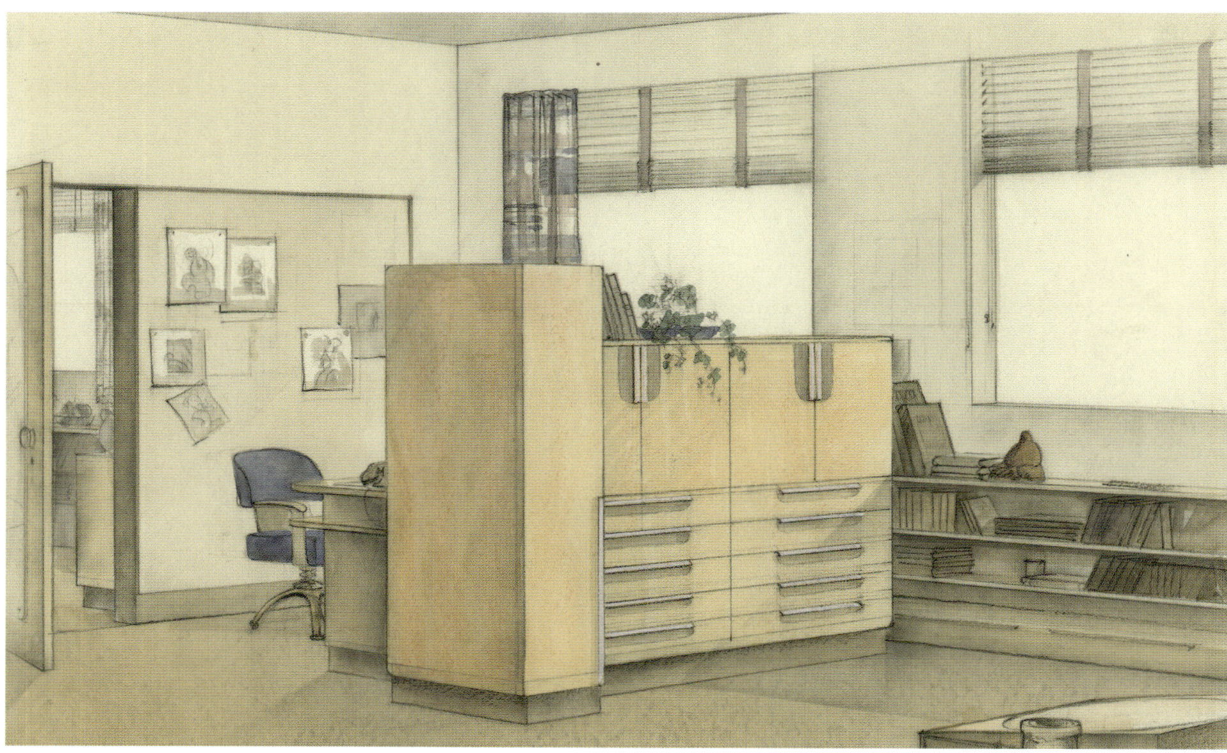

Kem Weber concept illustration of layout storage room with flat files. ©UCSB

of the cork board and was not only functional but also a structural support keeping the unit rigid. On the left side of the upper unit is a set of four raked shelves that were progressively stepped back slightly from bottom to top.

The desk was perfect for the layout artists. "The surface is big and you could do 24 Field setups [oversized rectangular paper] and three field pans [three foot or longer piece of paper],"[64] said Karen Keller, former Disney layout artist. The large drawing surface also allowed the layout artist to see the entire scene and to be able to plot out the camera move across the artwork much like a cinematographer plans out camera placement in a live action film.

The layout desk also was set higher than the animation desks and even with that, some layout artists had their desks on risers so that they could stand or sit throughout

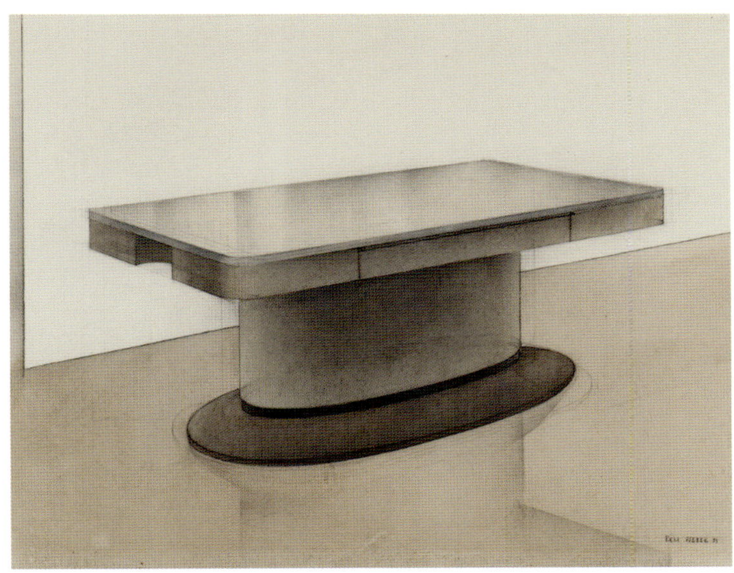

Kem Weber concept
for a layout center table.
©UCSB

the day. "Sometimes you just step back to look at the layout and it was much easier than sitting," said Keller. It is one thing to be animating on a small piece of paper, it is entirely different when you are drawing a large interior or exterior of the entire scene. "Being able to stand, especially when you were doing wide strokes on a large drawing, was much more comfortable," said Keller.[65]

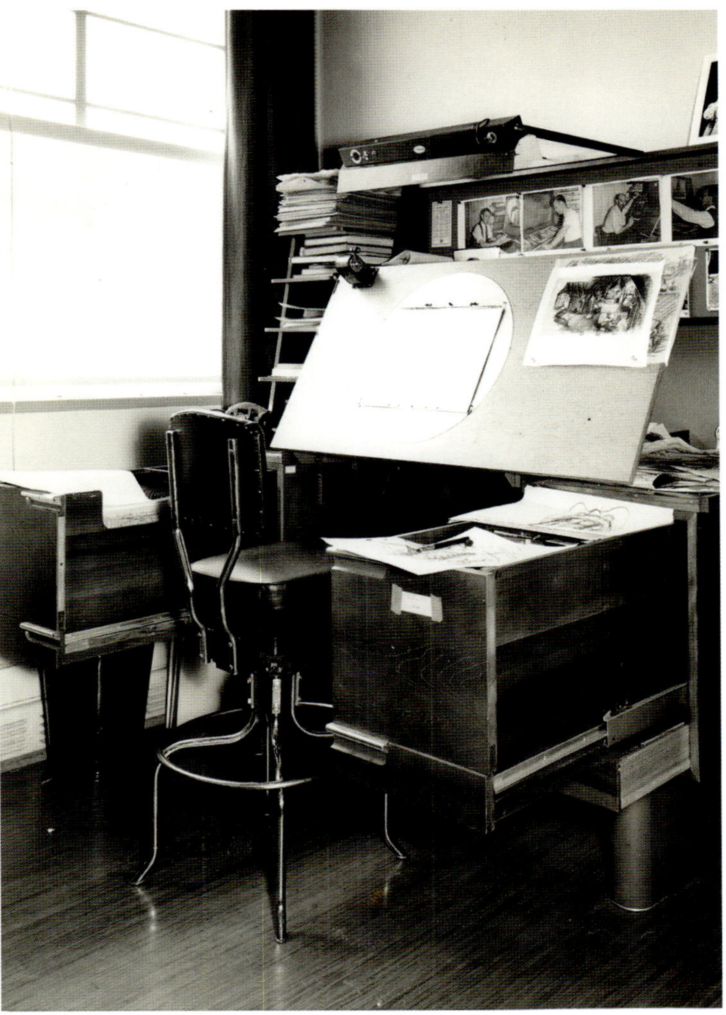

A typical Disney layout artist's desk and chair setup, circa 1939.
Photo by Baskerville. ©UCSB

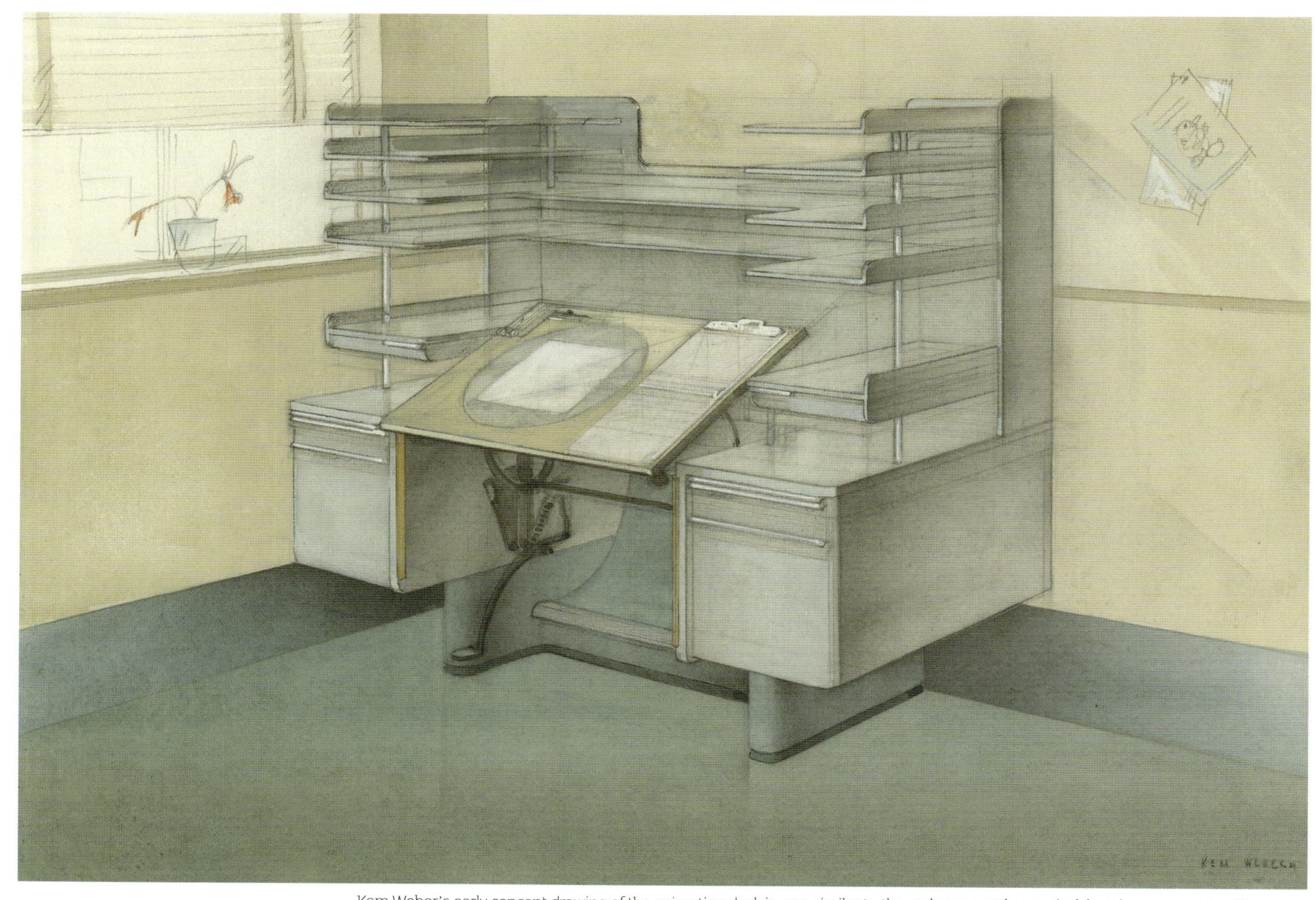

Kem Weber's early concept drawing of the animation desk is very similar to the early concept layout desk but there are subtle differences. This animation desk has much more shelving space along the back and sides around the drawing table; circa 1939.©UCSB

CHAPTER 8
THE VERSATILE ANIMATION DESK

"Design is not just what it looks like and feels like. Design is how it works."

-Steve Jobs, Co-founder of Apple

After the layout artist completed drawing the background and related elements for a scene, it was ready for the character animators. The animators used the background and the loosely suggested character poses supplied by the layout artists to create the character animation.

The animation desk is probably the most versatile piece that was designed by Kem Weber for The Walt Disney Studios. He had come up with a brilliant modular design that gave choices as to what kind of lower section of the desk an artist might want, as well as the upper portion based on a particular discipline. The desk sections were built with an interlocking channel so that the upper portion of the desk, which had a recessed channel, fit onto a corresponding raised channel on the lower portion of the desk. This allowed the two sections to lock together as one unit with the upper and lower sections being mixed and matched.

The various lower sections could be used with different upper sections that allowed the artists to customize their particular desk. "You could have one door just open into one big empty space,"[66] said animator Andreas Deja, "or you could have a set of drawers." The choices accommodated the variety of preferences of the artists allowing for that portion of individual customization. There is an old wives' tale at the studio that the cabinet/drawer size was designed by whether "a fifth of gin or whiskey could stand upright in the deep drawer"[67] in those desks so that the artist could have their favorite bottle of libation handy. "Ever notice how the handles of your Weber desk drawers can open a bottle of beer perfectly? And your lower cabinet is exactly the height of a bottle of Scotch? Don't think that is by accident. Everything was designed for a purpose," said animator Tom Sito. The drawer handles were indeed handy bottle openers. I opened many a bottle on my drawer pulls.

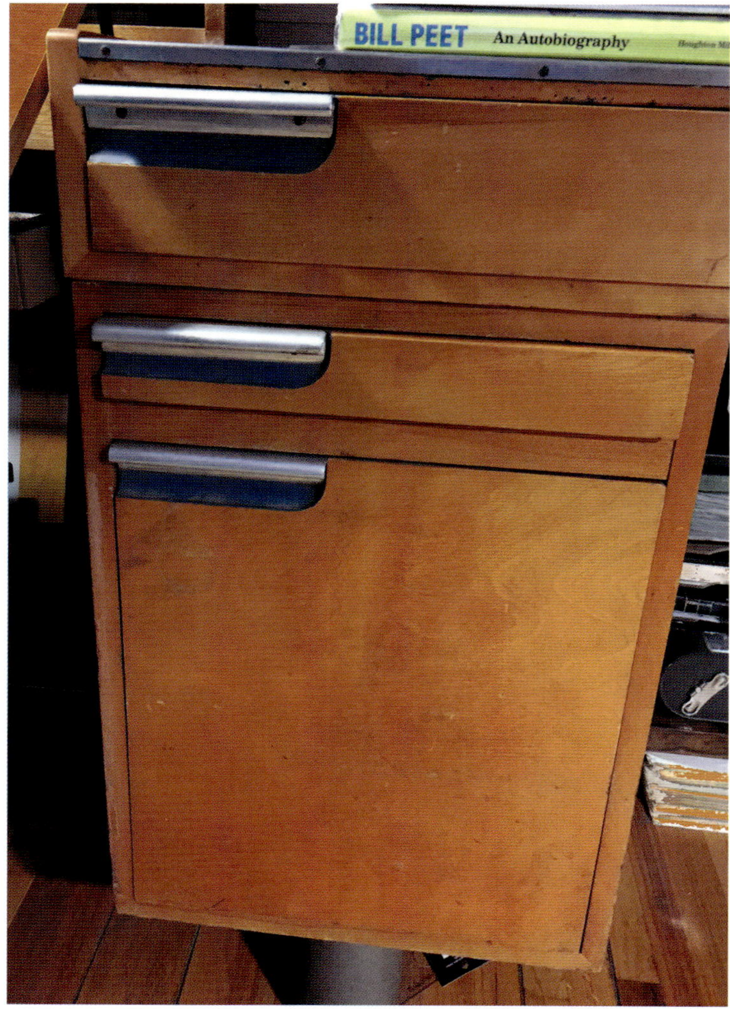

Desk drawer detail of Ollie Johnston's modified animator's desk.
Courtesy of Mark Kirkland. Photo ©Dave Bossert

Because of the size and weight, these desks are heavy, the modular nature made it easier and more manageable to move them in pieces. Even separated, these desks required at least two or more studio movers to transfer the desk from one space to another, including the invariable wiggling of the desk through a doorway or tight passage. When the furniture was first placed in the office of the new Animation Building on the studio lot, it was there for good. When asked if the artists moved around a lot, Don Hahn, producer and director, commented, "No, they didn't really. People were in their rooms for decades."[68] If an artist moved the furniture stayed and the artist boxed up his personal stuff and went into another office with the same furniture and then just setup their space as they had it previously. That did change over the years to where the artists did move with their furniture. I dragged my compact animator's desk with me to various buildings during my tenure.

The prototype desk had rounded edges and a painted finish; further adjustments were made to the design of the animation desk before the first batch was manufactured at the Petersen Show Case & Fixture Co., Inc. in Los Angeles. Both Weber and Walt Disney visited the Petersen facility to inspect the progress of

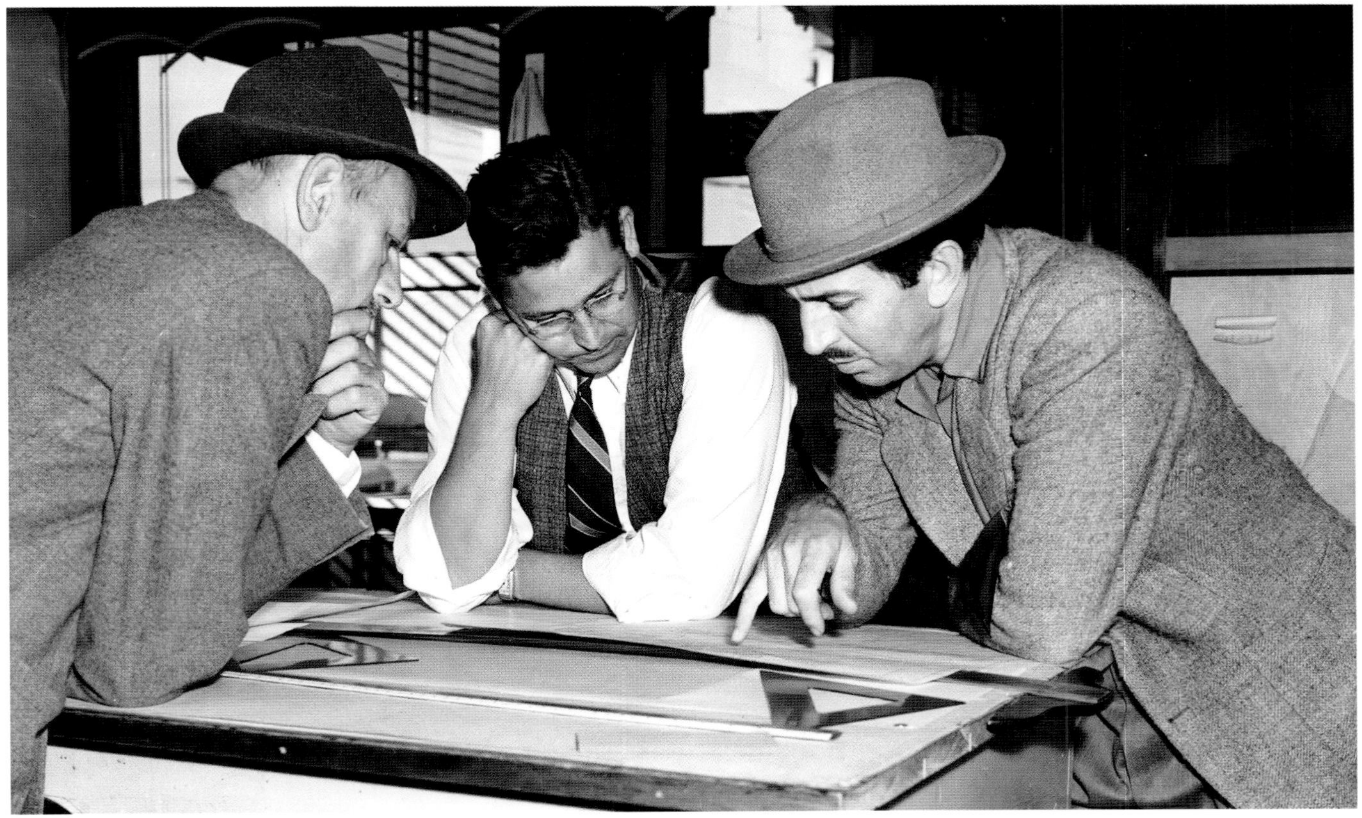

A prototype animation desk designed by Kem Weber with input from animator Frank Thomas was custom built and used at the Hyperion facility. While Thomas animated on the desk during Pinocchio (1940) further notes and adjustments were suggested.
(L to R) Kem Weber, Howard Petersen and Walt Disney discussing the furniture plans at The Petersen Show Case and Fixture Company in Los Angeles. 1939. ©UCSB

the furniture as it was being manufactured. The simple purchase order from Walt Disney Productions stated that, "Furnish all furniture & items in strict accordance with plans, specifications & models, subject to inspection & acceptance of the Owner's agent, as preschedule attached." It further indicated that, "All shop drawings to be made by you are to be corrected & okehed [sic] by Owner's agent before proceeding with work," the owner's agent being Weber, the purchase order specifically states, "Your plant to be open at all times to Owner's agent for inspection of work."[69]

To give a sense of the modularity of this animation

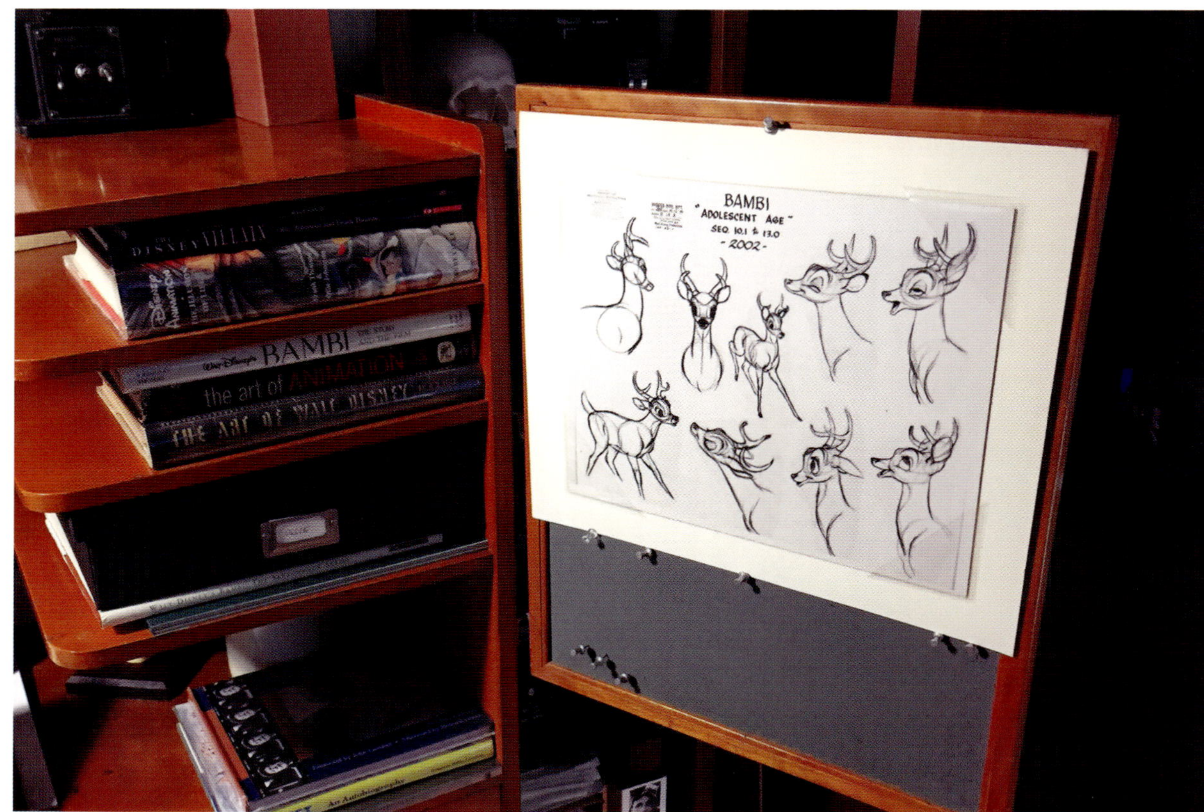

Ollie Johnston's desk detail of movable bulletin board with Bambi (1942) model sheet. Courtesy of Mark Kirkland. Photo ©Dave Bossert

desk, it consisted of a base noted as UNIT No.1 with drawers or cabinets on either side and UNIT No.2 which was the upper portion of the desk consisting of an adjustable drawing table that held the animation disc with a single drawer on either side, recessed raked shelving on either side, behind and above the tabletop and disc. As an option, there was an extended base that would raise the desk up so that the artist could stand or sit on a high stool. There was also a spacer that went in between UNIT No.1 and UNIT No.2 which accomplished the same thing as the extended base but gave it a different look. I can say with certainty that the extended base or wood blocks was the most common way of raising the animation desk. I have never seen the spacers between UNIT No.1 and UNIT No.2 used at the studio during my tenure there.

Up until this point, the animators had worked on a hodgepodge of desks with drawing boards seated on top either fixed in place or just sitting on the flat desk and moveable. Animators at other studios were used to this type of set-up or something that was homemade. "I started my career in Europe," said animator Ken Duncan, "so a lot of studios were smaller, put together without a lot of funds, and sometimes you just had a simple plexiglass disc on a piece of wood that sat on top of a desk."[70] This is similar to what the artists worked on at Disney's studio on Hyperion. "When I got to Disney and to see the Weber desks, they were kind of the Rolls-Royce of desks," said Duncan, "Weber really thought about how it was gonna work for the animator."[71]

"I started out in that room next to Eric Larson [Disney legend and one of Walt's Nine Old Men] in that kind of bullpen at the end of the hall. It was me and Brad Bird [*The Incredibles*], Henry Selick [*Tim Burton's The Nightmare Before Christmas, Coraline*], Dan Haskett [animator, character designer] and Bill Kroyer [*FernGully: The Last

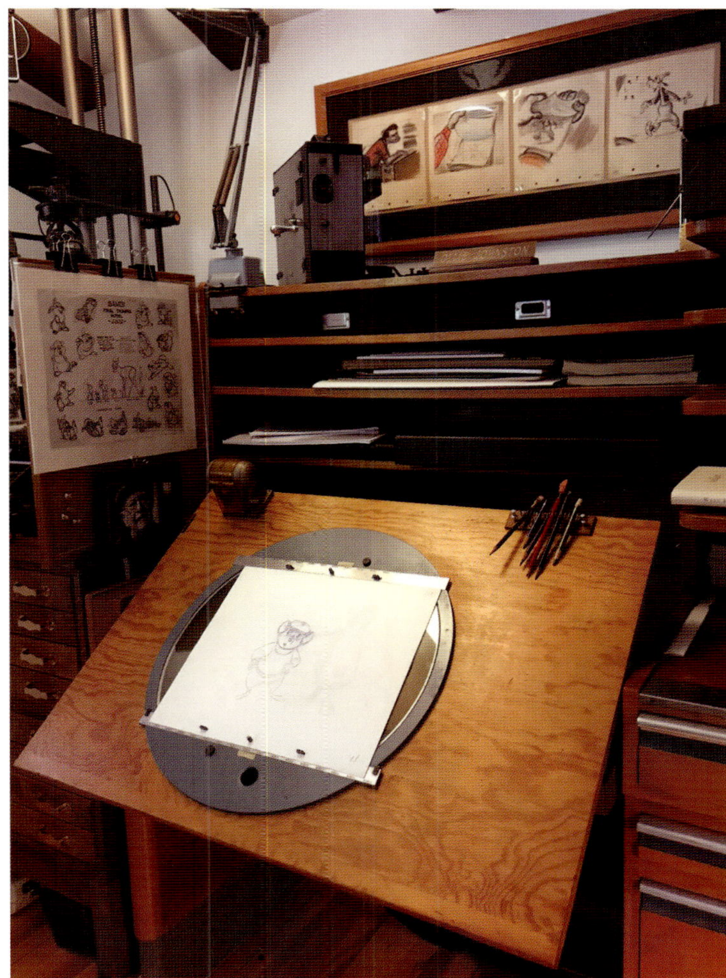

Ollie Johnston's modified animator' desk that he used at home.
Courtesy of Mark Kirkland. Photo ©Dave Bossert

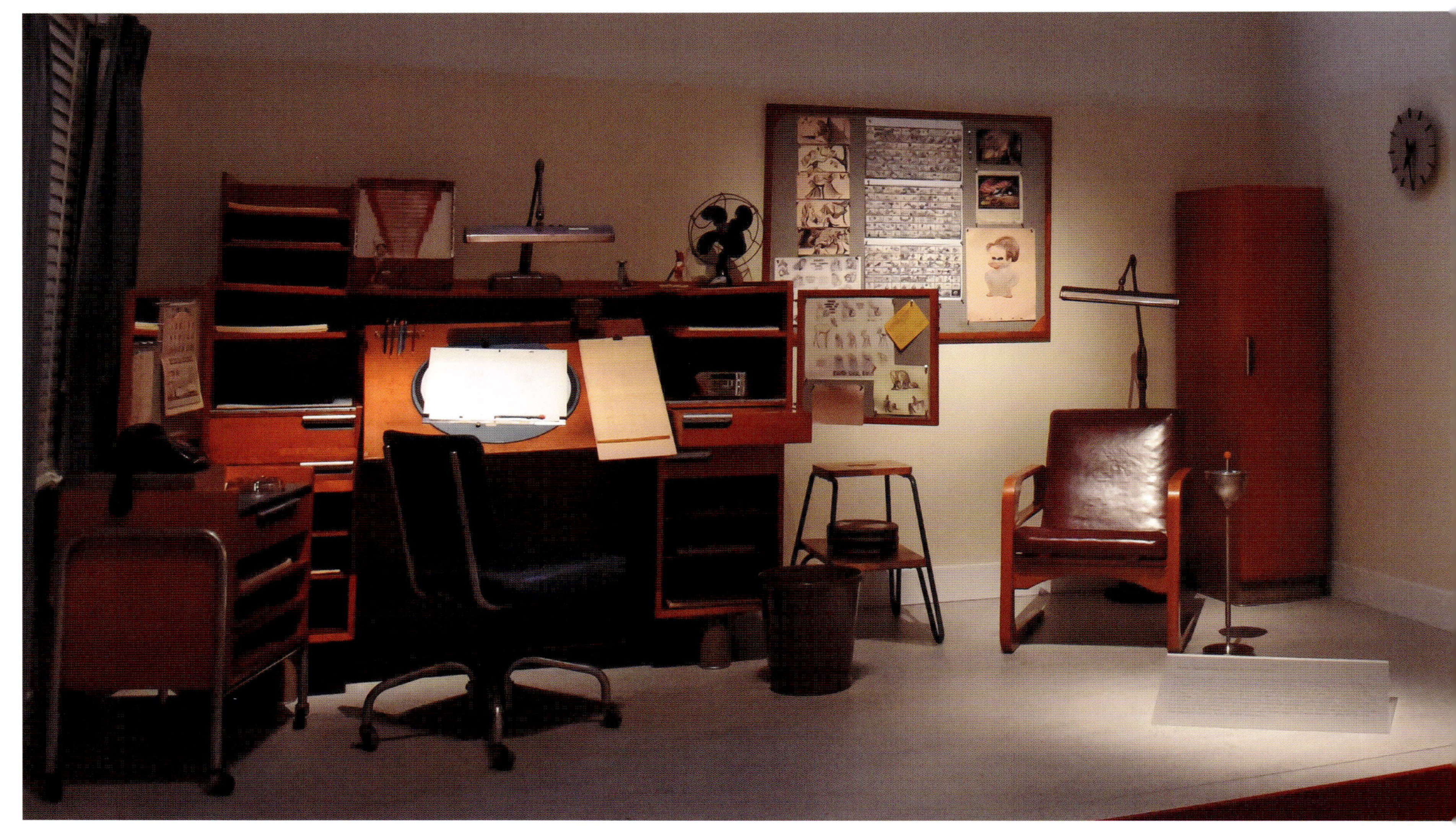

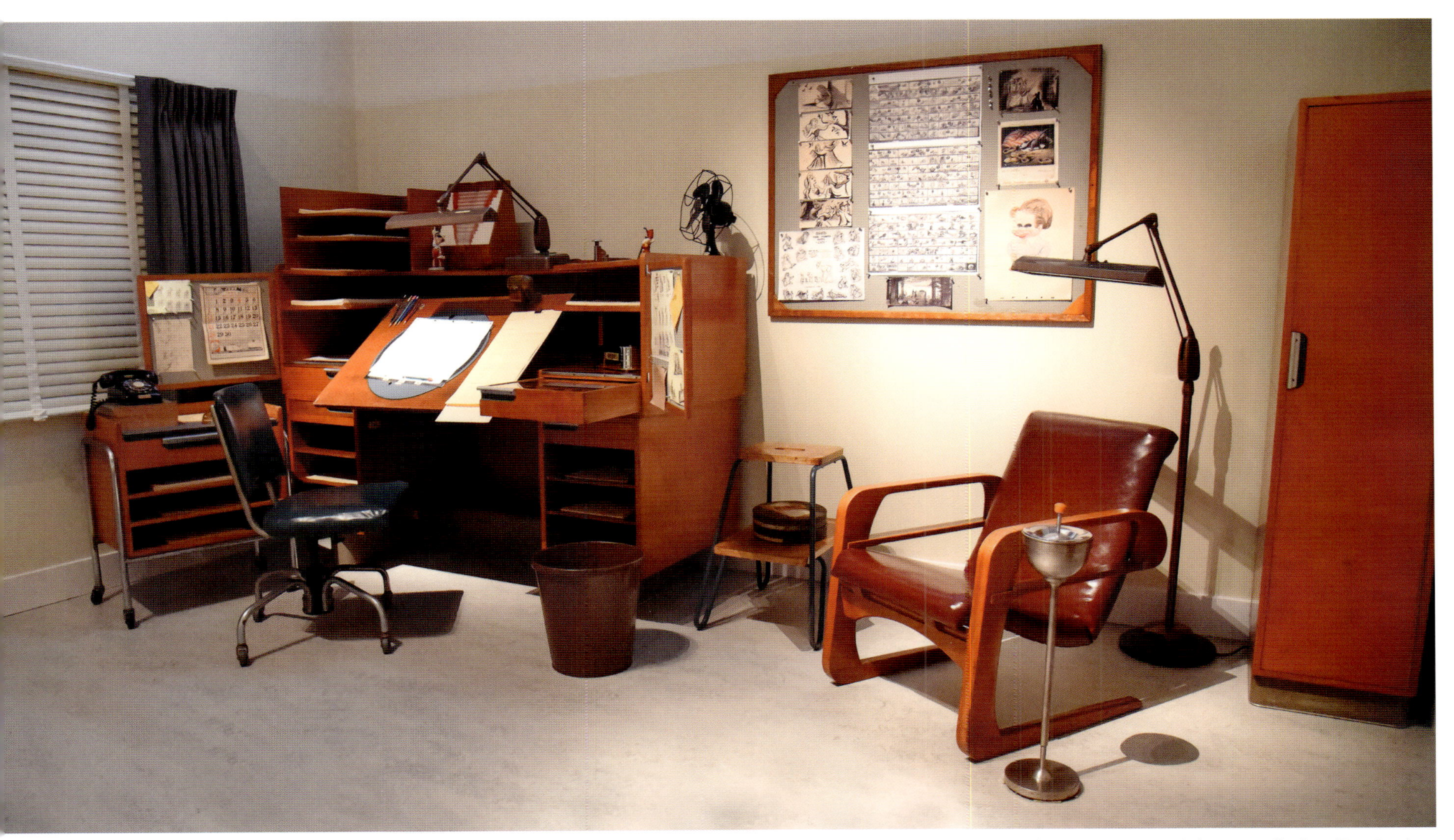

Left and right: A typical Disney Animator's office set-up with Kem Weber designed furniture. Animator's desk set-up, collection of Tony Anselmo; photo by Frank Anzalone, courtesy The Walt Disney Family Museum.

Rainforest] all working at those desks. Right away you got a feeling of the Disney tradition," said John Musker. "It was really like we were stepping up from a VW to a Cadillac in terms of the bells and whistles of the desk—the different drawers, the shelves, the way it could tilt and move and the features, the whole thing. Occasionally people knew whose desk it was and they were like 'this is Ollie's desk or this is Milt's desk' or whatever."[72] Some artists tracked down desks that belonged to Disney legends in hopes of something rubbing off, some kind of aura. "You got just a sense that the desks had a lived-in feel to it, like wow, I'm part of this tradition that goes back years and years. Who knows who used this desk? Who knows what scenes crossed this disc and you don't really know but you can only imagine," said Musker.[73]

Weber also thought about the efficient and streamlined use of the furniture by making some of the pieces interchangeable. Base UNIT No.1 has a variant noted as UNIT No.1B that had drawers for the checkers, the group that literally checked the art for each frame of animation and called out what levels needed to be combined for cel painting. There was a limit of four cel levels against a background being photographed under a camera. Any more than four levels and the clarity of images would degrade.

The checkers made sure that each set-up for each frame was going to work the way the animator had listed the art onto the exposure sheets. Think of the exposure sheet, often called the x-sheet, as a road map to how a scene of artwork was put together—the order of levels and the drawings used for each frame of film.

UNIT No.1 or No.1B could also have a flat desk top added creating a layout work table or with UNIT No.3 turned into an animator's work table, which could then use cabinet and/or shelving UNITS No.6, No.7, No.9, No.10, and No.11, in a customizable configuration stacked onto the rear shelf of the worktable top. A short base could be added to any of these cabinet and shelving sections turning them into freestanding pieces of furniture.

The modified animator's desk, UNIT No.19, was a more compact desk that had drawers or a cabinet on the right side of the desk. The left side of the desk was a 3 inch wide wood support structure with a rounded face. Some of the legendary Disney animators had these desks at their homes because they took up much less space than the much wider UNIT No.1 and No.2 animator's desks. This modified animation desk also had a work table top,

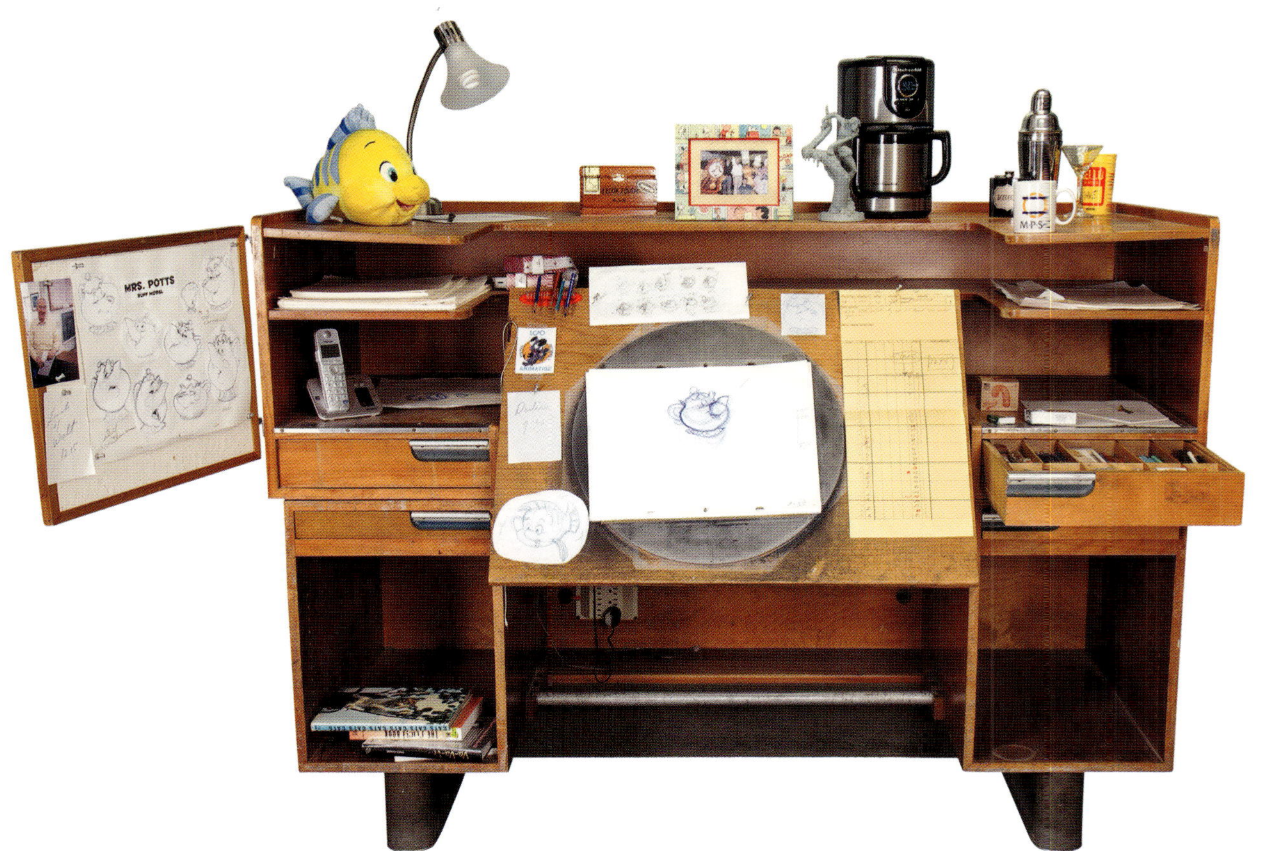

A typical Disney animation desk complete with personal items. The drawing board has more space on the right side to accommodate an animation exposure sheet. There is also a ring stain in the lower right cabinet opening no doubt from a bottle or coffee mug. Courtesy of Heritage Auctions, HA.com.

noted as UNIT No.20, that consisted of a flat top with a vertical shelving unit at the back. This allowed the animator to spread out the artwork for whatever scene he/she might be working on.

Another variant of the animator's desk was UNIT No.22, the assistant animator's and inbetweener's desk. It is similar to the animator's desk but with more shelf space, which the assistants and inbetweener's needed to spread out the animation drawings. There were also additional separate shelving units that sat on top of the upper most shelf and could be used as an end table by standing it vertically. It was all about versatility and efficiency for each step in the animation process.

One of the more interesting features on the top portion of the animator's desk is the metal cigarette protector, which is noted on the blueprint elevations of the assistant animator's and inbetweener's desks, but was also on the animator's and compact animator's desks. It is a two-and-a-half inch by sixteen-and-a-quarter inch piece of metal with a quarter inch lip that is screwed to the top surface of the single drawer on the upper section of the desk. It was an amenity that prevented the wood from being burned when an artist laid a cigarette down for a moment to draw. It would burn the wood if left unattended, which appears to have been common enough to warrant the design of this metal guard.

The animator's desk as well as the other desks that had adjustable drawing boards all shared a mechanism under the drawing board that allowed for easy adjustment simply by pulling a lever and moving the board to the desired angle. On most commercially available drawing tables today, there is usually a knob that is loosened on each side of the table top to adjust the angle then tightened. It is a bit cumbersome to make adjustments that way. The Weber desks had thought that through thoroughly to make it as easy as possible. On an early concept sketch of the animator's desk there is an indication of a foot pedal operated adjustment mechanism. It was likely simplified to the hand lever to keep costs down.

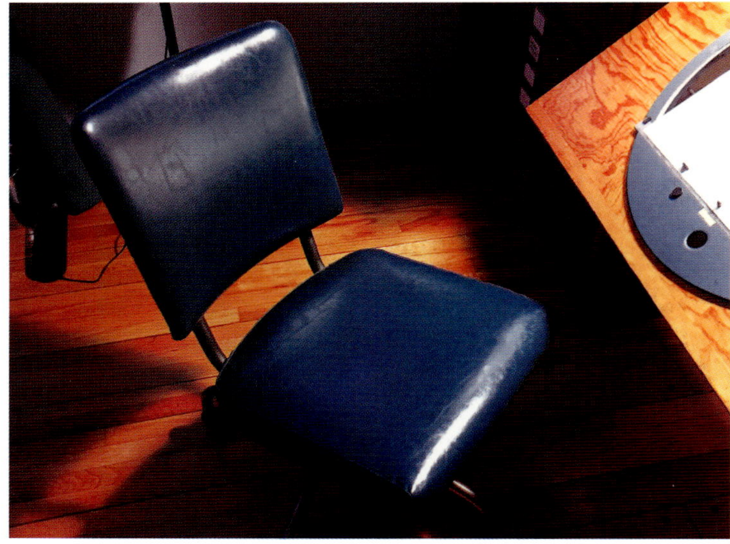

The Kem Weber designed animator's chair was made from tubular chrome with automobile upholstery Naugahyde for the seat and back cushions. Courtesy of Mark Kirkland. Photo ©Dave Bossert

Although not part of the original design, some animators added a bulletin-board to one or both side of their desk. The bulletin-board was fastened to the front side of the upper unit using a simple barrel hinge or small butt hinge. This gave the artist a place to pin character model sheets, a sheet of paper with multiple views and poses of a character, and other reference material for easy access.

All of the Weber furniture had a unique handle design for all the drawers—an elongated recessed soft channel rounded on the interior side and painted a muted blue with a metal handle pull mounted flush with the top of the wooden drawer face. The drawer pull itself was a sleek design in keeping with the philosophy of stripping away ornamentation and streamlining the shape. There has been some speculation that these drawer pulls are an early example of extruded metal but this has not been verified. It is possible that the drawer pulls were machined as a channel stock and then the pulls cut and finished. There is no written record, that I could find, of how or where these pulls where made.

It was that care—that thoughtfulness that went into designing and building these animation desks that created a sense of permanency for the new animation studio that Walt envisioned. "You knew what you were doing, it was an art form and it was a craft. And the desks emphasized that as much as anything in that they were so solidly built," said Musker.[74] "They weren't gonna crack or break or give way and withstood years and years of filmmaking and who knows what abuse from cigarette stains and bottles of gin in the drawer. But, you definitely got a feeling that you were one in a line of artists. You were part of the Knights of the Roundtable, the roundtable being the disc. I don't know, you just were part of a tradition and that was cool."[75]

In the 1990s, Walt Disney Animation Studios expanded by adding satellite studios in Orlando, Florida and Paris, France. New furniture was created based on the Kem Weber designs and was manufactured in Canada. The new desks used similar design elements indicative to the Weber furniture including the clean horizontal lines, rounded corners on the shelves, and recessed painted channel with the drawer pulls. However, these reproductions lack the rich, warm patina of the original vintage desks, and the aura of the legends that inhabited them.

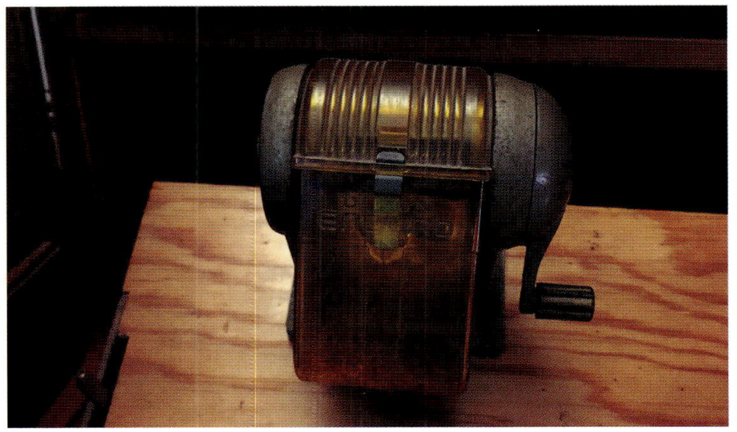

The original pencil sharpener mounted to the Ollie Johnson modified animator's desk. Courtesy of Mark Kirkland. Photo ©Dave Bossert.

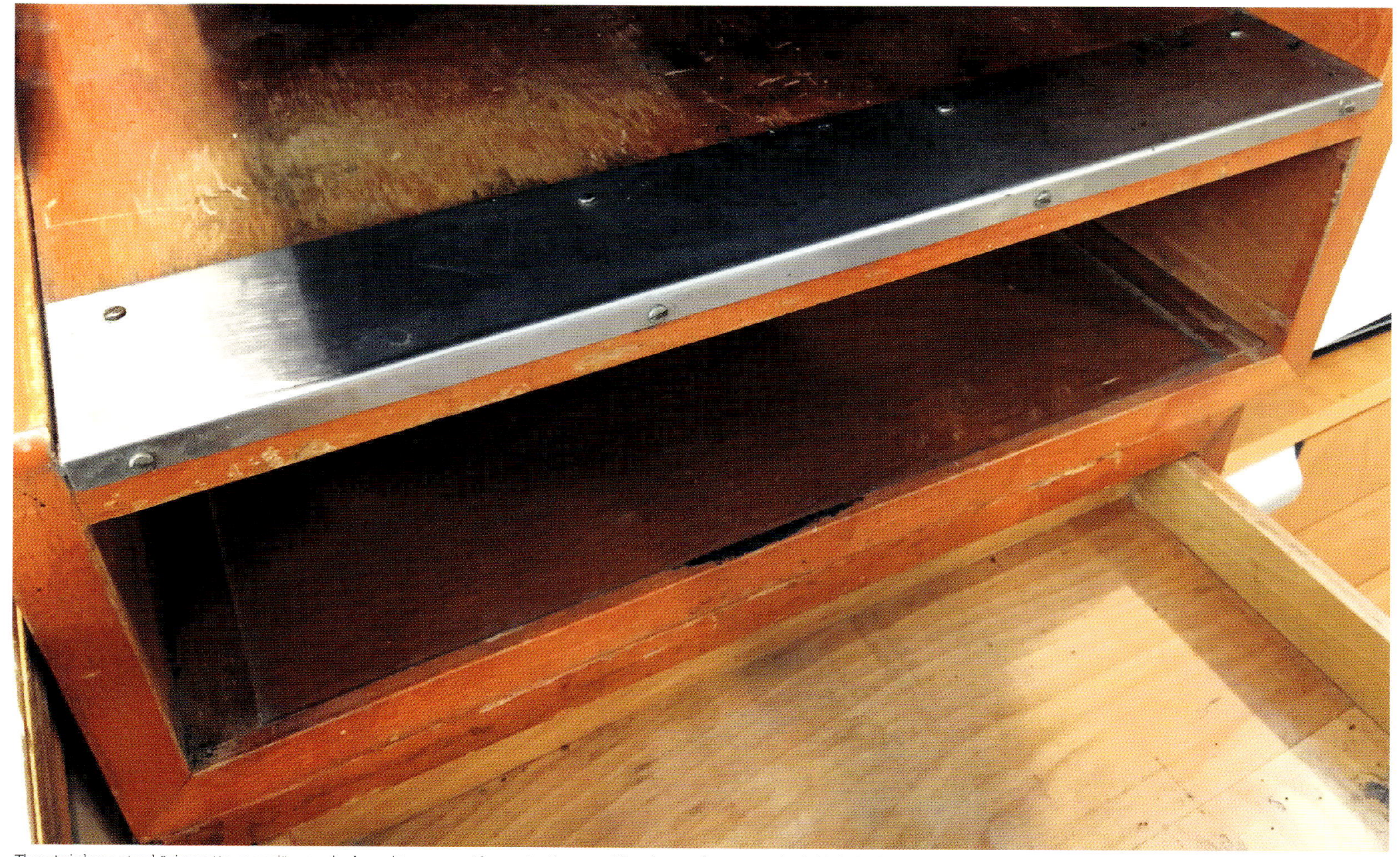

The stainless-steel "cigarette guard" was designed to prevent burns to the wood furniture when an artist laid their cigarette down while drawing. Although there were plenty of ashtrays around the studio, laying a cigarette on the edge of animation desks appears to have been common enough at the Hyperion facility to warrant this protective guard for the new animation furniture at the Burbank studio. It was important enough that it was indicated prominently on the blueprints for the desks. Photo ©Dave Bossert.

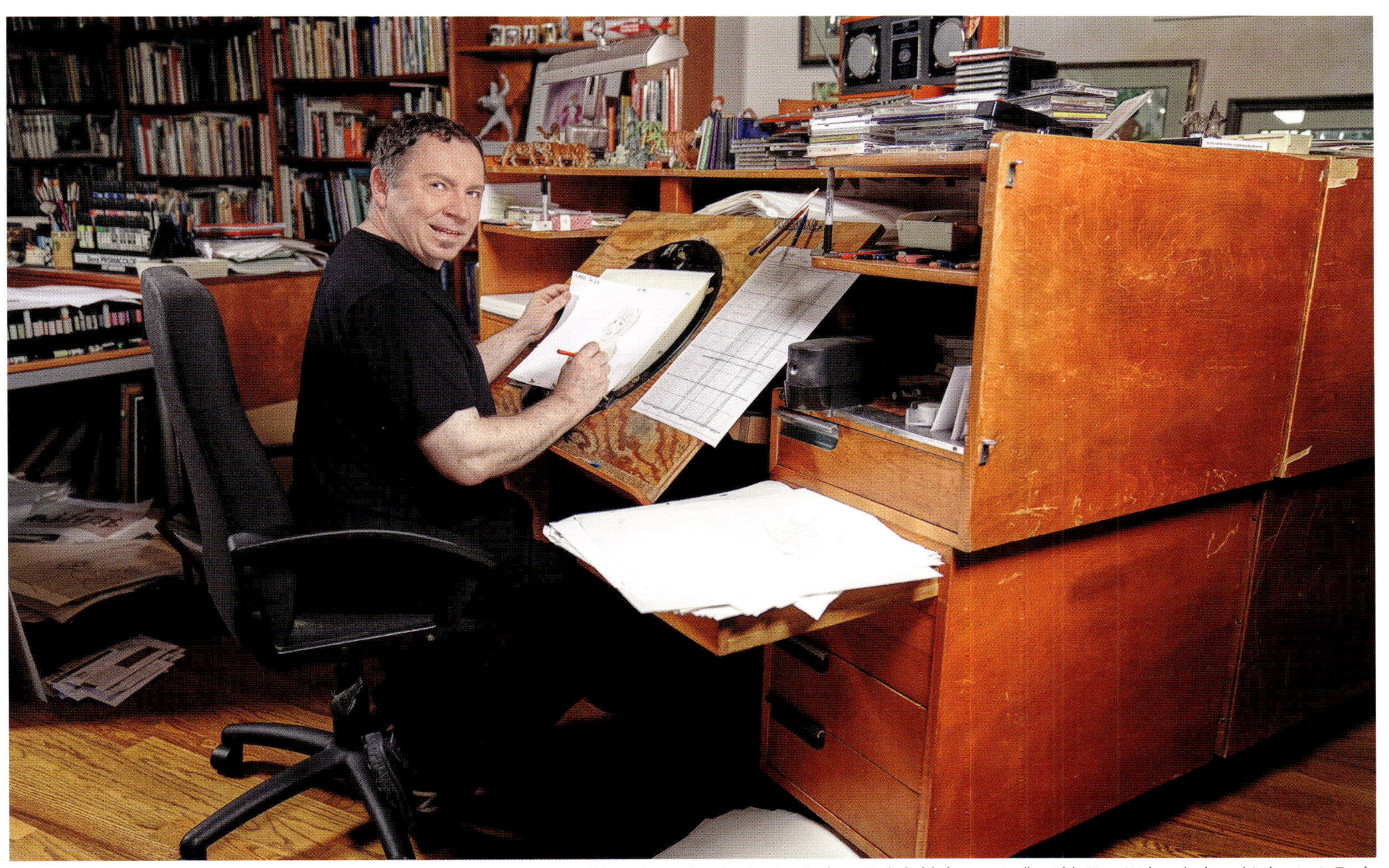

Disney legend and animator Andreas Deja in his home studio at his Kem Weber designed Animator's Desk. This desk used to belong to Milt Kahl, one of Walt's Nine Old Men. Photo by Roger Viloria.

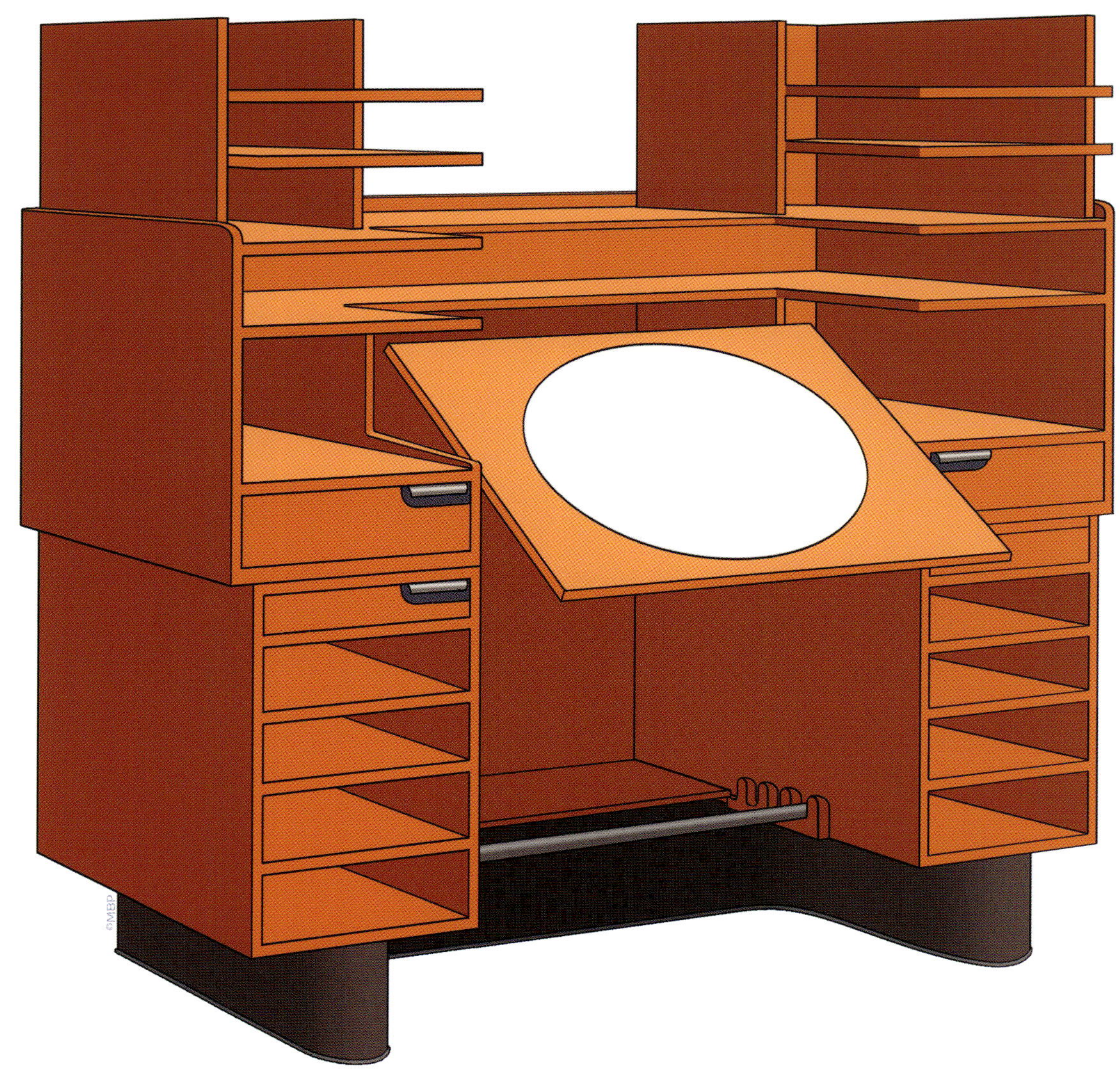

The Assistant's and Inbetweener's desk. UNIT No. 22

CHAPTER 9
THE ASSISTANT'S AND INBETWEENER'S DESK

"Form follows function - that has been misunderstood.
Form and function should be one, joined in a spiritual union."
-Frank Lloyd Wright, Architect/Interior Designer

"You suddenly felt not only like a professional but you're working on history," said Tony Anselmo, voice of Donald Duck and former Disney animation artist. "Because every one of those Disney animated films was drawn on the desks we were drawing on. So I thought about that a lot."[76]

The Assistant's and In-betweener's [sic] desk, UNIT No.22, is similar to the animator's desk except that it has more shelf space on both the upper and lower sections. It should be noted that on the Weber blueprints, *in-betweener* is indicated with a hyphen but the position's name is spelled *inbetweener*. It has the same overall dimensions of 30 inches by 72 inches. The cabinet and/or drawers on the lower section of the animator's desk are replaced on this desk with shelving allowing for the assistant or inbetweener to spread a scene out more, creating their own work flow on the desk. It has the same adjustable drawing board with a disc mounted in it and the stainless steel pipe below as a foot rest.

The desk also had two additional shelving units, measuring thirteen-and-half inches high twenty-eight inches long and fifteen inches wide, that sat on the uppermost shelf of the top section of the desk. These separate shelf units, when not in use, also doubled as a small side table. In fact, one was sold at auction in 2016 for $3,125.00.[77] For me, they were always additional shelving for your desk. I never used those extra shelves as a side table—maybe others did.

"What artists needed, north light, natural light, not incandescent or fluorescent, and the workflow on the desk, if you have all these shelves, you can have your scene broken up to inbetweens, roughs, cleanups," said Anselmo. "You know, everybody had their own system of working. So, there was just this flow that you didn't have to move from your seat."[78] In fact, Weber designed the animation production building oriented along a precise north/south axis to give the animators that consistent northern light.

The assistant's and inbetweener's job was to fill in the drawings needed between the animator's key poses. So, if an animator was working on a scene and did a drawing for frame one and frame sixteen, the assistant would create drawings for say, frame four, eight and twelve. The scene would then go to the inbetweener who would add drawings two, six, ten and fourteen there by filling in the drawings needed for a smooth action of the animation. If the scene needed drawings for every frame, then the additional drawings or inbetweens would be completed by the inbetweener. Typically the scene might be split up amongst an assistant and several inbetweeners, so the desk required a lot of shelf space to spread out the scene for completion.

Compared to other studios, the Weber desks had significantly more shelving space for the artists to do their particular job more efficiently, and the desk itself was inspiring to many of the artists that came to Disney to do animation. "I think it helped you work 'cause you thought you were part of something that was a legacy," said Anselmo. "And I also have been impressed with the synergy that went between the design of the building with all of those windows with north light. The way the work flowed between all the buildings and that the furniture matched. They went through the process between the Disney Brothers Studios on Kingswell and Hyperion, they figured out what worked and what didn't work."[79]

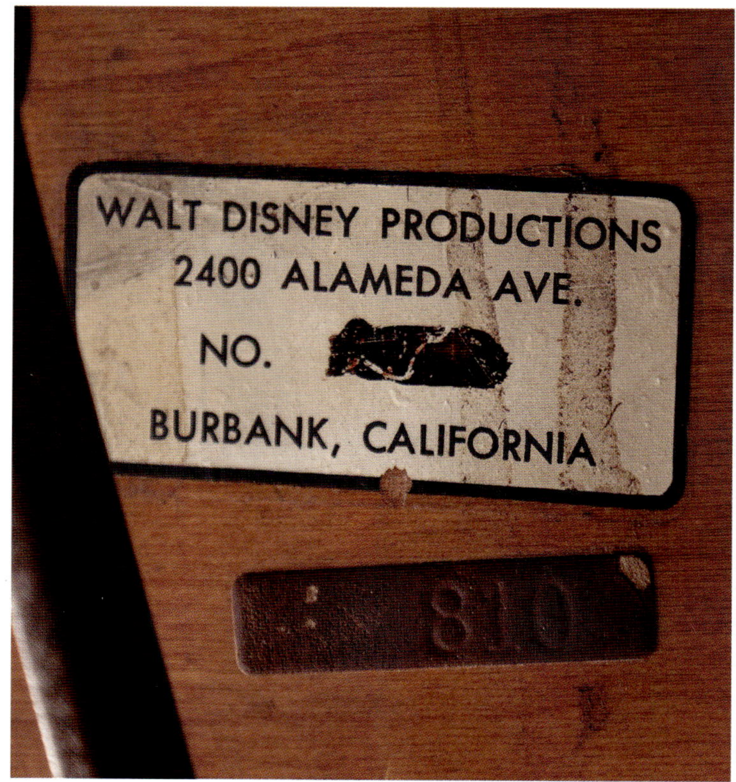

The Walt Disney Studios inventory registration tag for desk 810.
Courtesy of Heritage Auctions, HA.com

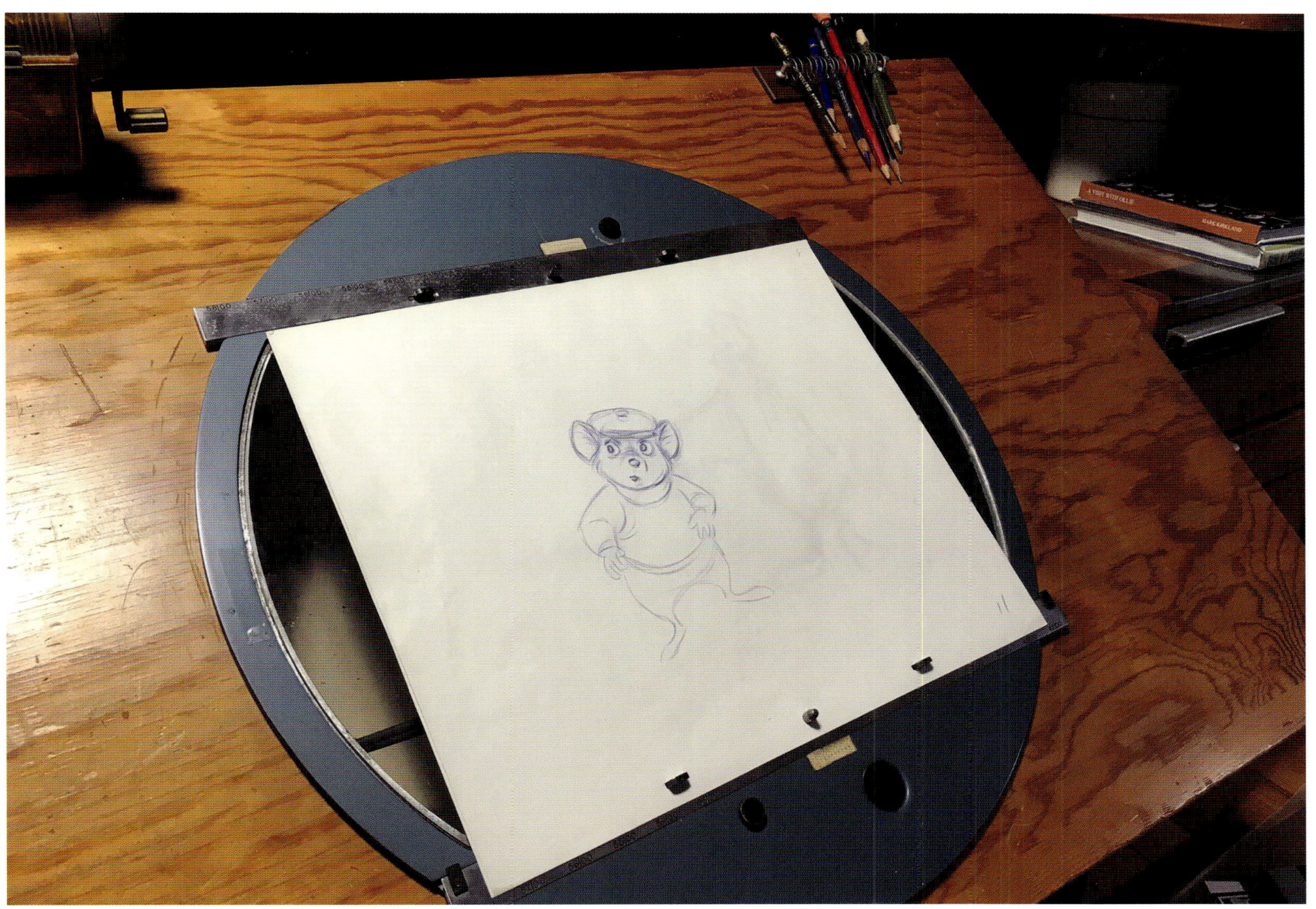

Animat on Disc for Ollie Johnston's home modified Animator's desk with his drawing of Bernard from The Rescuers (1977).
Courtesy of Mark Kirkland. Photo ©Dave Bossert

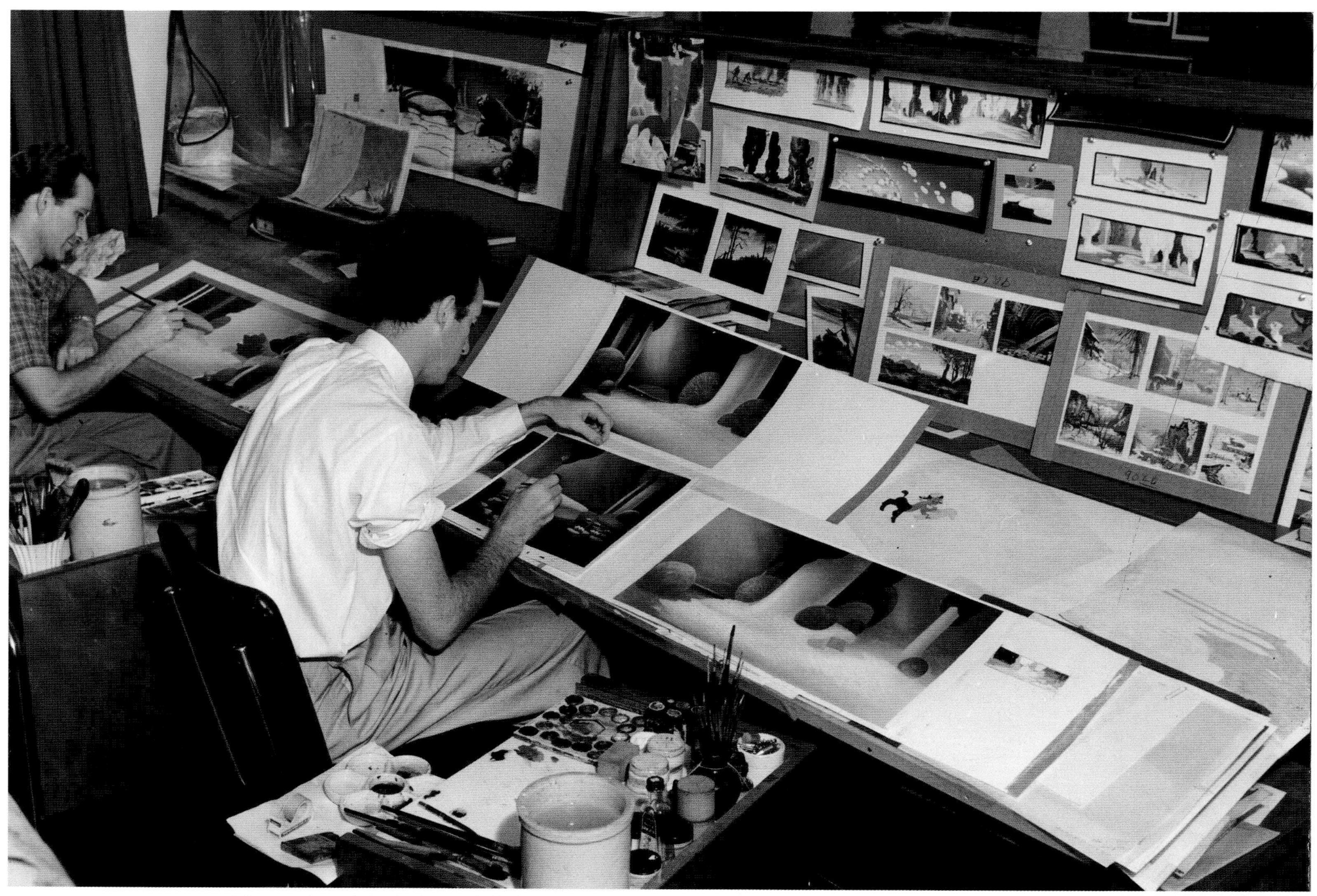

Disney artists painting backgrounds for the Pastoral sequence in Fantasia (1940) at Weber designed background pan desks. Photo by Baskerville. ©UCSB

CHAPTER 10
THE BACKGROUND DESK / COLOR KEYING DESK

"I dream of painting and then I paint my dream."
-Vincent Van Gogh, Artist

"I just remember the furniture always seemed so special. Because as a young artist, I looked at those desks and just said how amazing it would be some day to be sitting there and actually be working on a film with one of these desks that all the great painters had used for many years," said James Coleman, former Walt Disney Animation Studios background supervisor. "When they moved me up from art props to work on *Winnie the Pooh and Tigger Too* (1974), it was like you want to just rub that desk 'cause you're thinking it's full of mojo somehow."[80] This is how many of the contemporary Disney artists felt about the Weber furniture, myself included, that there was something...yes, magical about it.

The background/color keying desk was one of the simpler pieces of furniture made for a discipline in the animation process. It measured 30 inches by 72 inches, with a tall back board that was lined with cork board material. There is a narrow shelf that runs the length of the backboard just above the adjustable solid table top where the background artist created the painted backgrounds for a film. As with all of the other desks for the various disciplines, the background/color keying desk had a stainless steel pipe as an adjustable foot rest. It could be moved into one of three slots based on the desired comfort of the artist.

Again, the desk designs were well thought-out because Walt asked the artists for their opinions when the furniture was being designed. "You can tell that everything had a place and every place had a thing for it. So, you couldn't help but know that somebody had some input that knew what they were doing," said Coleman. "It wasn't just someone saying well, you know, we are gonna need water, so maybe we need to cut a hole here for a water crock. It was just set up that way and it all worked."[81]

Some of the background artists migrated to the layout desk for painting backgrounds because there was more

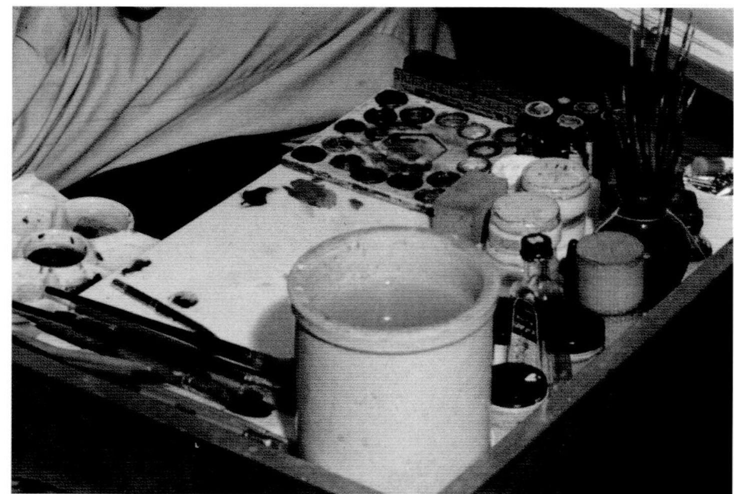

Detail of the ceramic crock of water, the paints, palettes and brushes. (1940). Photo by Baskerville. ©UCSB

shelf space and the lower section had pullout drawers that made it easier to have paints, palettes, and brushes in easy proximity. Both the layout and background desks were interchangeable and could be used for either discipline. "The shelves and everything were there, it was all figured out, and you'd say, okay, I'm gonna stack this here, I'm gonna put that there," said Coleman. "There was also a circle cut in the top of the drawer on the right-hand side for a ceramic crock of water."[82]

It is not hard to imagine that at the Hyperion studio, a crock or tub of water was spilled because it was sitting, unsecured, on a desk surface. "You know, depending on the artist. If they're clumsy, like me, there would be no doubt that they would have spilled the water every so often,"[83] said Coleman with a laugh. Adding a cut out on the top of the drawer was a simple solution to a minor issue that most artists experienced from time to time, yet a furniture designer would not think of it unless they collaborated with the artist on the desk design.

Next to the water crock was a recessed space with a piece of white glass that was a used as a palette. The artist could squeeze out paint onto the glass. Some background artists put a cel down on top of the glass to put paint on because it made for easier cleanup. "Everybody used it in different ways. Then they made, separate from the desk, a small wooden device to set the paints upside down in. The poster paints, so that you wouldn't have to shake them to get the paint out," said Coleman.[84]

For those who didn't use the layout desk and stayed with the background desk, there was a separate Paint Table, UNIT No.23, that was a small wooden cabinet with a recessed top for the paint palette and paints, two pull out drawers underneath where the palette is and the three shelves under the drawers. The unit was on wheels, making it easy for the artist to position it in the most efficient and comfortable way for painting. The basic attributes of this small paint table were also incorporated into the drawer design of the layout desk lower unit.

The cork backboard was specifically designed for both layout and background/color keying desk so that the artists could pin up reference art, photos and other relevant material. The backside of the vertical back of the desk was also covered with corking so that more reference or other backgrounds could be pinned up. Although, often times two background/color keying desks would be butted up against each other if artists were sharing an office. The layout desks also had the same cork bulletin-board on the vertical desk back for the same reasons, pinning up reference material.

"When I think of all the artists who had that desk. It could have been Merle Cox, it could have been Claude Coats, it could be anybody," said Coleman. "So, it's almost like there's an aura surrounding it. And, I used to think if I could get Al Dempster's brushes and paint with them, you'd be better."[85] (Merle Cox, Claude Coats and Al Dempster were all background artists.) It didn't work that way but the desks served as one of many an inspiration at the Disney Studios complex. Once again, there is reverence accorded to the Weber designed animation furniture at Disney. It was a badge of honor to have a desk that belonged to a legendary artist from the previous generation. The background desks that I recall seeing around the studio were splattered with paint from years of backgrounds being painted on them. I always viewed that as part of the desk's patina.

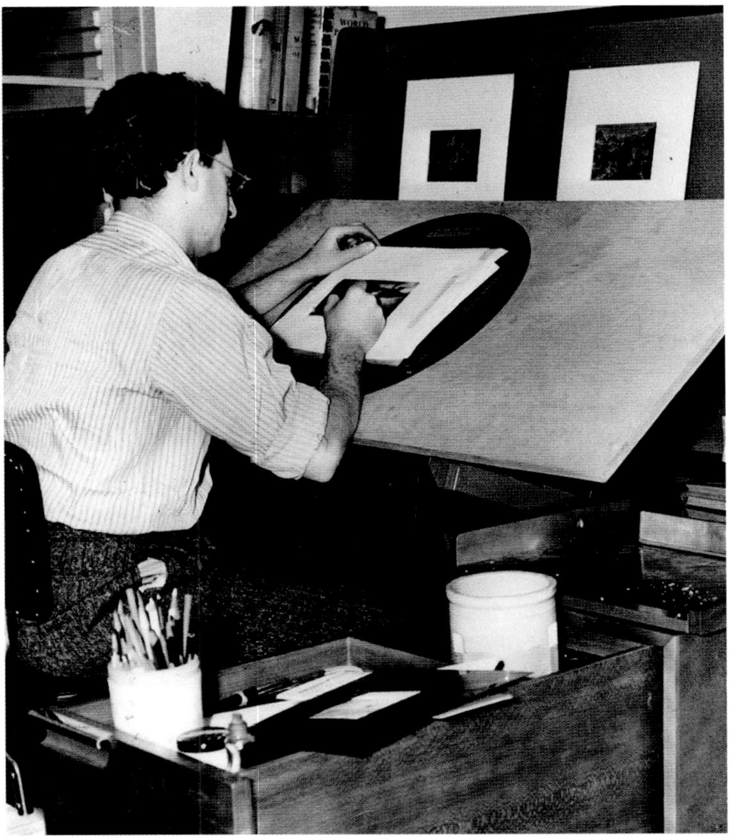

Disney artist working on Fantasia (1940) at a Kem Weber designed background desk. Photo by Baskerville. ©UCSB

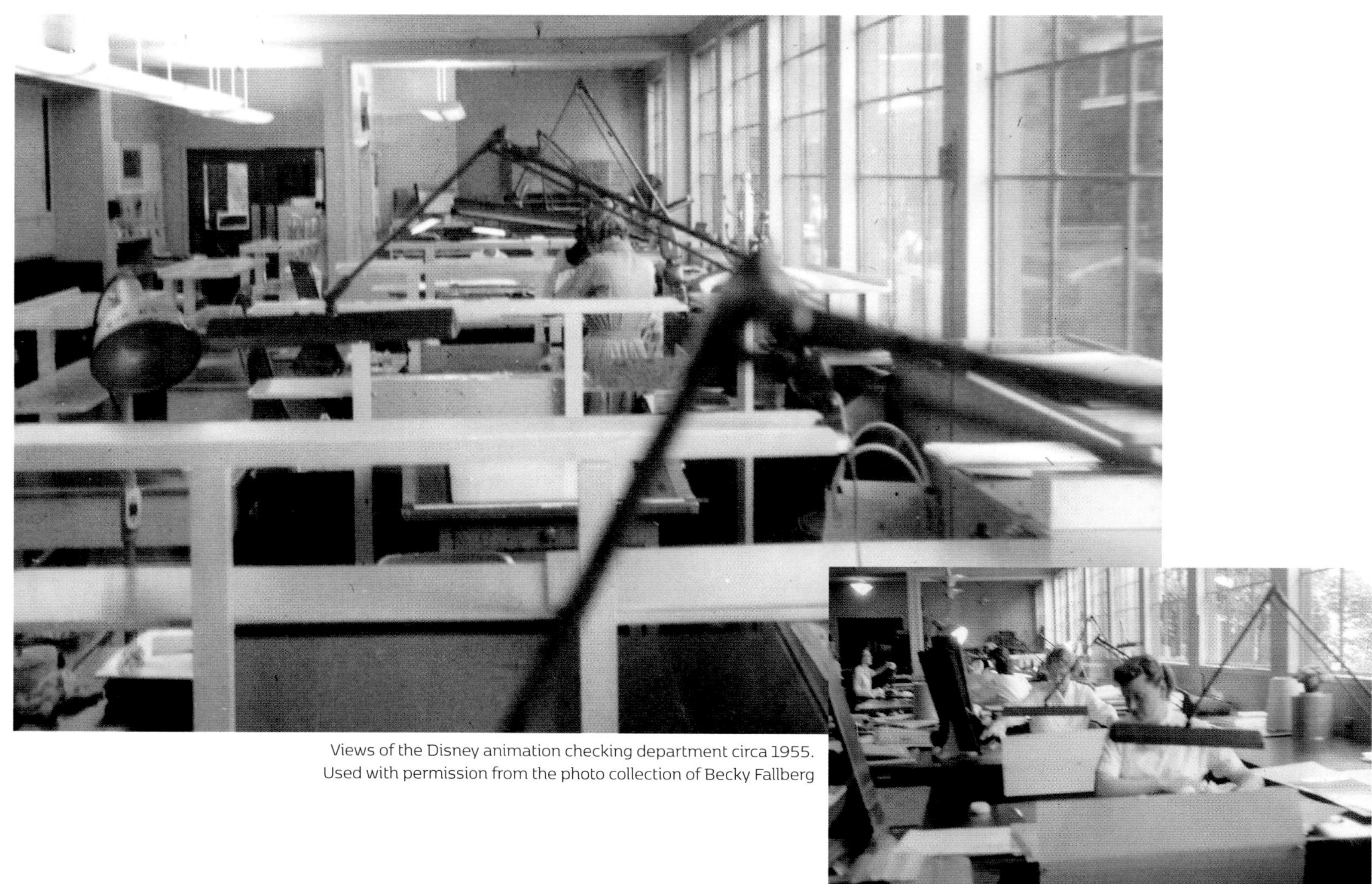

Views of the Disney animation checking department circa 1955.
Used with permission from the photo collection of Becky Fallberg

CHAPTER 11
THE CHECKER'S DESK

"Simplicity is the ultimate form of sophistication."
-Leonardo Di Vinci, Painter, Sculptor, Inventor

The checker is the first stop after a scene of animation, both character and special effects, and layout are completed. The checker's job was to create a set-up of each frame of the scene and "check" it to make sure that it will work properly in the continuity of the overall scene. During the days of hand-drawn animation, the checkers also made notations to combine animation levels because the traditional animation process allowed for only four cel levels under the camera. This is because the cel density beyond the four levels begins to darken and distort what could be photographed through the animation camera. So, if multiple characters were animated on separate levels or sheets of paper, some of those levels would need to be combined onto one cel level and the checker called out those instructions for the ink and paint department.

The Checker's Desk, UNIT No.2B, had a large drawing board that measured 72 inches long and was equipped with an equally long peg bar that allowed the checker to setup each frame including pan scenes. The desk, as with all the animation furniture, had an adjustable stainless steel pipe footrest on the bottom section. Behind the drawing board was a short back with three shelves that ran the full seventy-two-inch length of the desk. The shelves were deep enough to handle the standard animation paper and pan length drawing as well.

There is also a Checker's Filing Cabinet, UNIT No.17, that was a raked shelving unit used to hold the various levels of animation in a scene. The unit had ten shelves that were raked back so that the shelves were on a slight upward angle for holding artwork securely. The entire shelving unit sat in a metal tubular frame with wheels for ease of movement and placement by the checker. Again, this was so that each checker could customize their own work space with having the unit on either side of their desk and at whatever angle worked best for them.

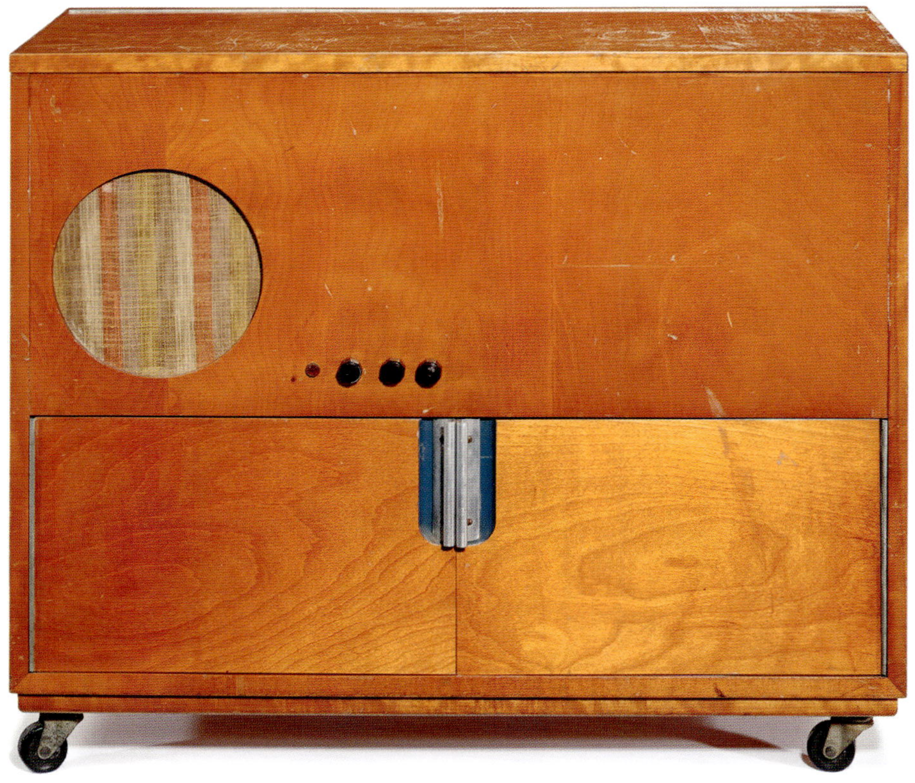

Kem Weber designed playback Unit No.8. Photograph by Los Angeles Modern Auctions

CHAPTER 12
ANCILLARY FURNITURE PIECES

"Style is very personal. It has nothing to do with fashion. Fashion is over quickly. Style is forever."

-Ralph Lauren, Designer

The remaining Weber designed office furniture pieces are mostly storage or filing cabinets, shelving units and worktables. Many of these pieces are designed as either free-standing floor units or, without a base, were used with the worktables in various combinations. These are all cabinet and shelving units that gave the artists extra space to spread out scenes or additional storage for reference and personal items.

One interesting piece is the Model Sheet & Layout Storage File, UNIT No.5, which looks like a regular three drawer filing cabinet, but is larger. It was designed to hold the oversized paper that is indicative of the animation process and for which an off the shelf filing cabinet did not work. Instead, one was designed to be twenty-inches by twenty-two inches and was made out of the same wood as the furniture using the same drawer-pulls mounted in the painted recessed channels.

There are also two different wardrobe closets. One is a single closet, UNIT No.12, and the other is a doublewide, UNIT No.12A. Each had a mirror on the inside of the door and a cross bar to hang garments with a hanger. Above the crossbar is a shelf for hats, which have gone in and out of fashion over the years. These were designed and built for the offices, which were bare spaces devoid of any ornamentation or built in closets. Again, the philosophy was one of streamlined simplicity and affording the artists inhabiting the offices to fully customize their workspace.

One of the most interesting and rare pieces of furniture is the Playback Unit with Record Storage, UNIT No.8, on rollers. The piece measures sixteen-inches by thirty-six inches and was used by the animators to listen to the dialogue of the character they were animating. This was a purpose built record player, which pre-dates reel-to-reel or cassette tapes. It played either wax or acetate records allowing the animators to have

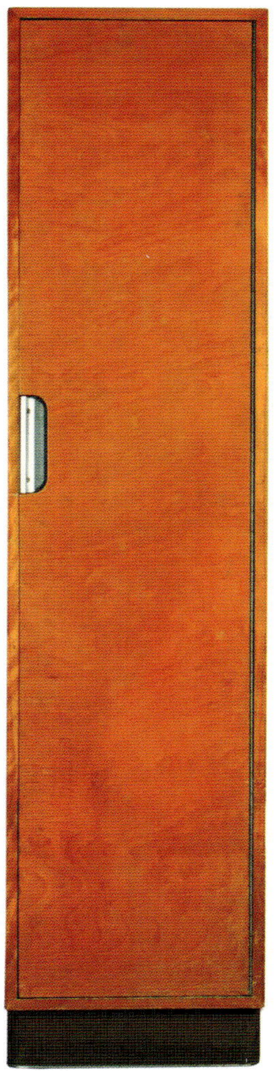

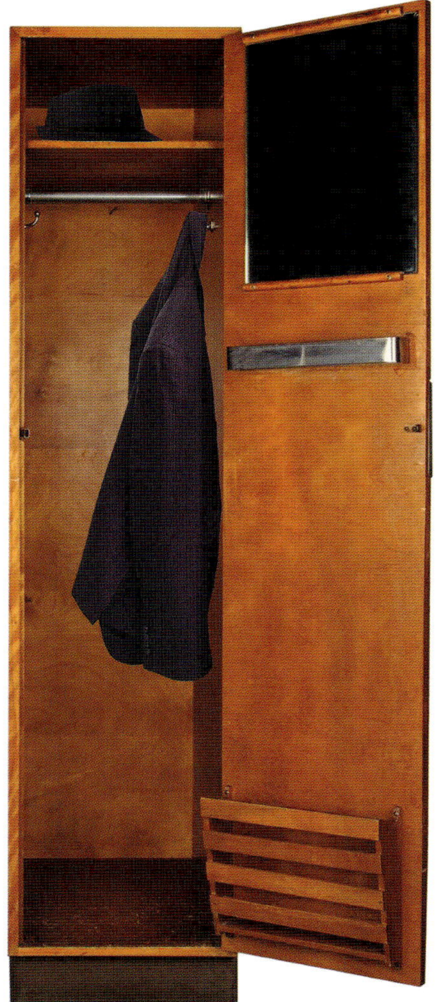

Kem Weber designed single wardrobe closet. ©Dave Bossert

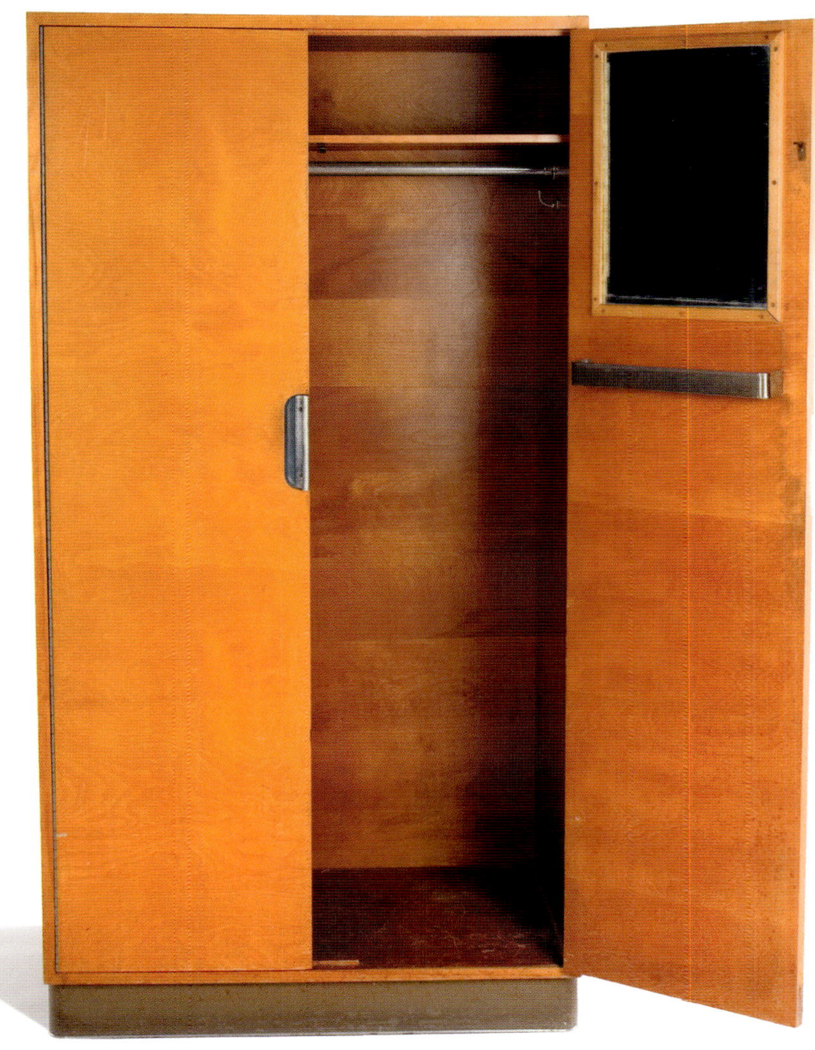

Kem Weber designed double wardrobe closet, Unit No.12A. Photograph by Los Angeles Modern Auctions

sound reference in their offices.

There were also two regular office desks created that had the same design attributes as all the other furniture pieces: a small office desk, and a standard office desk. The standard office desk had drawers on both sides with a thin center drawer and measured thirty-four-inches by sixty-inches. On the left side were three drawers and a thin pullout pencil/pen tray. On the right side was also another thin pullout pencil/pen tray, a regular single drawer and a standard filing drawer below. The small desk only had drawers on the left side and did not have the thin center drawer. The small desk measured thirty-four-inches by forty-five-inches. On the left side there is a thin pullout pencil/pen tray, a regular single drawer and a standard filing drawer below.

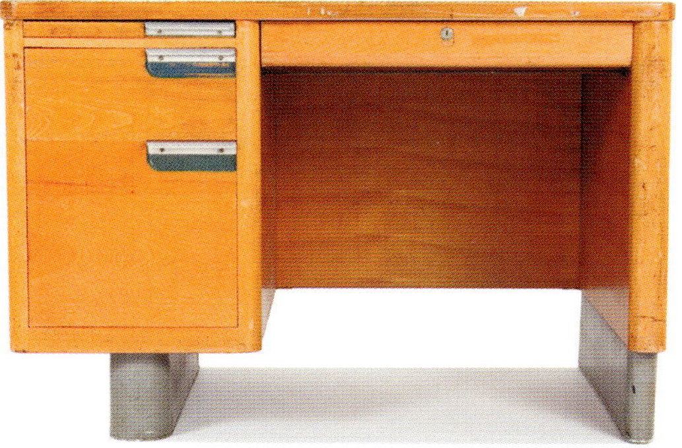

Above: Kem Weber designed small office desk, Unit No.24. Photograph by Los Angeles Modern Auctions

Bottom left: Kem Weber designed wall clock. Courtesy of Michael Jedlicka

Bottom middle: Kem Weber designed step stool used especially for pinning storyboards. Courtesy of Jorgen Klubien

Bottom right: Kem Weber designed paint table with shelving. Courtesy of Jorgen Klubien

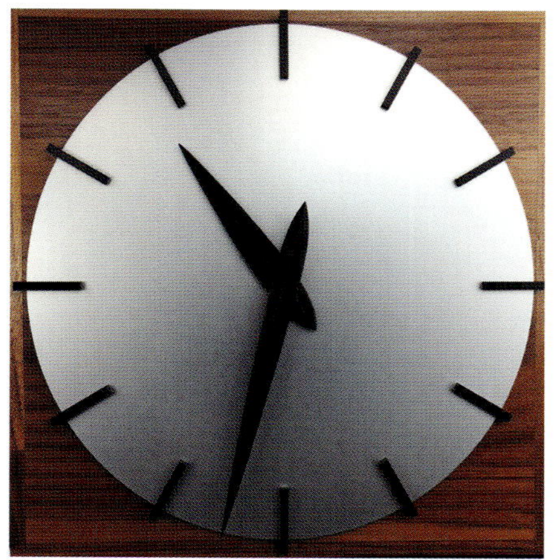

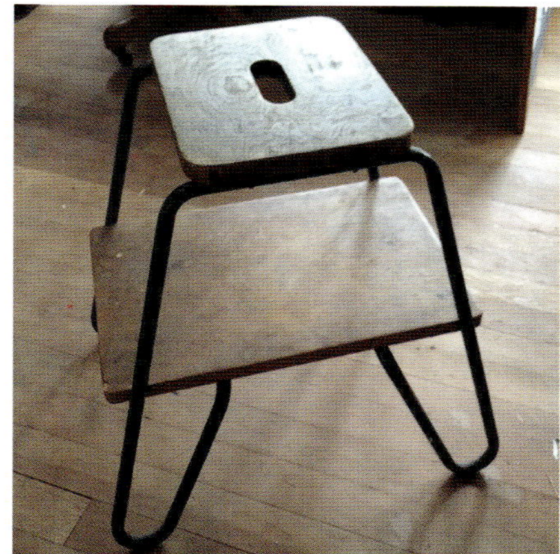

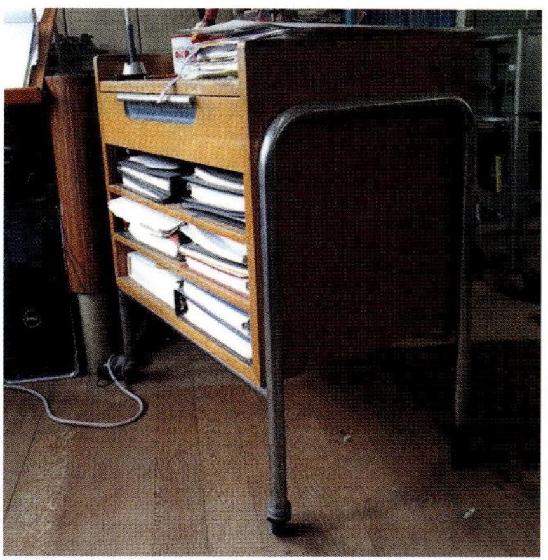

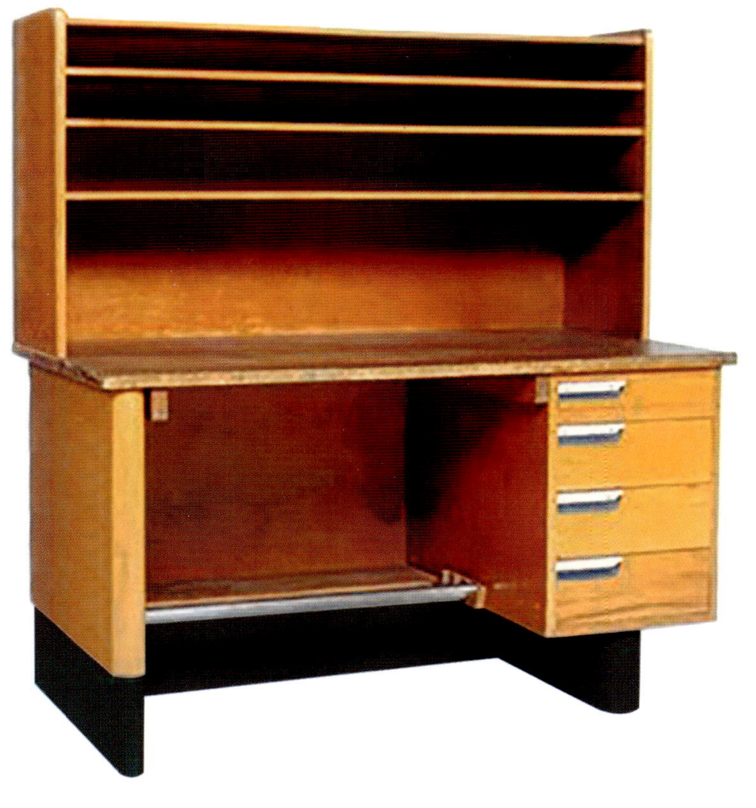

Left:
Kem Weber designed Modified animator's work table, Unit No.20 used by the author for many years at Walt Disney Animation Studios. Note that the original Armstrong linoleum #26 is painted black. ©Dave Bossert

Right:
Kem Weber designed extra shelving unit which sat on the very top shelf of the animator's and assistant animator's desk providing additional space to spread a scene out. Some artists also used the unit as an end table as indicated in this photo. Photograph by Los Angeles Modern Auctions

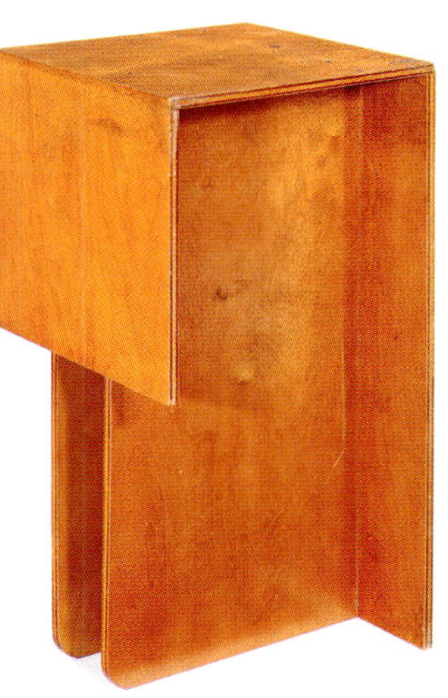

EPILOGUE

> "Of all the things I've done, the most vital is coordinating those who work with me and aiming their effort at a certain goal."
>
> -Walt Disney

When the animation department was moved off the studio lot in 1985 to a warehouse on Flower Street in Glendale, the Weber furniture, which was big, really felt too big for the size of the offices. The luxury of the spacious offices in the animation production building on the studio lot was forever gone and the new office spaces were a harbinger of things to come.

With the advent of digital technology and Walt Disney Animation Studios switch to computer generated animation, the need for spacious offices diminished as artists were working on computer terminals and there was no longer a need to spread a scene out on a large desk. The computers, especially with the flat panel monitors, needed little space and there was specialized furniture for computer use. The Weber animation desks started to become obsolete.

The storage cost for the animation furniture was expensive and management looked for ways to reduce the Weber animation furniture inventory. They began to sell off some of the furniture through warehouse sales to employees. Animators that retired or were laid off were offered their desks for free as a parting gift. Some of those desks had a provenance to them—they may have belonged to Disney Legends and had a lineage. An animation desk belonging to one of Disney's Nine Old Men, Eric Larson, sold at a Heritage Auction in 2017 for $13,145.00.[86]

Walt Disney and his artists refined the animation process, setting standards that were adapted industrywide and continued to be on the leading-edge of analog technology. Today, the artists at Walt Disney Animation Studios continue that tradition of artistry and innovation in the digital age. As with all new advancements, what came before eventually becomes outdated, outmoded, and no longer practical to use as the art form evolves. That is the case for the Weber animation furniture.

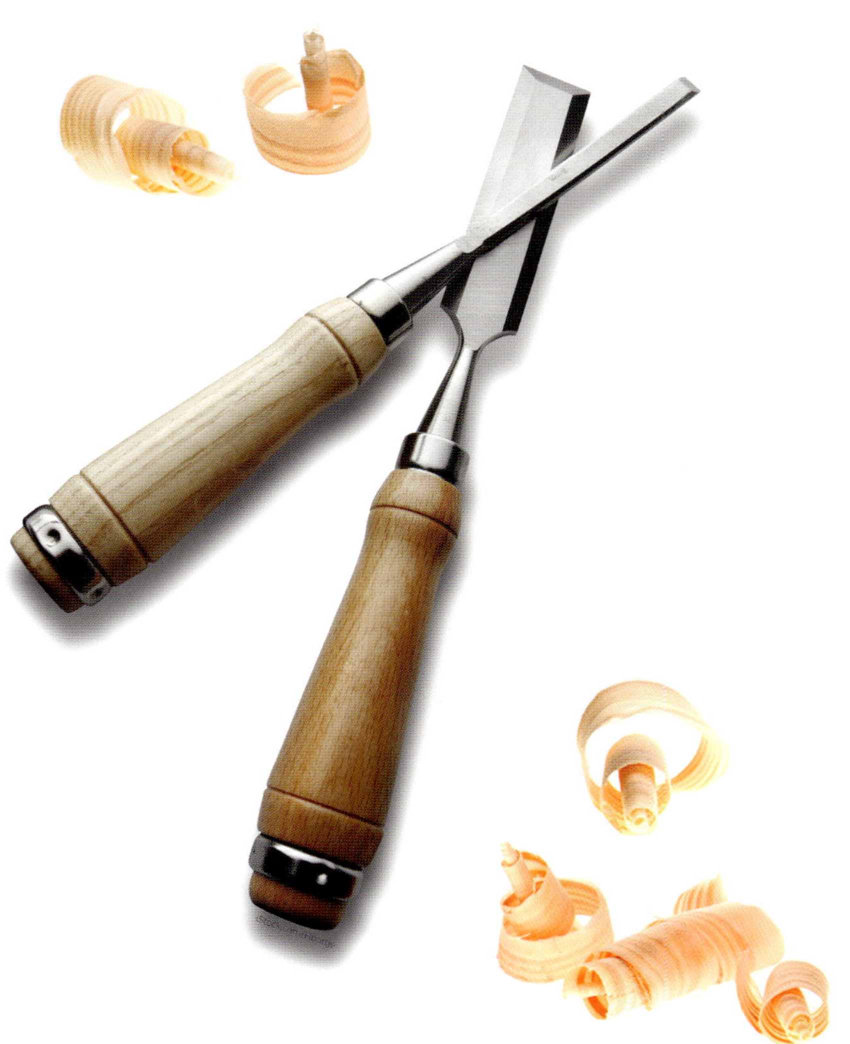

The Kem Weber animation furniture served its purpose well and the animation art crafted on it is a testament to that service. As with tools of any trade it is time to preserve and celebrate this furniture: to remember those legendary artists and the magnificent films that they created at The Walt Disney Studios on this very furniture.

Although, I would argue that some of this furniture is ripe for adaptation—a repurposing, which is what I have done with my Kem Weber animation desk. It has become my writing desk and a beautiful one at that. As has been stated by others, there is an aura to it that is hard to describe other than to say, you can feel the history, the mojo, the spiritual quality and the soul, that is embedded in these desks. I feel it every day when I sit at my Weber desk, which I've been doing now for nearly three and half decades. Though, as I stated before, instead of drawing, now I'm writing.

Like a beautifully restored antique car that is lovingly cared for, there are many more miles left in my desk and plenty of more stories to tell along the writing highway.

CONSTRUCTION NOTES

> "To create something exceptional, your mindset must be relentlessly focused on the smallest details."
>
> -Giorgio Armani, designer

It is worth noting a few points about the construction of the Kem Weber designed animation furniture for The Walt Disney Studios. The main structure of the desks is made primarily of solid core plywood also known as "lumber core plywood." This is a type of plywood in which lumber is "edge glued into a solid slab" and then sandwiched on the face and back with veneers. The ability of this solid core plywood "to bounce back makes it an excellent choice when constructing long or wide shelves in cabinets or closets."[87]

Weber incorporated long horizontal shelves on the animation desks, again as a design element that can be seen throughout the studio complex. The shelves are likely glued and doweled into the side panels of the desks. The only sure way to know is to deconstruct a desk, which we wouldn't do. The one flaw of these long shelves was that they did sag over time in the middle, especially if weighted down with stacks of animation paper or books.

Weber chose solid core birch plywood for the bulk of the furniture construction. Birch is a hardwood that has a generally straight grain and even texture. It varies in color from a near white sapwood to a more reddish tone that, when finished with a varnish, will tend to take on a warm golden hue that darkens slightly over time. You can see this coloration in the animation furniture today with a beautiful golden patina more than seventy years since the furniture was manufactured. Birch is very similar to maple, which many have mistaken as the wood from which the furniture was made, but the construction drawings indicate birch plywood. We know it is solid core plywood from firsthand inspection and it was a typical use for furniture during that time period.

The flat surface drawing board with the animation disc seated in it was fitted with a custom-designed metal mechanism allowing for the board tilt to be changed. A lever underneath the board, when pulled, adjusted the drawing board to whatever angle suited the artist. The underside of the drawing board was also fitted with a light box that, when illuminated, created the under-lighting needed in animation to see through multiple levels of animation paper. There was a clever light dampening device that covered the lights to regulate the luminosity. I guess they didn't have dimmer switches back then!

The drawers are constructed using a mortise and tenon style joint. The face of the drawers is solid birch and the side-rails of the drawers appear to be either ash or a light birch. The side-rails are 5/16" thick except for at the bottom where it flairs out to 3/8." There are no drawer glides or any hardware for the drawer to sit in the desk. They likely used bees wax as a lubricant for the drawer to slide freely.[88] Each drawer pull is made from stainless steel and is fastened with screws to a recessed channel in the drawer face that is curved on the interior end and painted a muted blue-gray color. This is the only area on the furniture that is painted a color. The rest of the furniture is varnished wood.

The single side supports and the black bases of the furniture that have the rounded ends are made out of birch plywood over a white pine frame. The bases of the small and large office desks are covered with Armstrong #26, standard grade Linoleum, which is gray in color. The bases for the animation furniture had the same but over time, many were painted black—no doubt to cover up decades of scuffs and damage to the linoleum.

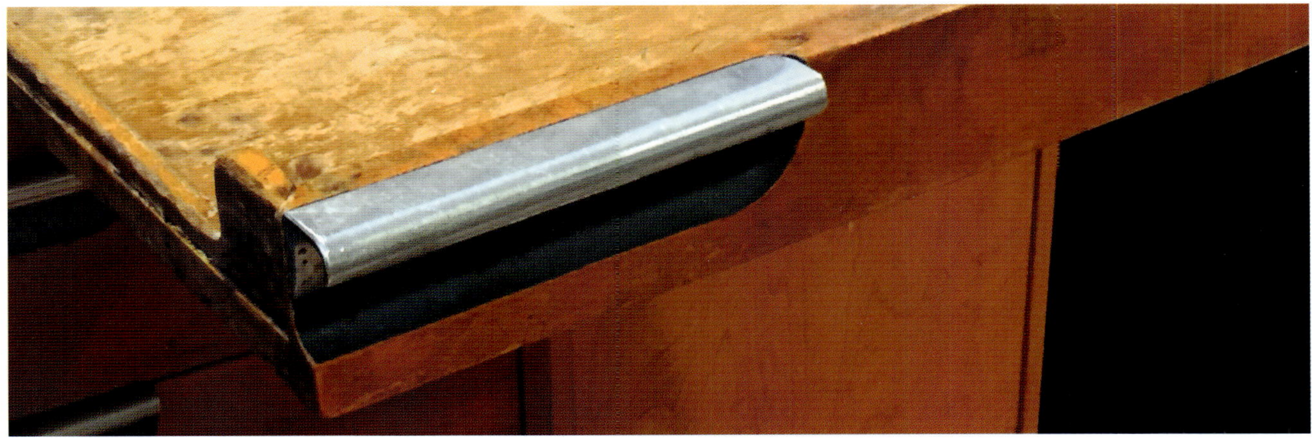

Construction detail of the "breadboard" drawer which was common on many of the Kem Weber designed Disney animation desks. It is a thin, long drawer that resembles a kitchen breadboard and allowed the artist additional space for drawing implements and paper. Note the beautiful workmanship involved in the recessed drawer pull accented by the only use of paint on the furniture. Photo ©Dave Bossert

QUICK REFERENCE GUIDE
TO THE DISNEY ANIMATION FURNITURE

1. UNIT No.1 (and UNIT 1B) - Drawers for Animation
2. UNIT No.2- Upper Animation Desk

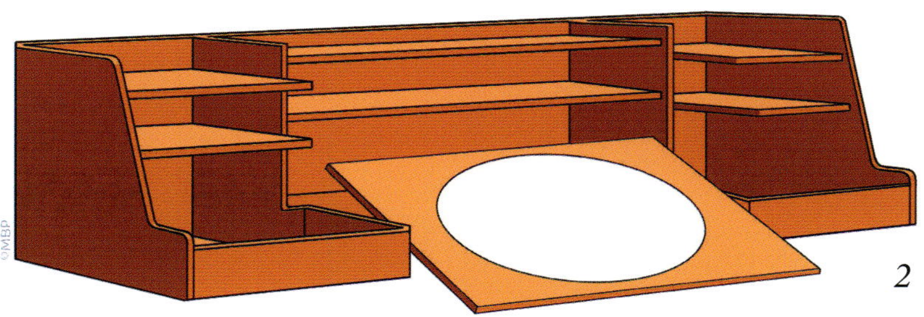

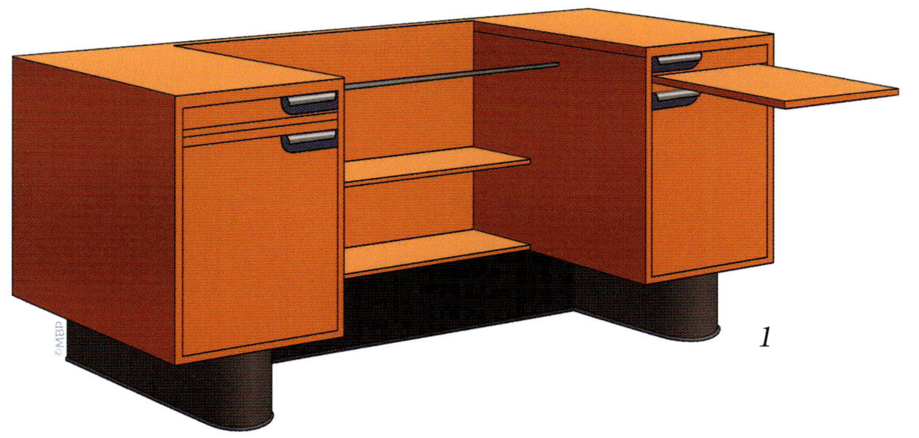

3. UNIT No.1, UNIT No.2 - Animation Desk
4. UNIT No.1, UNIT No.2 - Animation Desk with base riser
5. UNIT No.1, Raised UNIT No.2 - Animation Desk

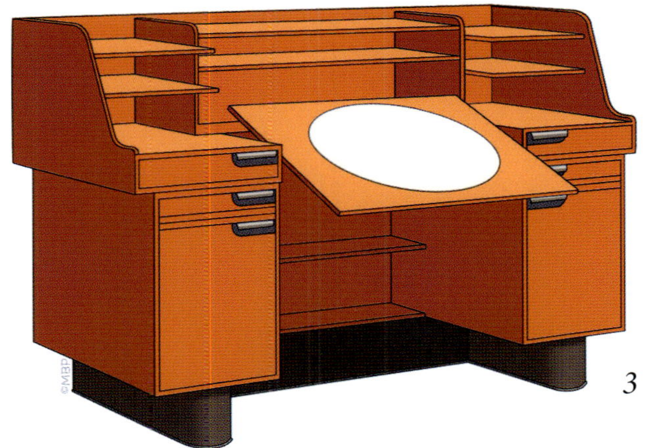

3

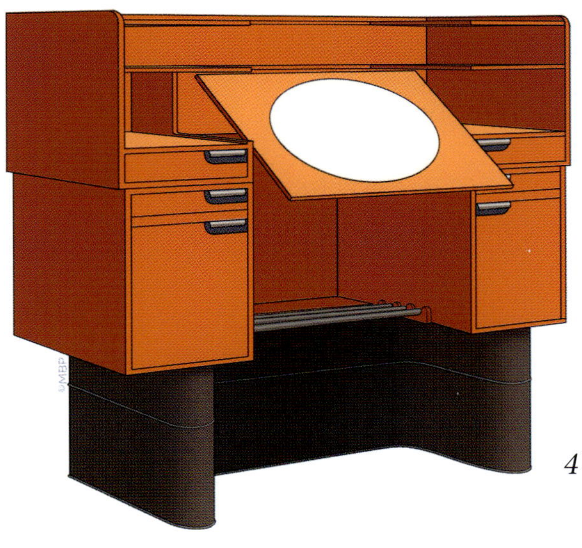

4

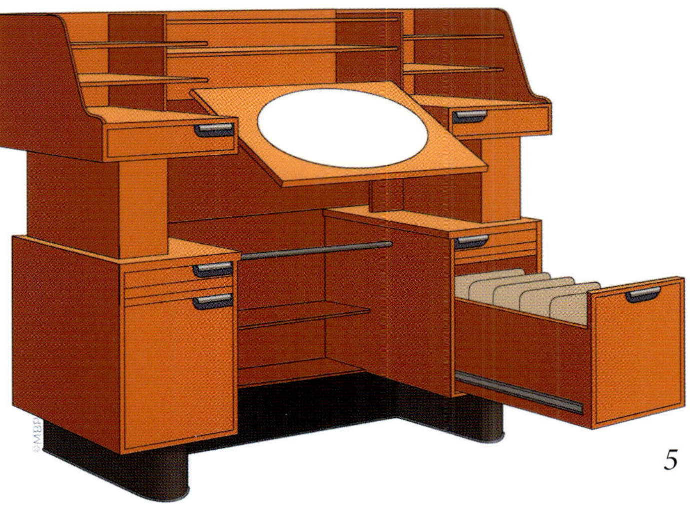

5

6. UNIT No.1A, UNIT No.2A- Layout Desk with base riser

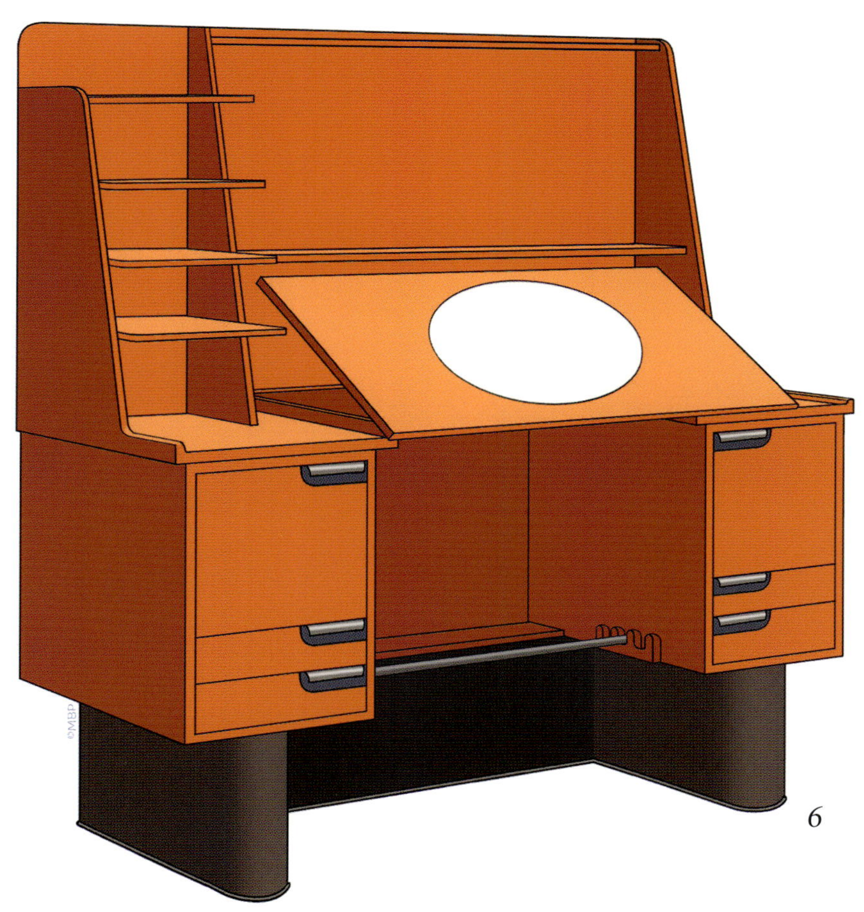

7. UNIT No.1A - Drawers for Layout
8. UNIT No.2A - Layout upper desk

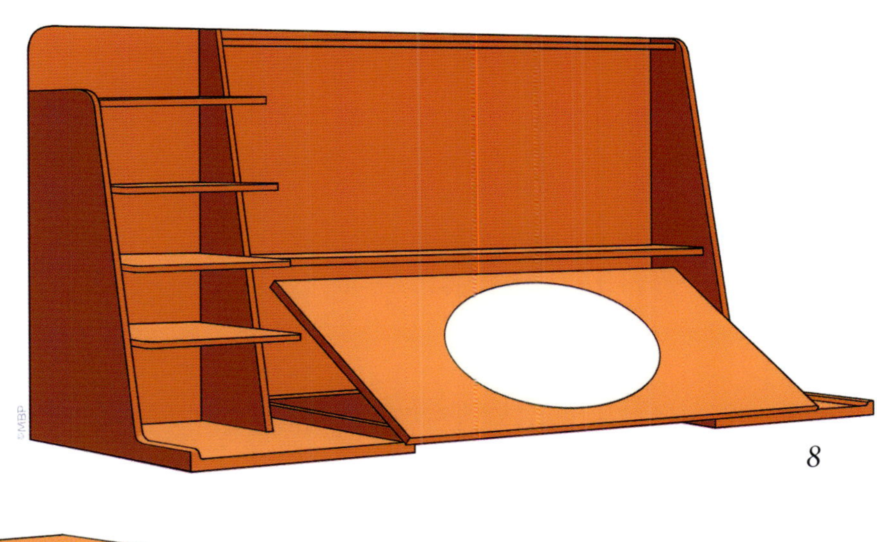

8

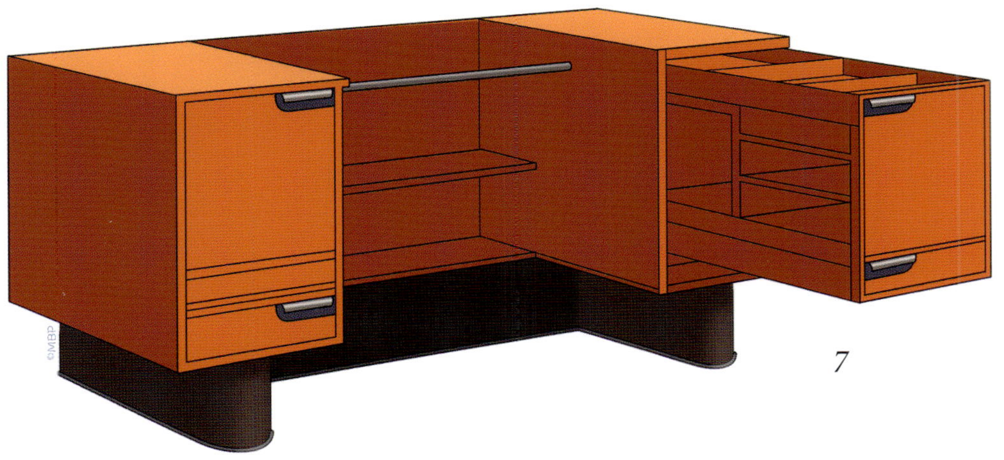

7

9. UNIT 2B- Checkers Desk

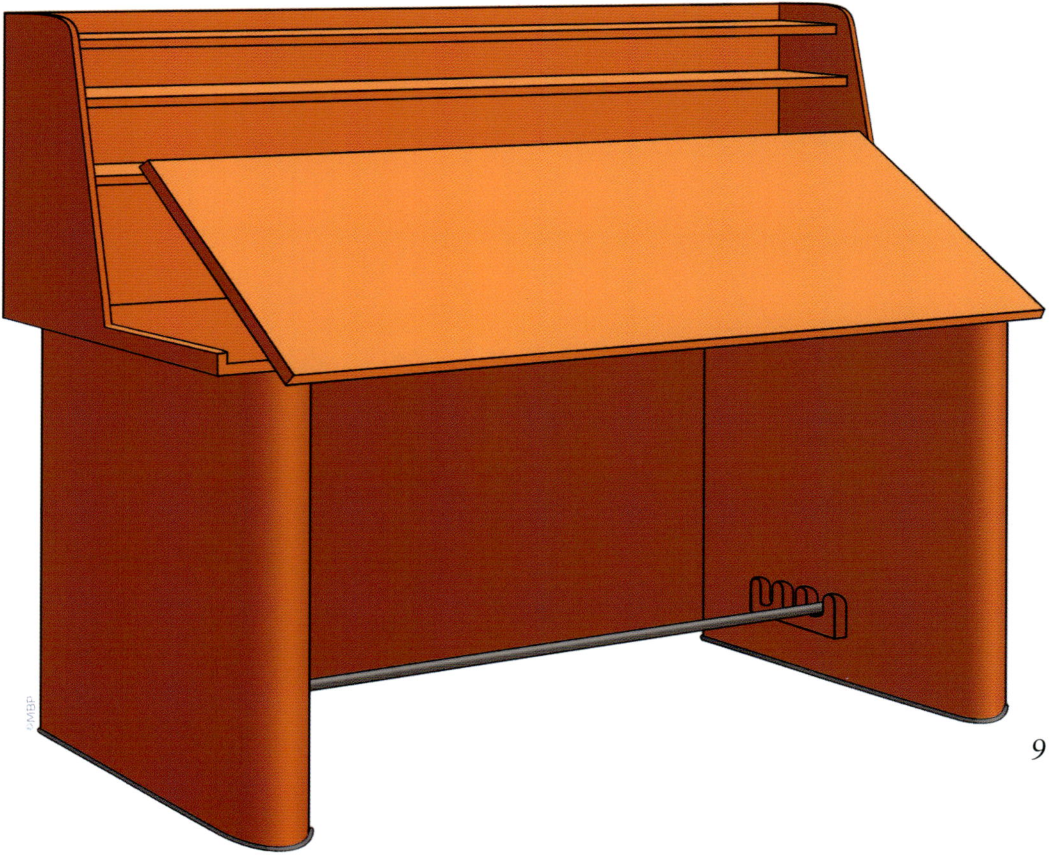

10. UNIT No.1B (and UNIT No.1) - Drawers for Checkers

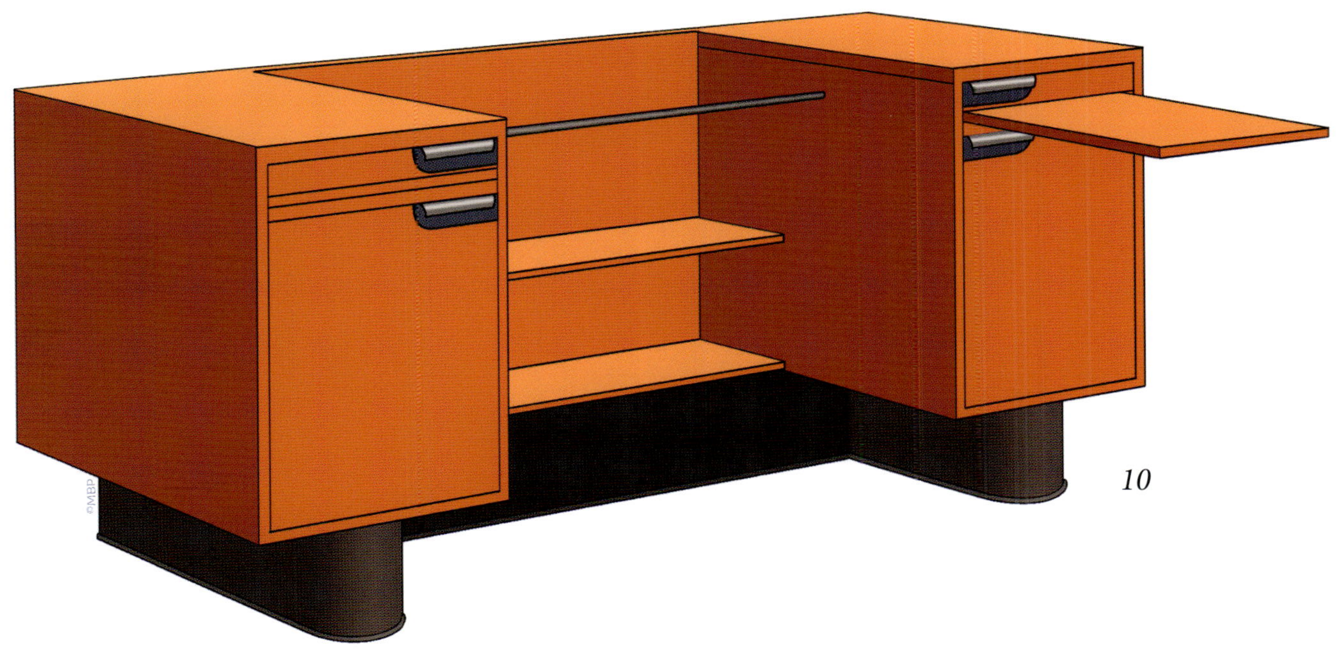

10

11. Animator's Work Table with interchangable upper units.
This one uses UNITS No.1, No.3 and No.9

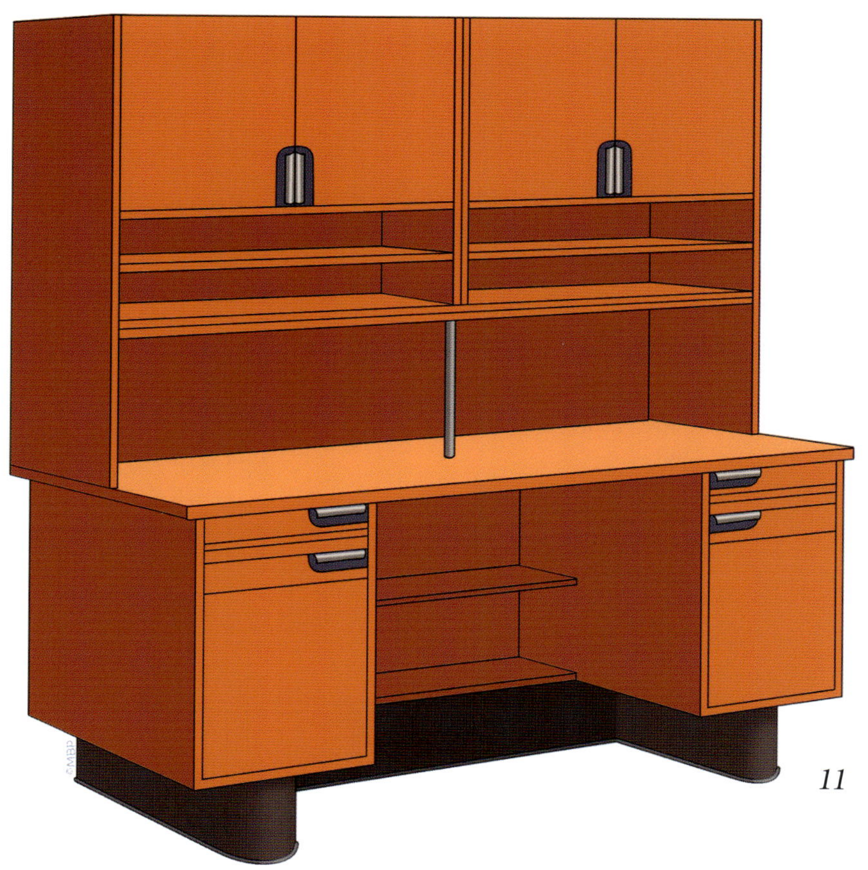

12. UNIT No.1 - base animation drawers
13. UNIT No.3 - shelving unit
14. UNIT No.9 - cabinet unit

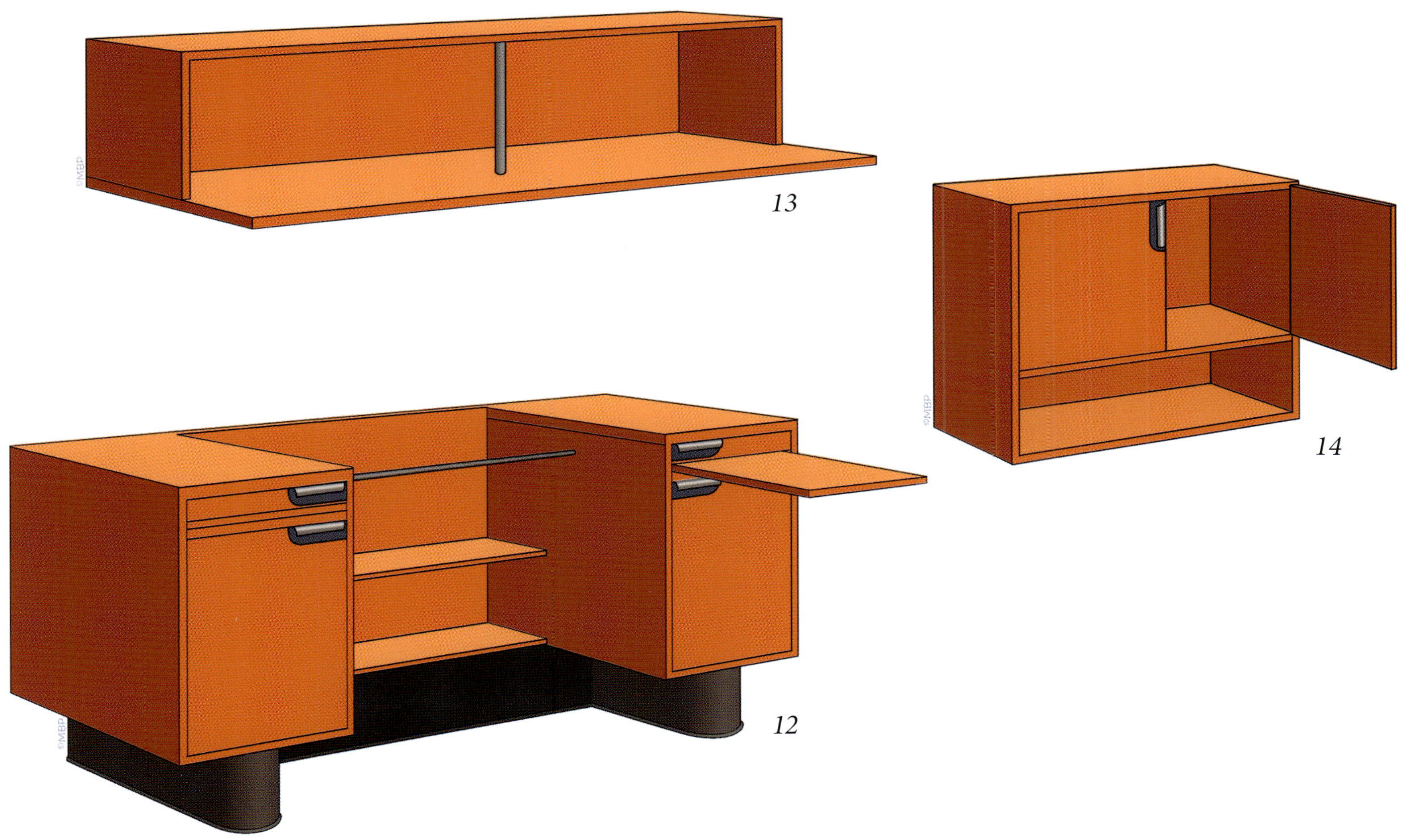

15. Layout Central Table using UNITS No.4 and No.9 with base UNIT No.13

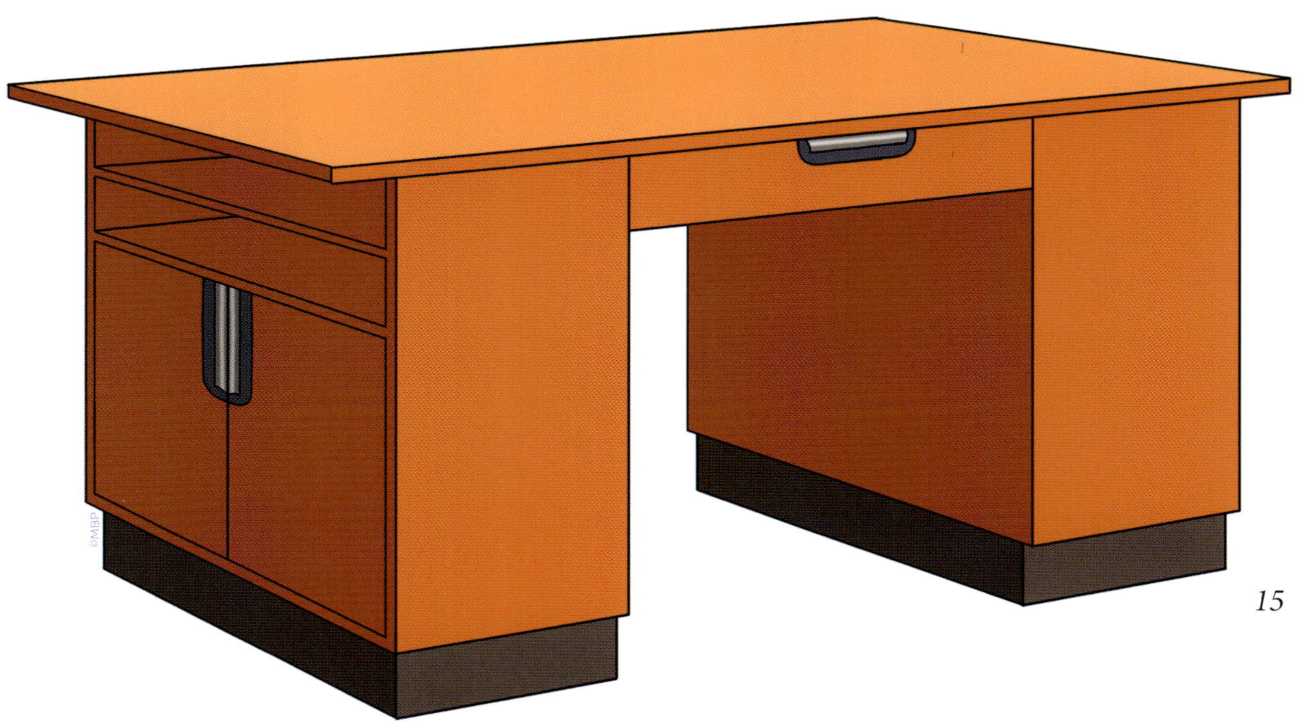

16. UNIT No.4 - Work table unit
17. UNIT No.9 - Cabinet Unit

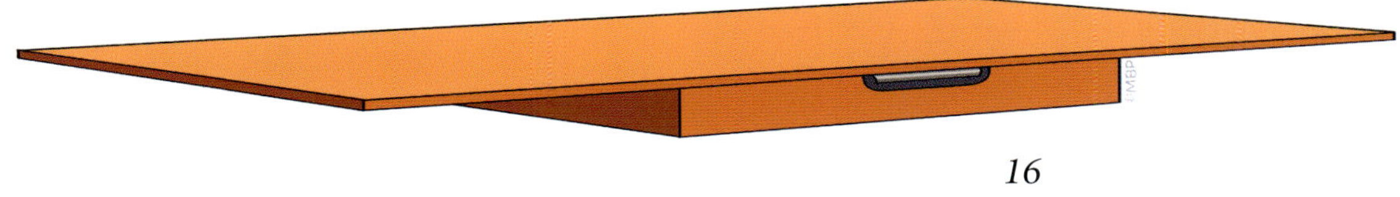

16

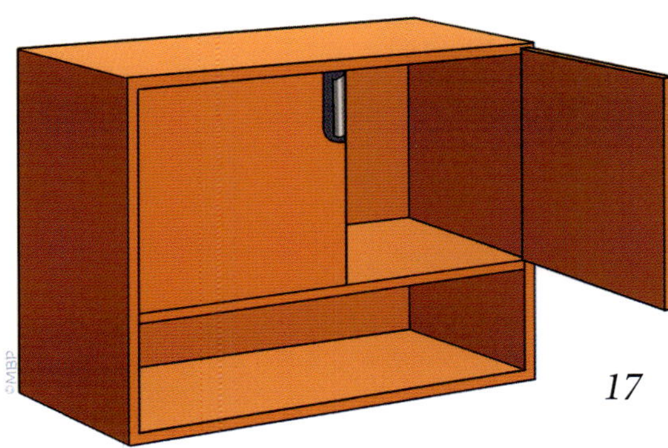

17

18. UNIT No.5 - Model Sheet & Layout Storage Unit
19. UNIT No.6 - Adjustable Shelf Unit
20. UNIT No.7 - Door Unit, Adjustable Shelf

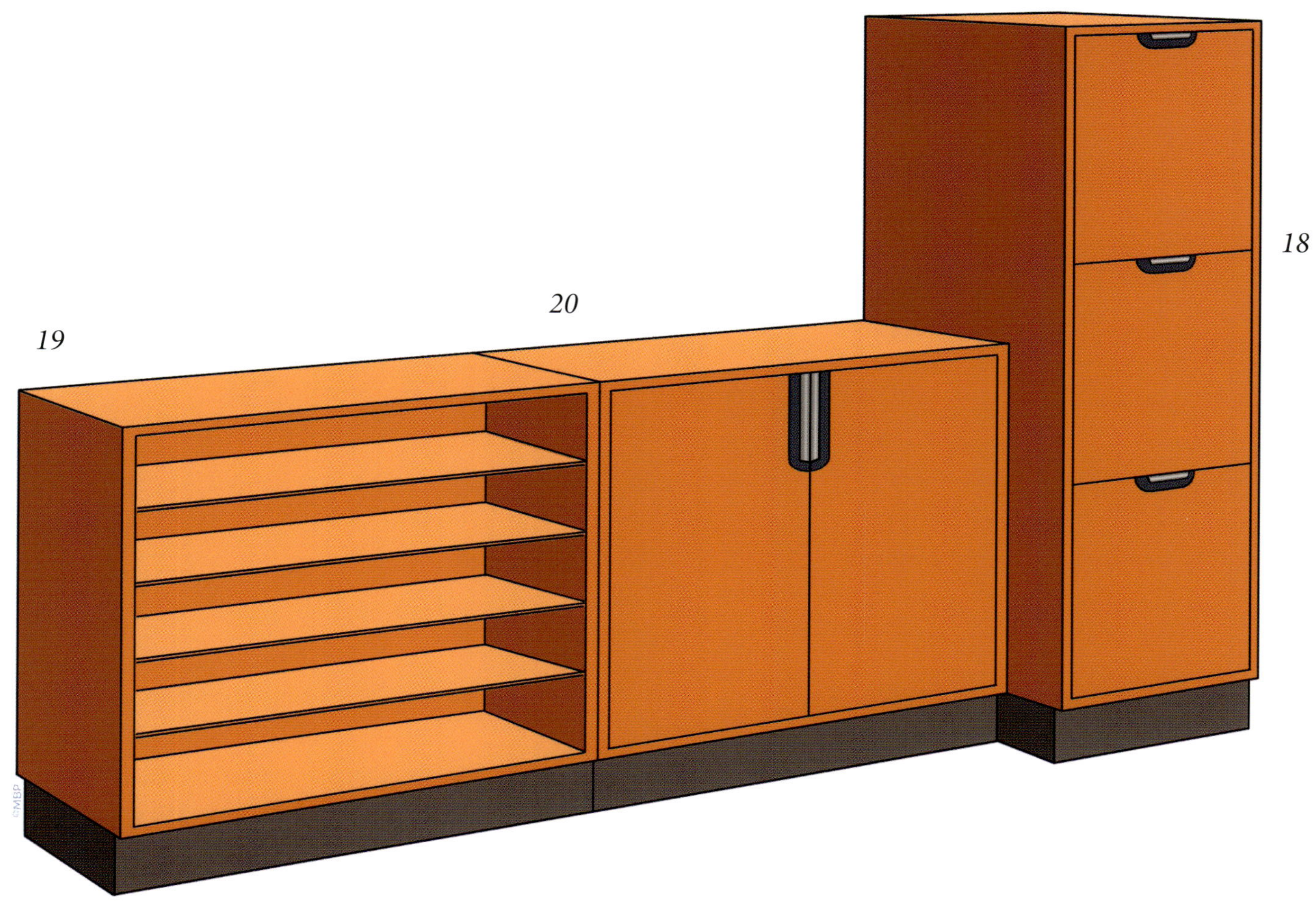

21. UNIT No.11 - closed and open (with UNIT No.13 base)
22. UNIT No.9 - Cabinet Unit
23. UNIT No.10 - Drawer Unit
24. UNIT No.8 - Playback Unit with Record storage

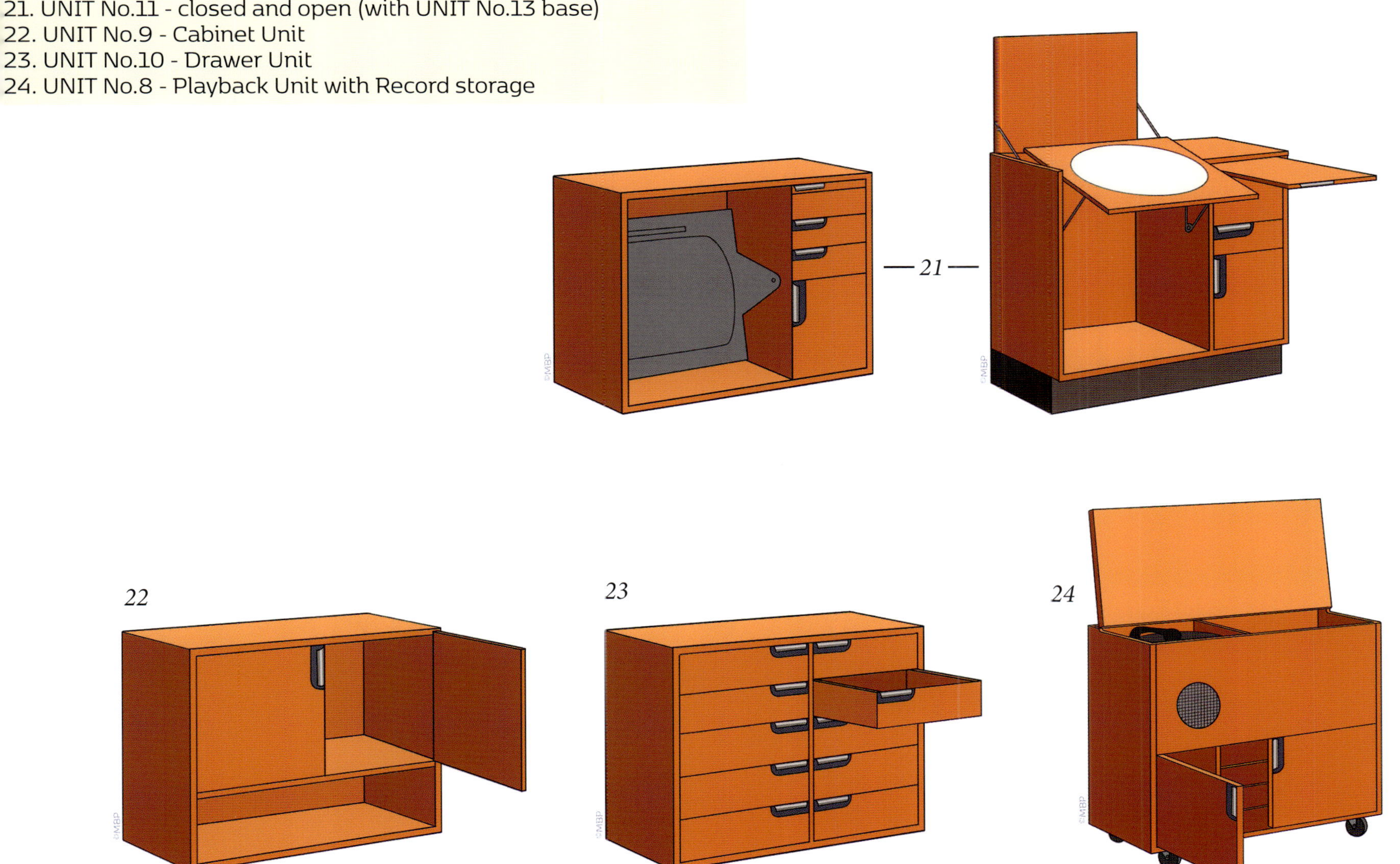

25. UNIT No.12- Single Wardrobe
26. UNIT No.12A- Double Wardrobe

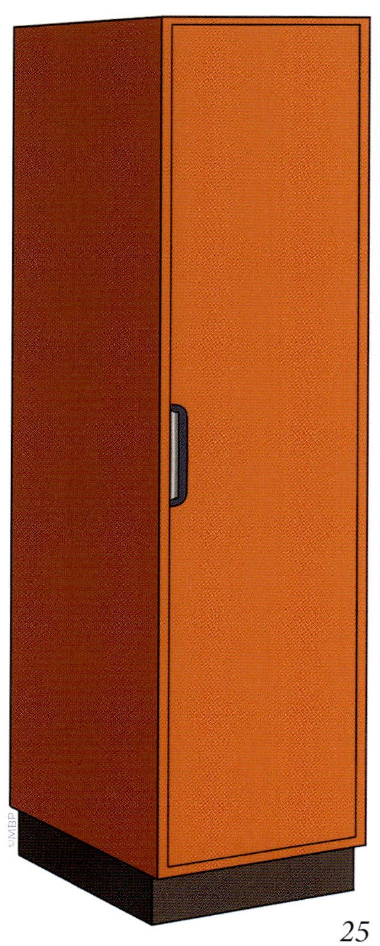

25

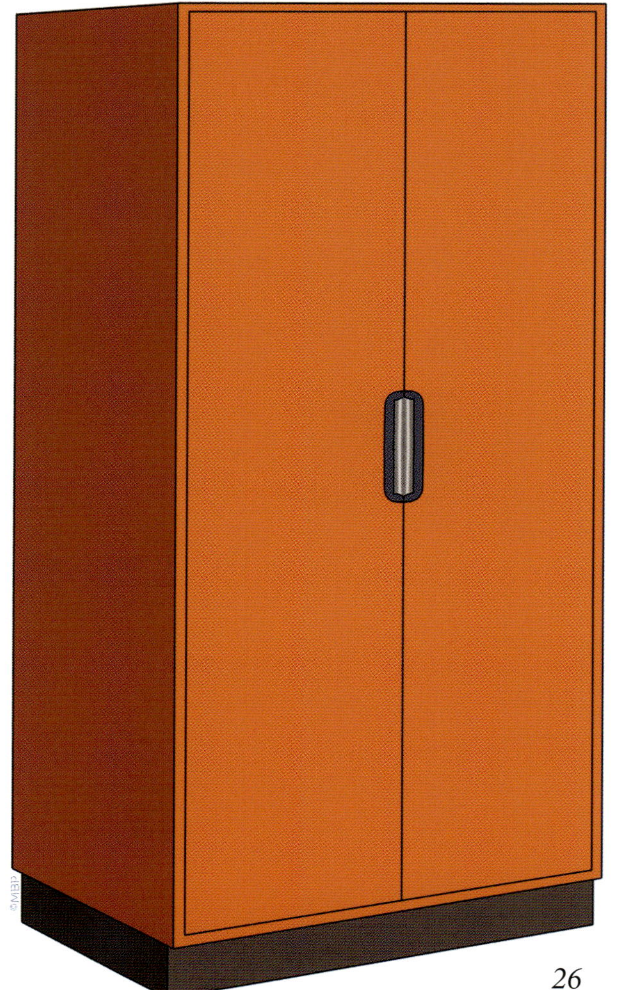

26

27. UNIT No.14 - Pan Table
28. UNIT No.9, UNIT No.10 and Unit No.12A

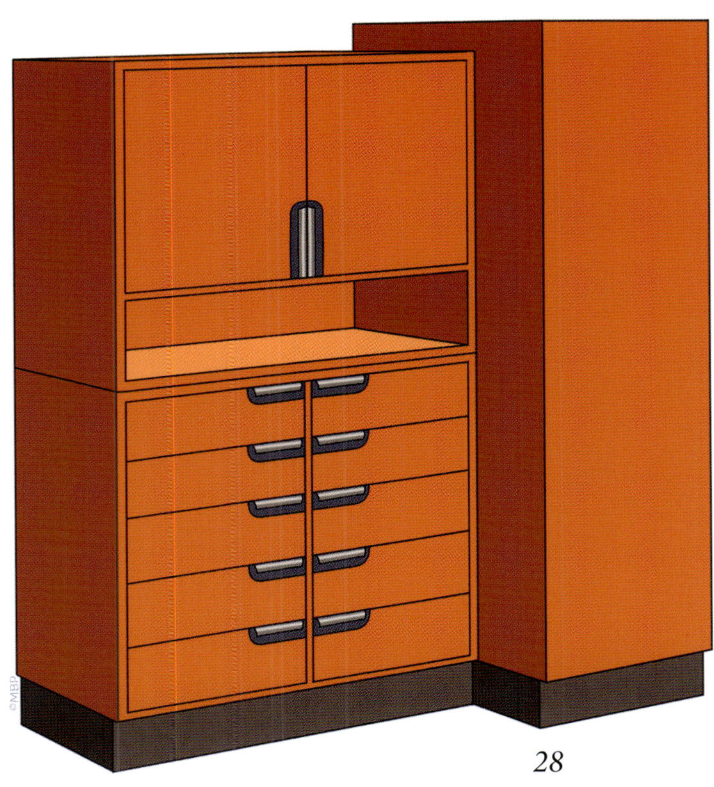

28

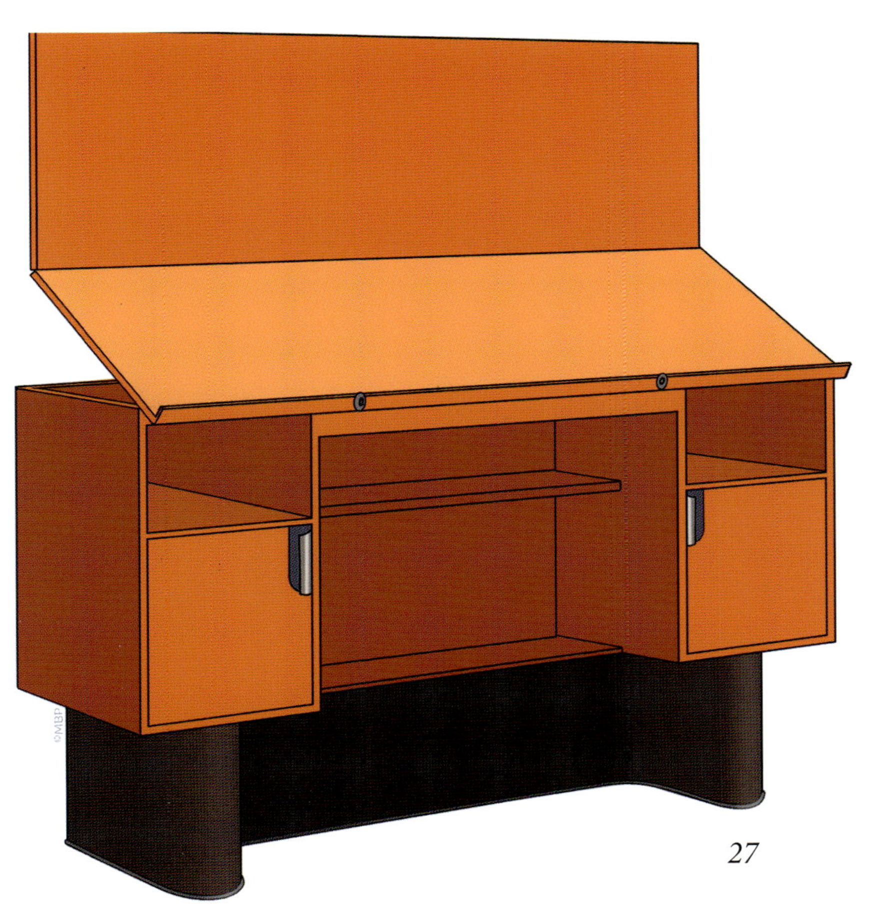

27

29. UNIT No.15 - Large Director's Center Table
30. UNIT No.15A - Small Director's Center Table

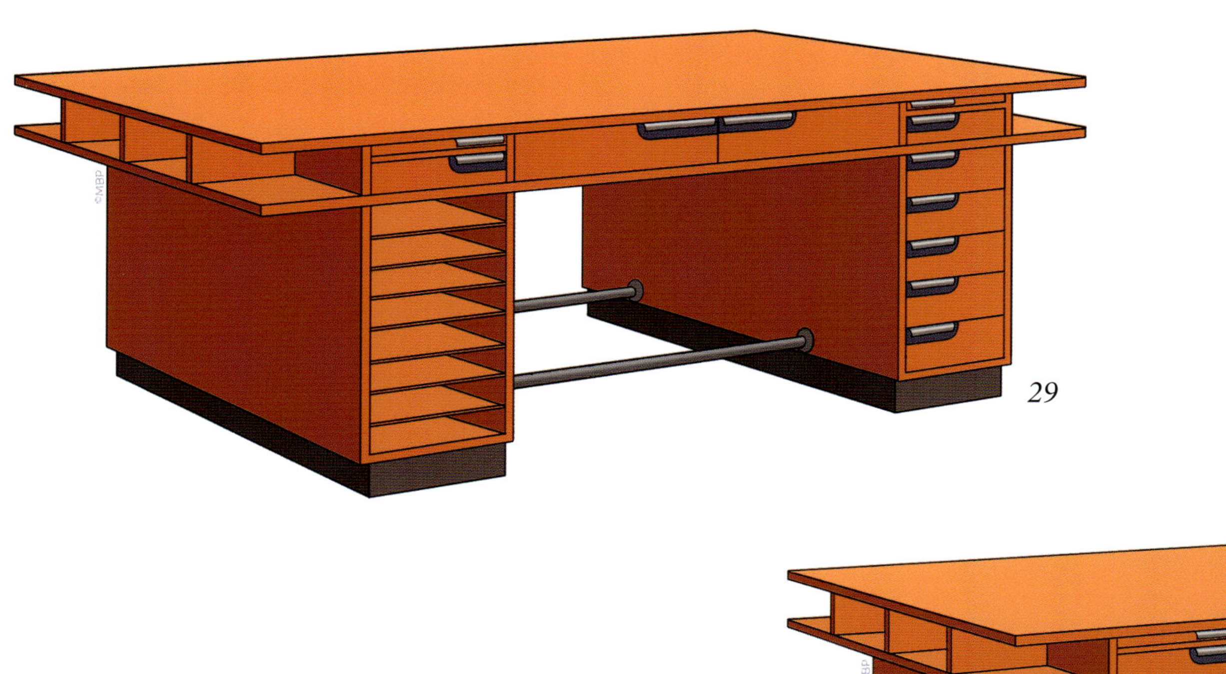

29

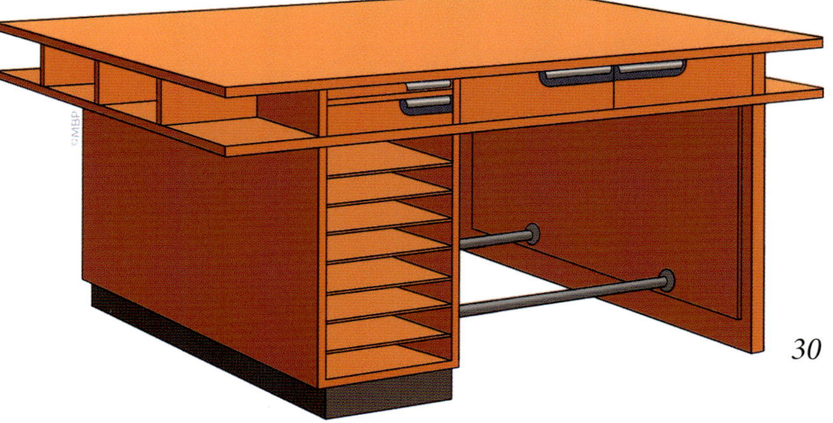

30

31. UNIT No.16 - Director's Moveable Animation Desk

32. UNIT No.17 - Checker's Filing Cabinet

*There is no UNIT No.18 listed in any reference.

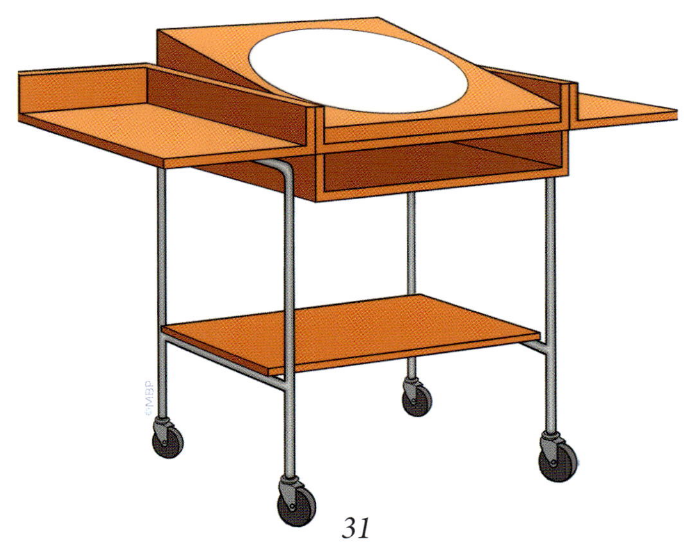

31

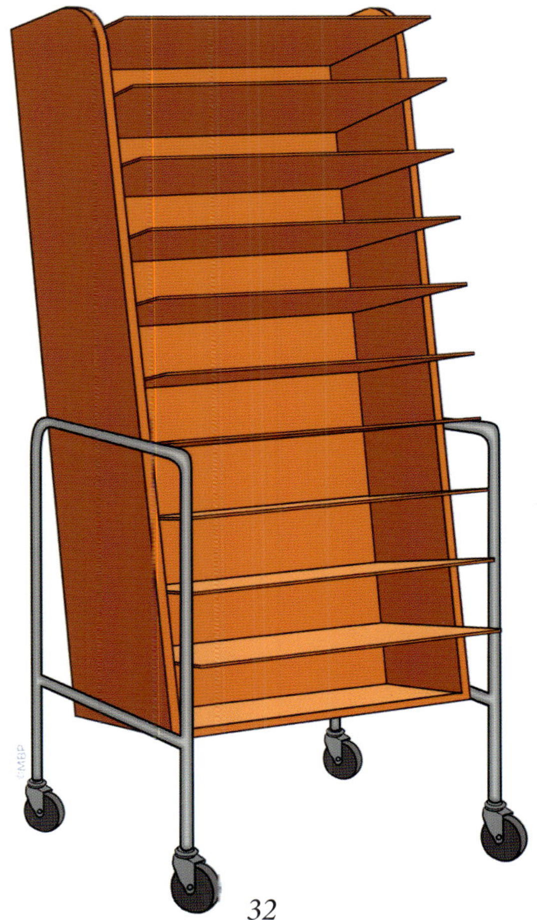

32

33. UNIT No.19 - Modified Animator's Desk

34. UNIT No.20 - Modified Animator's Work Table

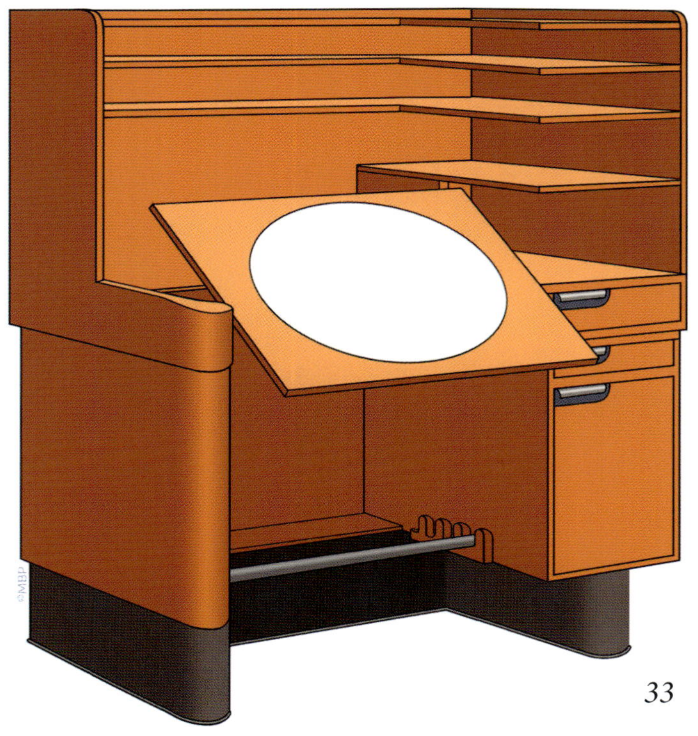

33

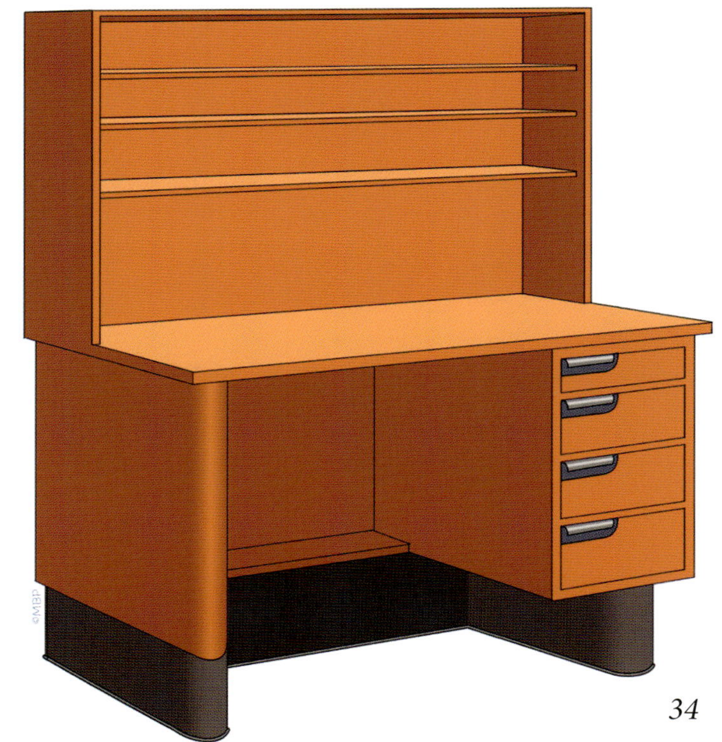

34

35. UNIT No.21 - Story Men's Sketch Desk (without disc)

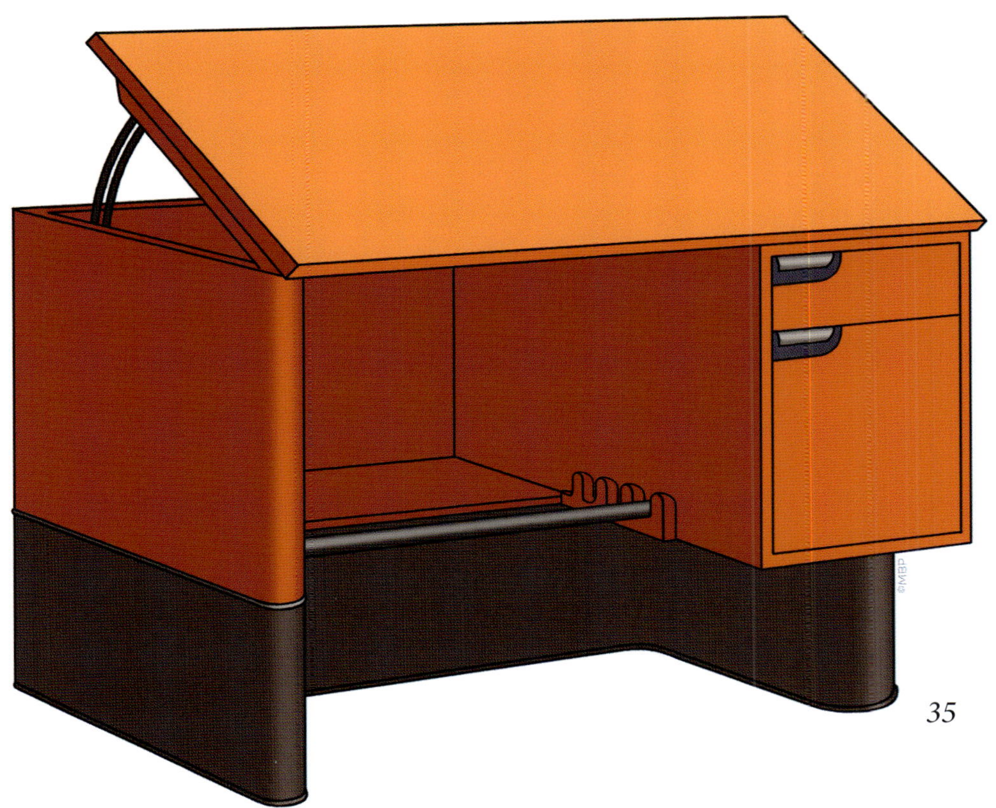

35

36. UNIT No.22 - Assistant Animator's and Inbetweener's Desk

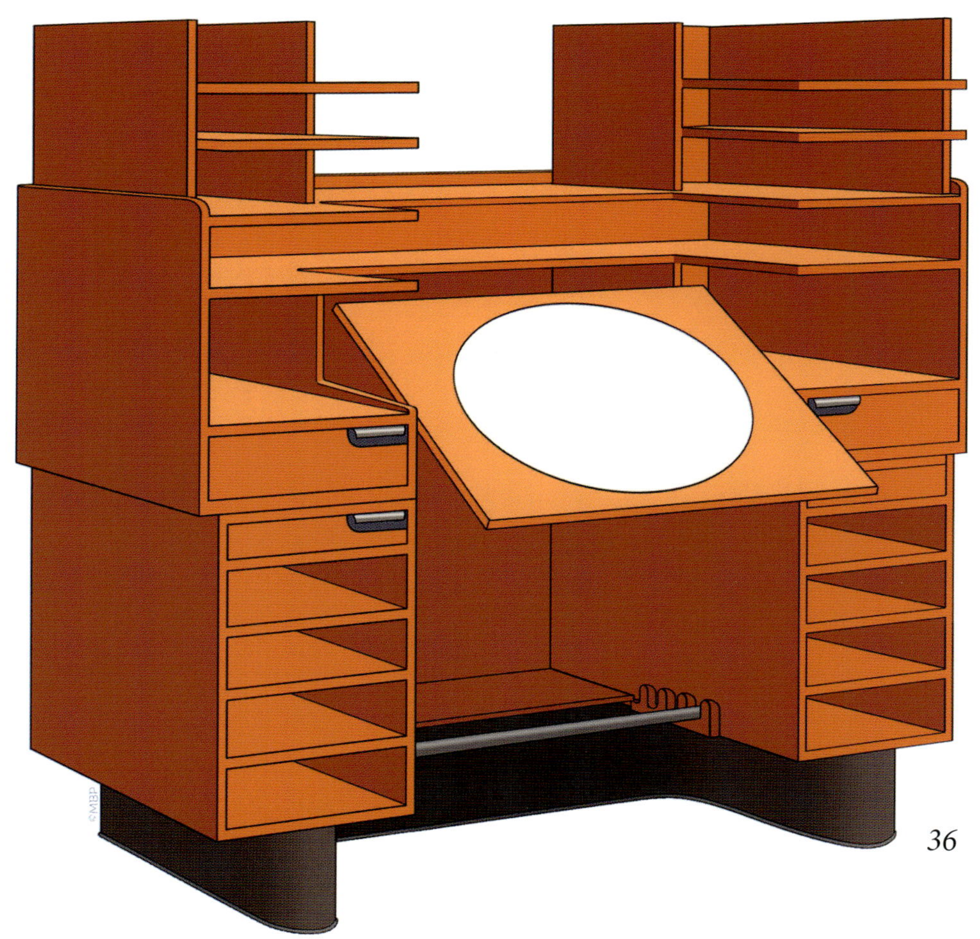

37. UNIT No.23 - Paint Table
38. Standard Office Desk
39. Small Office Desk

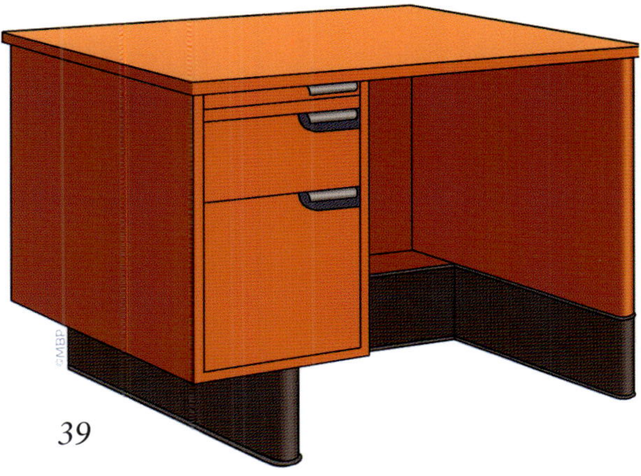

39

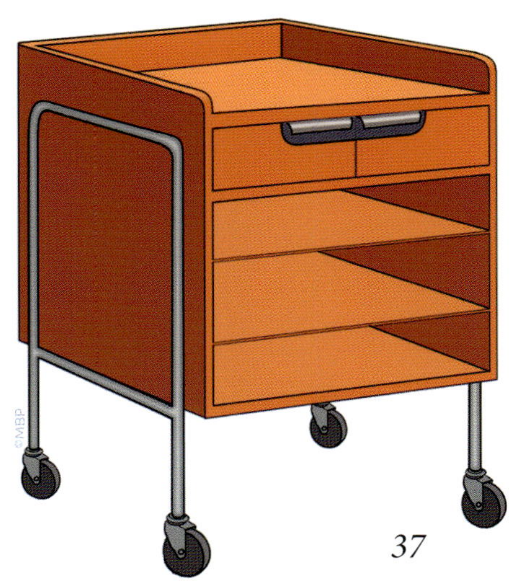

37

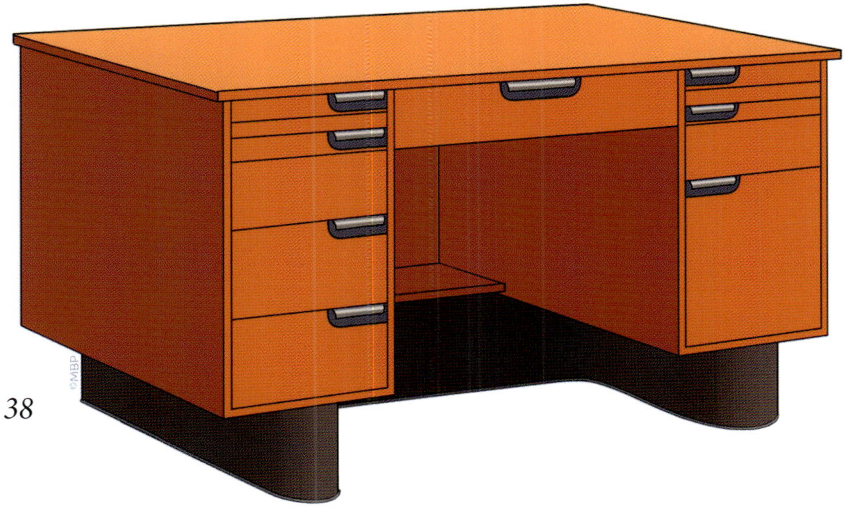

38

GALLERY

> "There is no magic in magic, it's all in the details."
>
> -Walt Disney

While working as the chief designer for The Walt Disney Studio complex in Burbank, Kem Weber not only designed the animation furniture that has been discussed in-depth thus far but also other "one-off" furniture pieces. He designed Walt Disney office including Walt's desk and piano as well as the private suite off of his main office.

One of Kem Weber's concept sketches for the private suite included a day bed presumably for afternoon naps. This was only a concept and never actually built that way. The private suite became more of "war room" for Walt where he could plan various projects without having to cover them up when guests came to visit. The private suite also became a brief residence when a member of the military stayed there due to a local housing shortage during WWII.

In 2015, to celebrate the 75th Anniversary of The Walt Disney Studio complex in Burbank, Bob Iger, CEO of The Walt Disney Company, dedicated the newly refurbished offices where Walt Disney worked up until his death in 1966. According to *Variety*, Iger said that the offices reminded him and many others of Walt's "devotion to his family, his curiosity and his relentless creative passion."

Kem Weber designed a variety of other spaces including the music room where Oliver Wallace, the Sherman Brothers and other composers would work with directors and story artists on the various films. There were story rooms for groups of story artists to work together on film sequences developing the story and action. The studio cutting or editorial suites, the Ink & Paint desks and color lab tables, even the physical plant for the studio. All of these spaces had the common design thread of the Streamline Moderne style.

The following pages are a sampling of some of those diverse common areas and work spaces designed by Kem Weber. It showcases The Walt Disney Studios as one of the original and preeminent creative campuses.

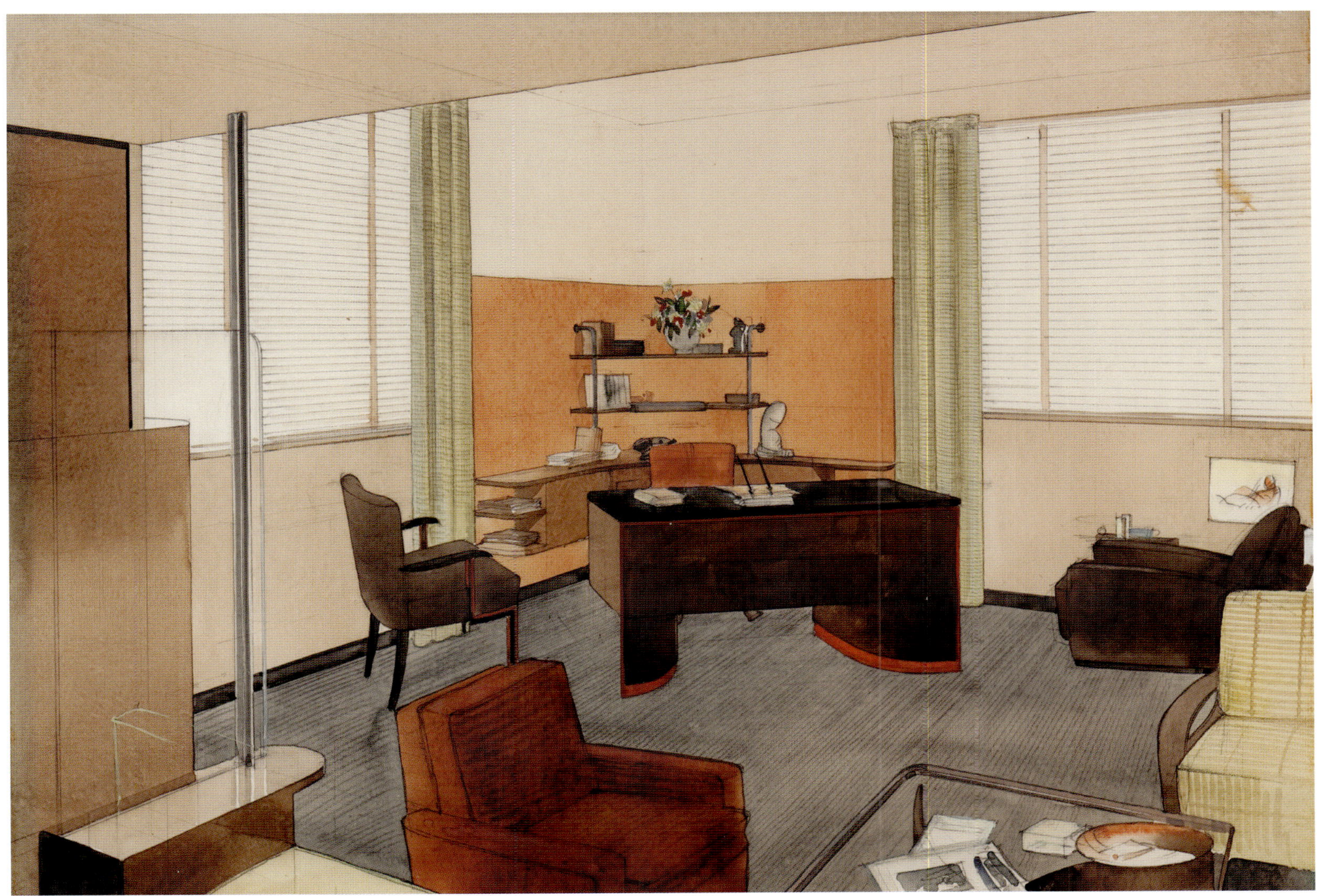

Kem Weber concept illustration of Walt Disney's office, circa 1939. ©UCSB

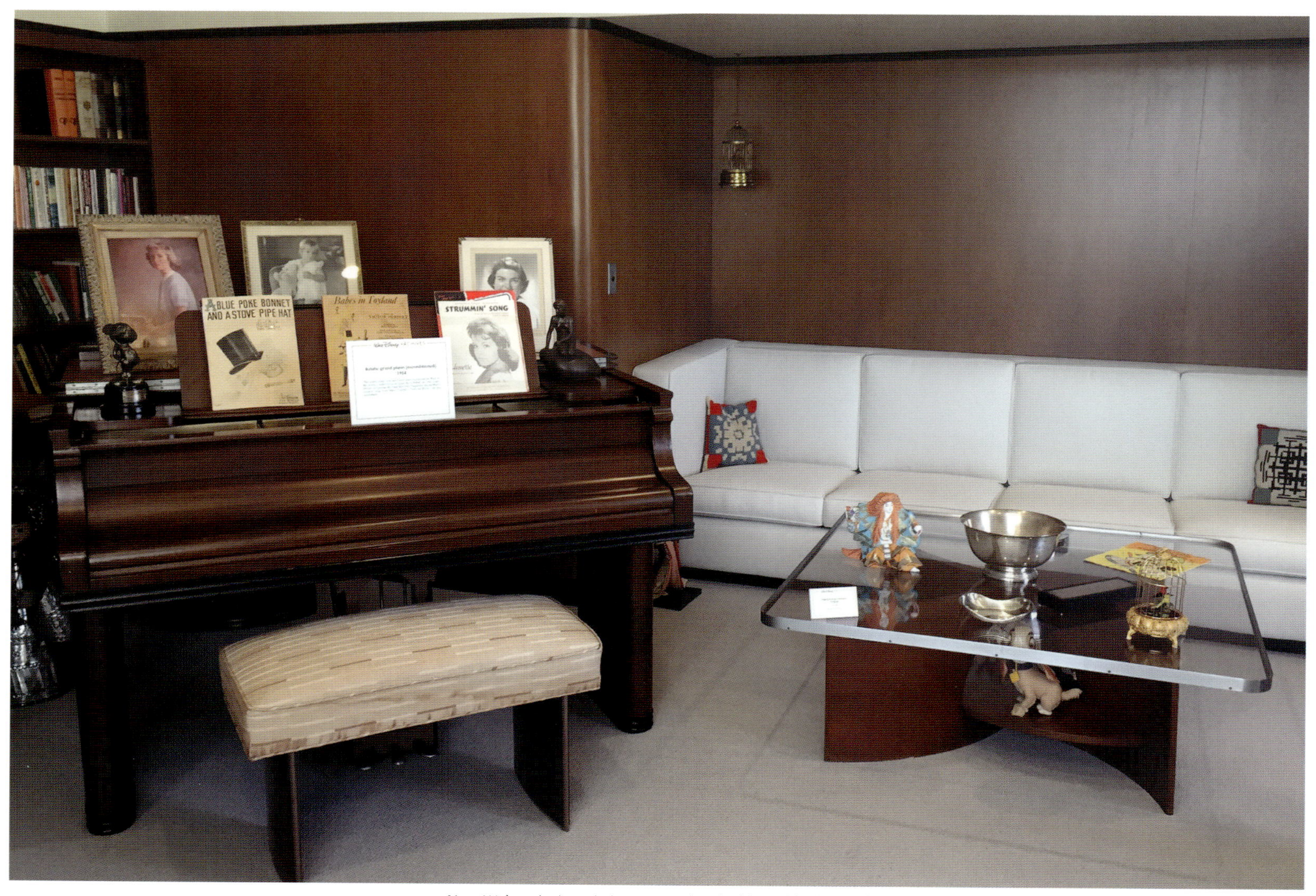

Kem Weber designed piano, occasional table and built-in sofa in Walt Disney's office. Photo courtesy of LaughingPlace.com

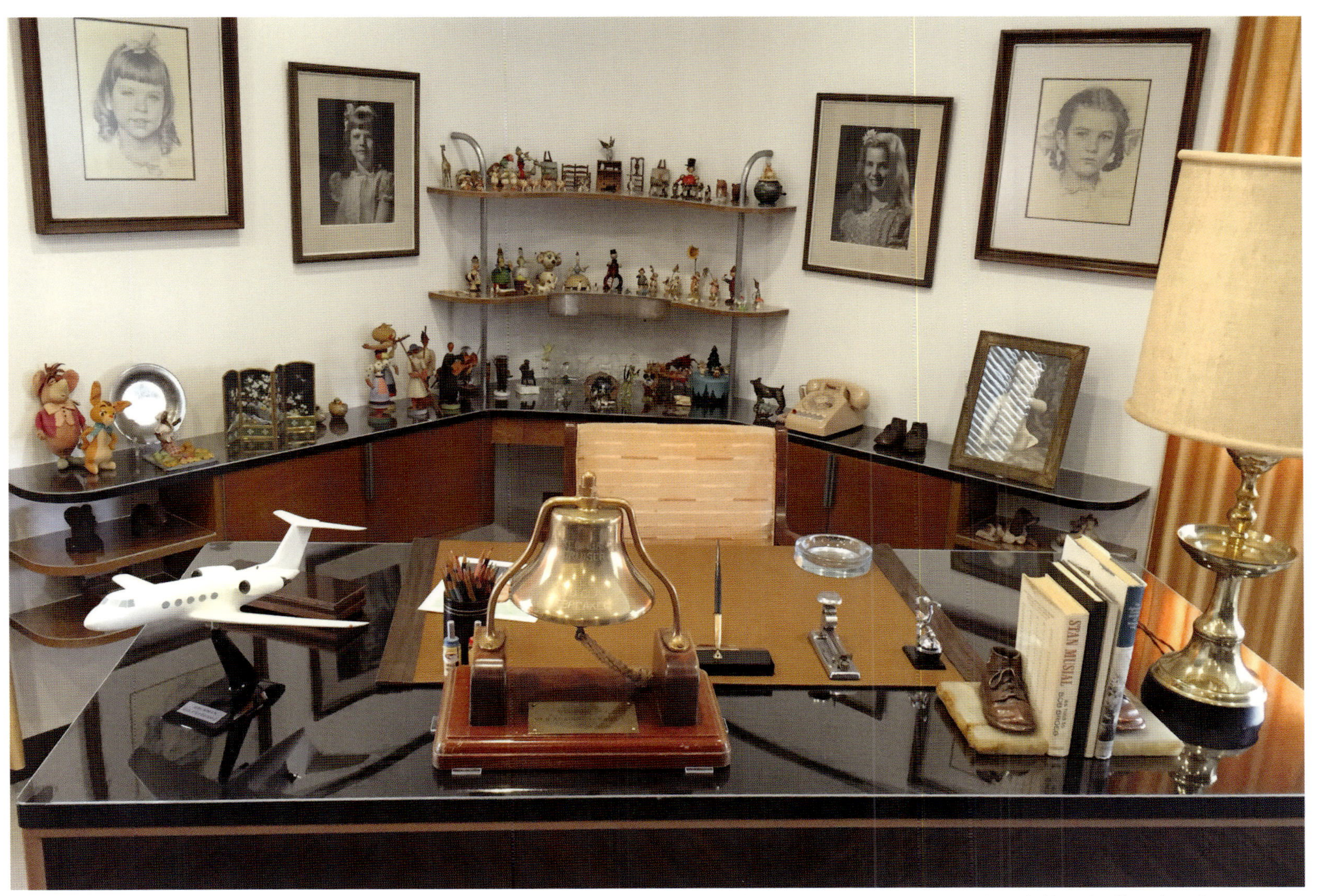

Contemporary shot of Walt Disney's desk and corner credenza in his main office. Photo ©Dave Bossert.

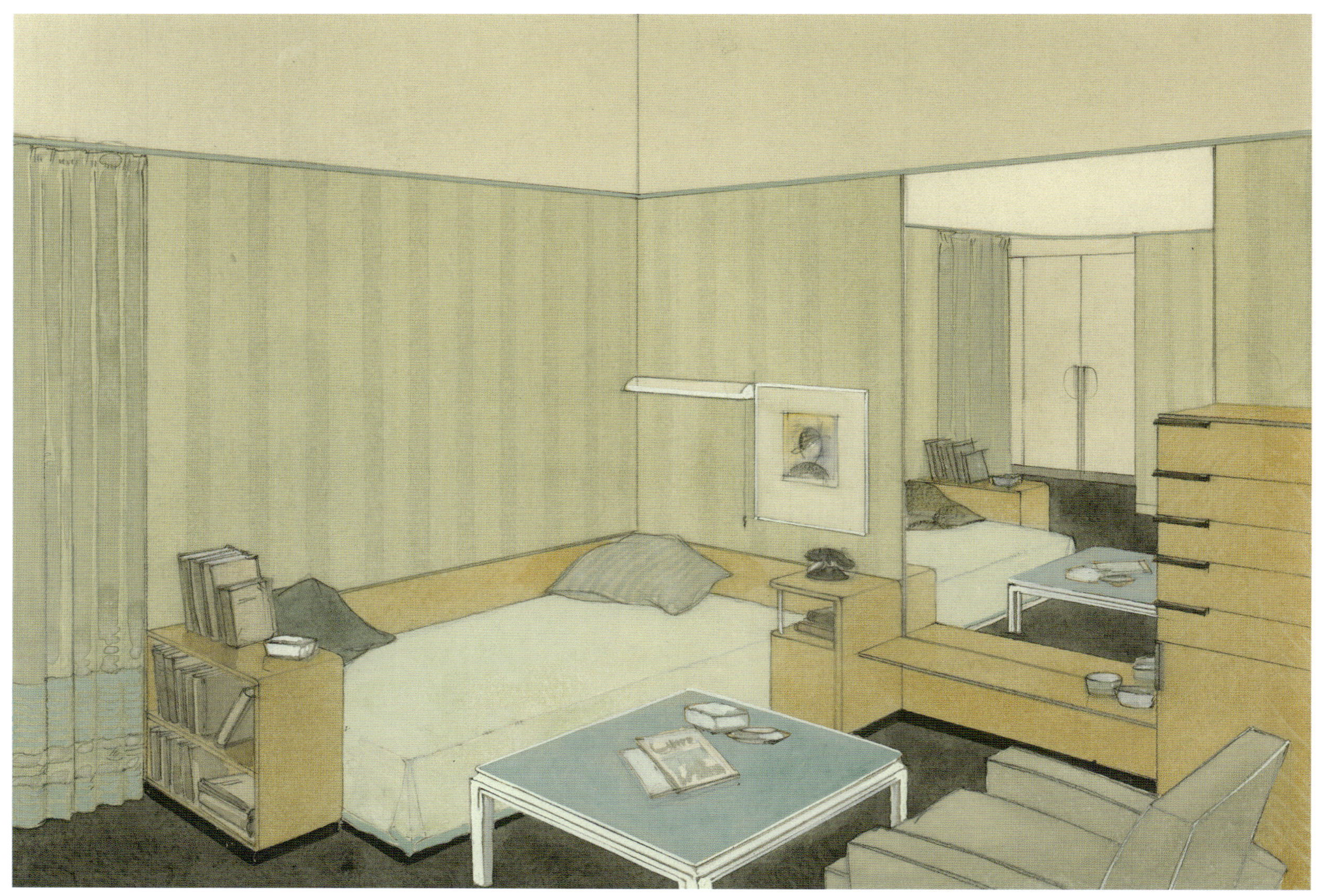

Kem Weber concept illustration of Walt Disney's private suite off his main office, circa 1939. ©UCSB

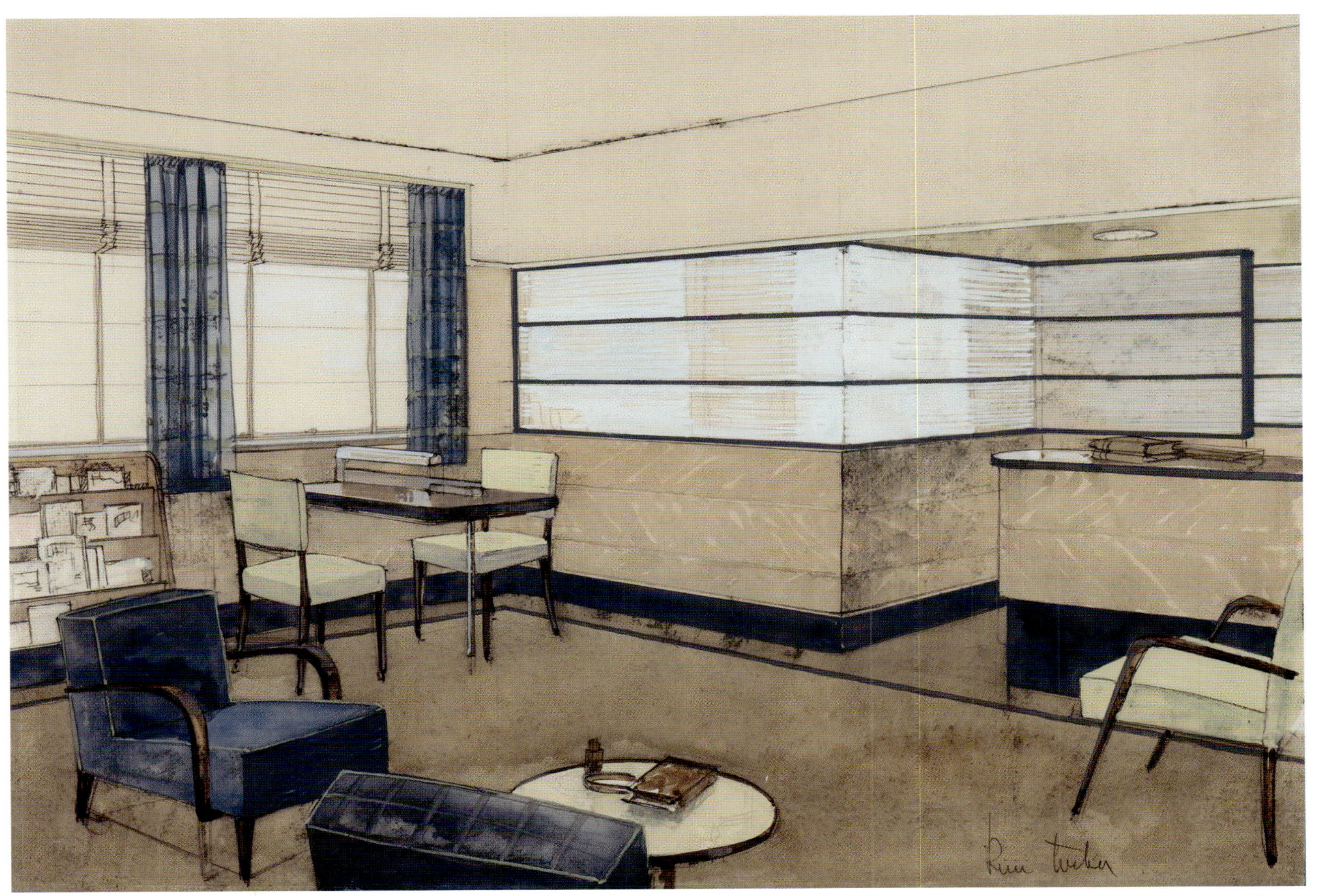

Kem Weber concept illustration of animation production building research library, circa 1939. ©UCSB

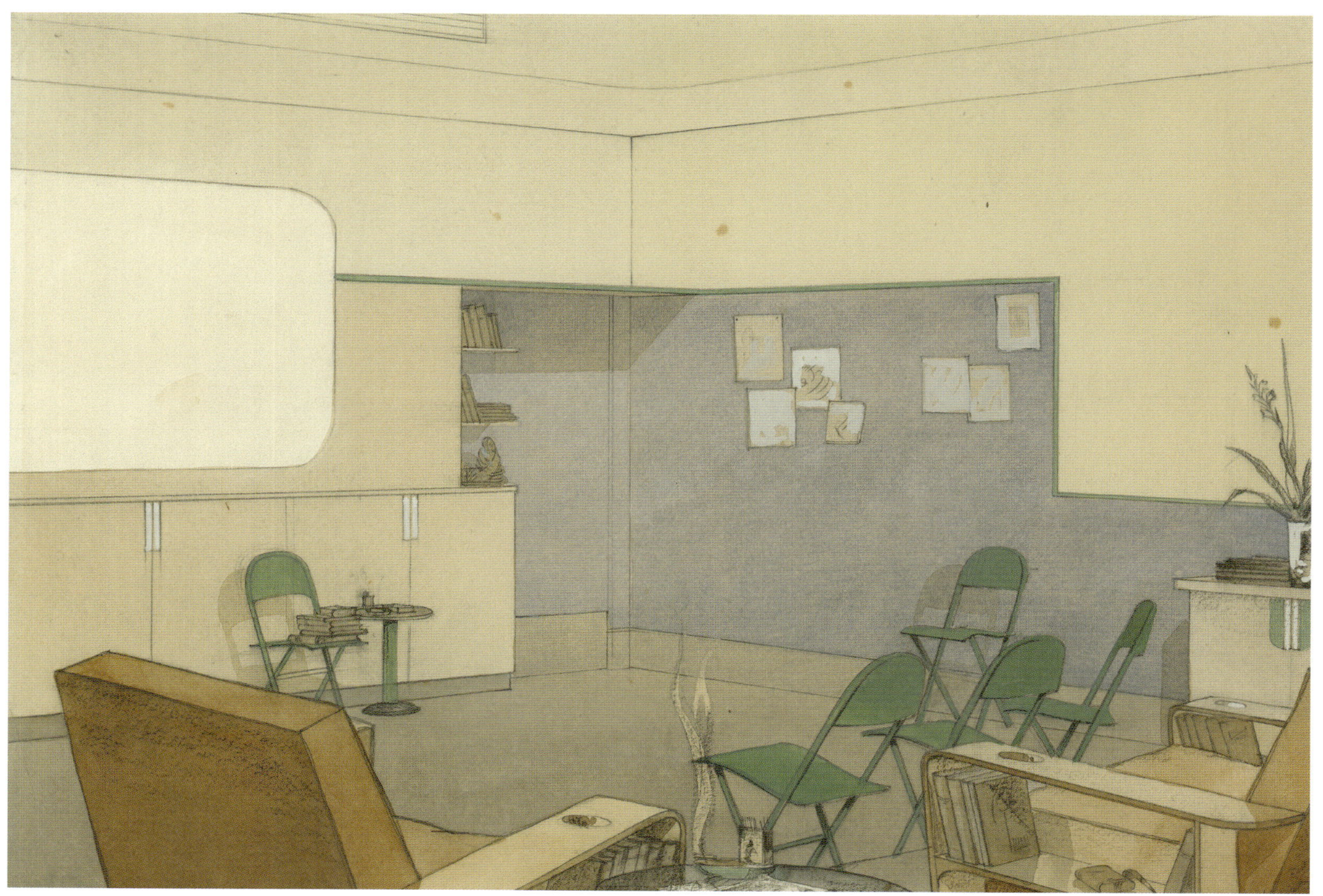

Kem Weber concept illustration of story room in animation production building, circa 1939. ©UCSB

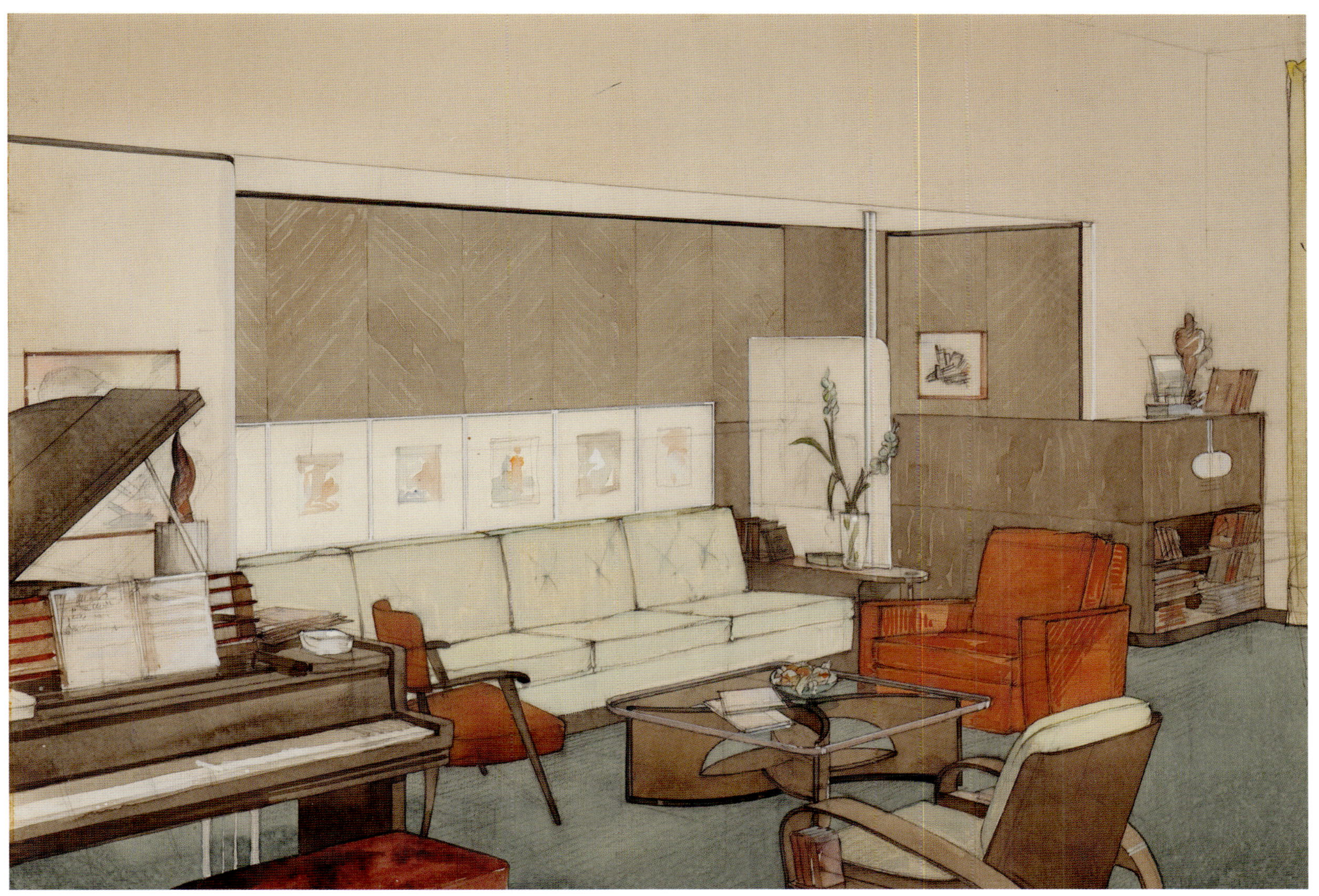

Kem Weber concept illustration of animation production building music room, circa 1939. ©UCSB

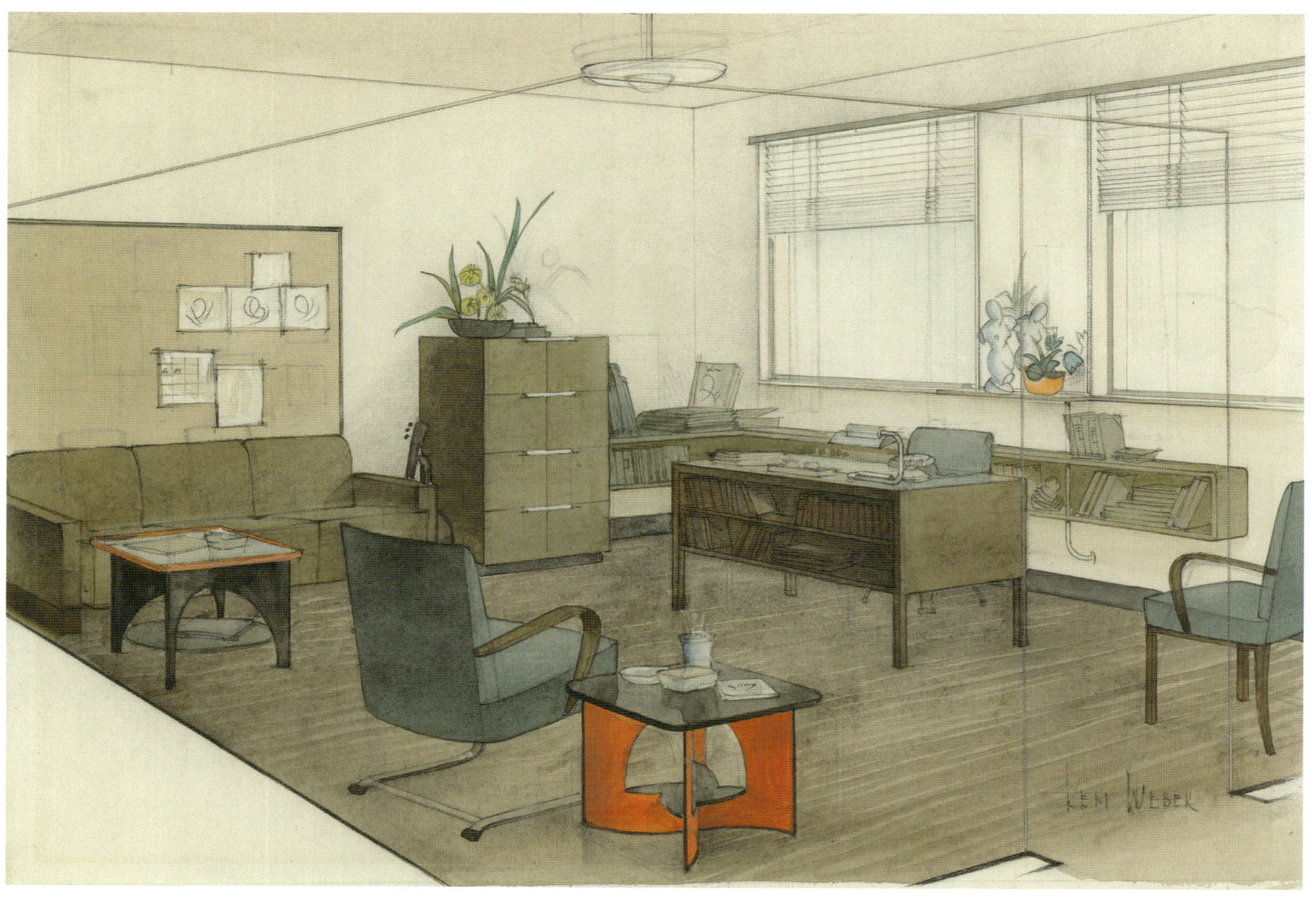

Kem Weber concept illustration of animation production building story artist office, circa 1939. ©UCSB

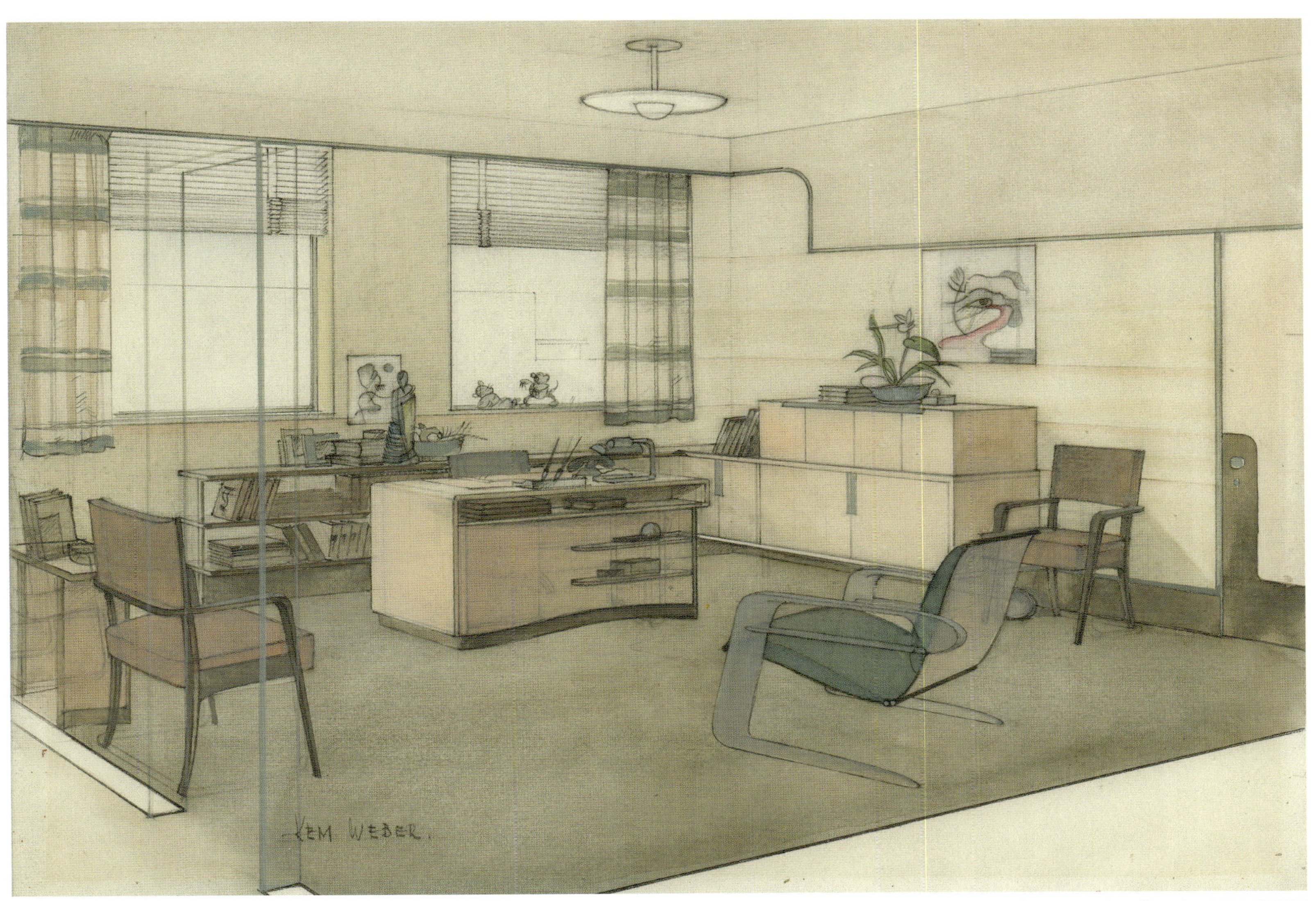

Kem Weber concept illustration of animation production building executive office, circa 1939. ©UCSB

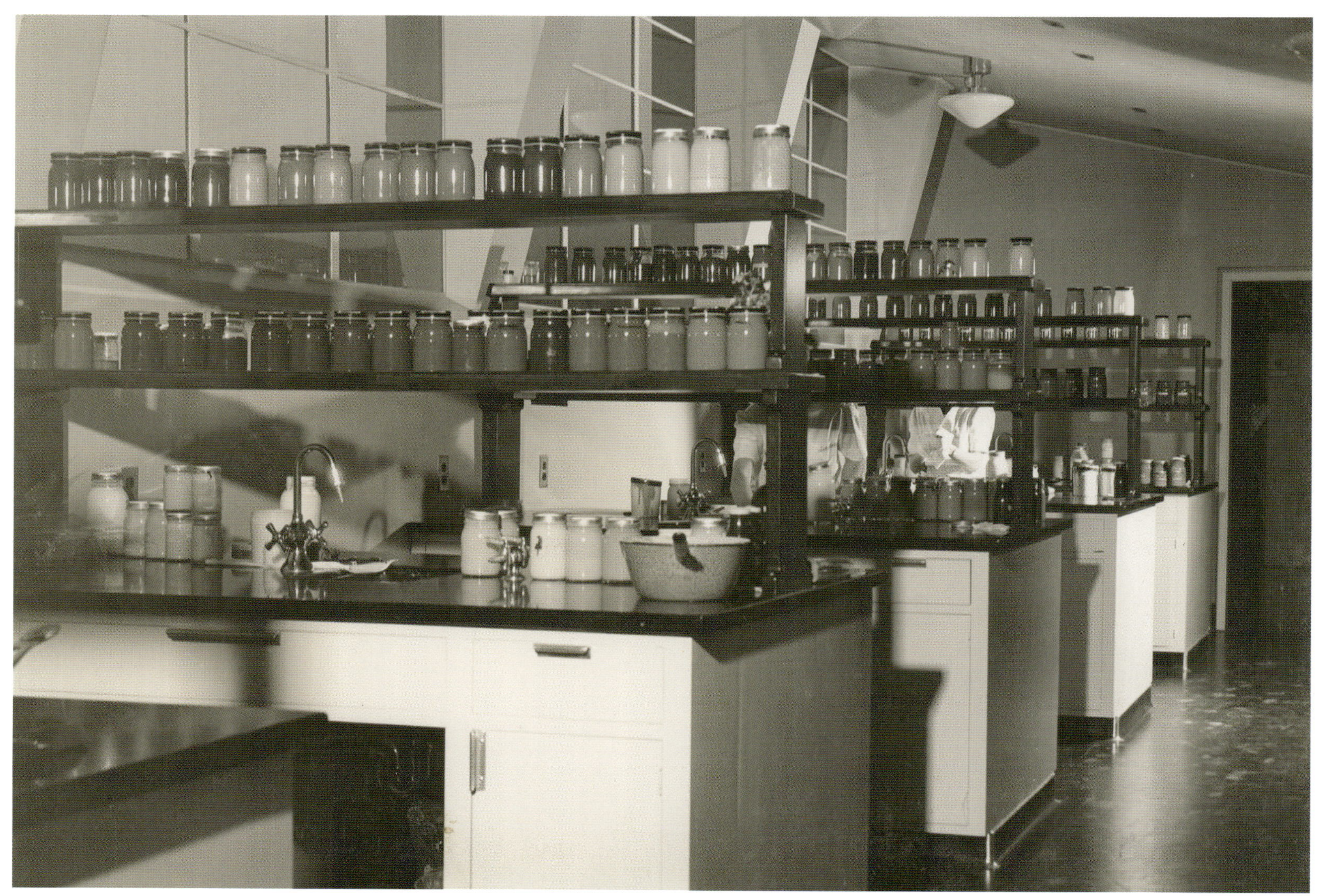

Kem Weber designed color lab desks for Ink and Paint building, circa 1939. Photo by Baskerville. ©UCSB

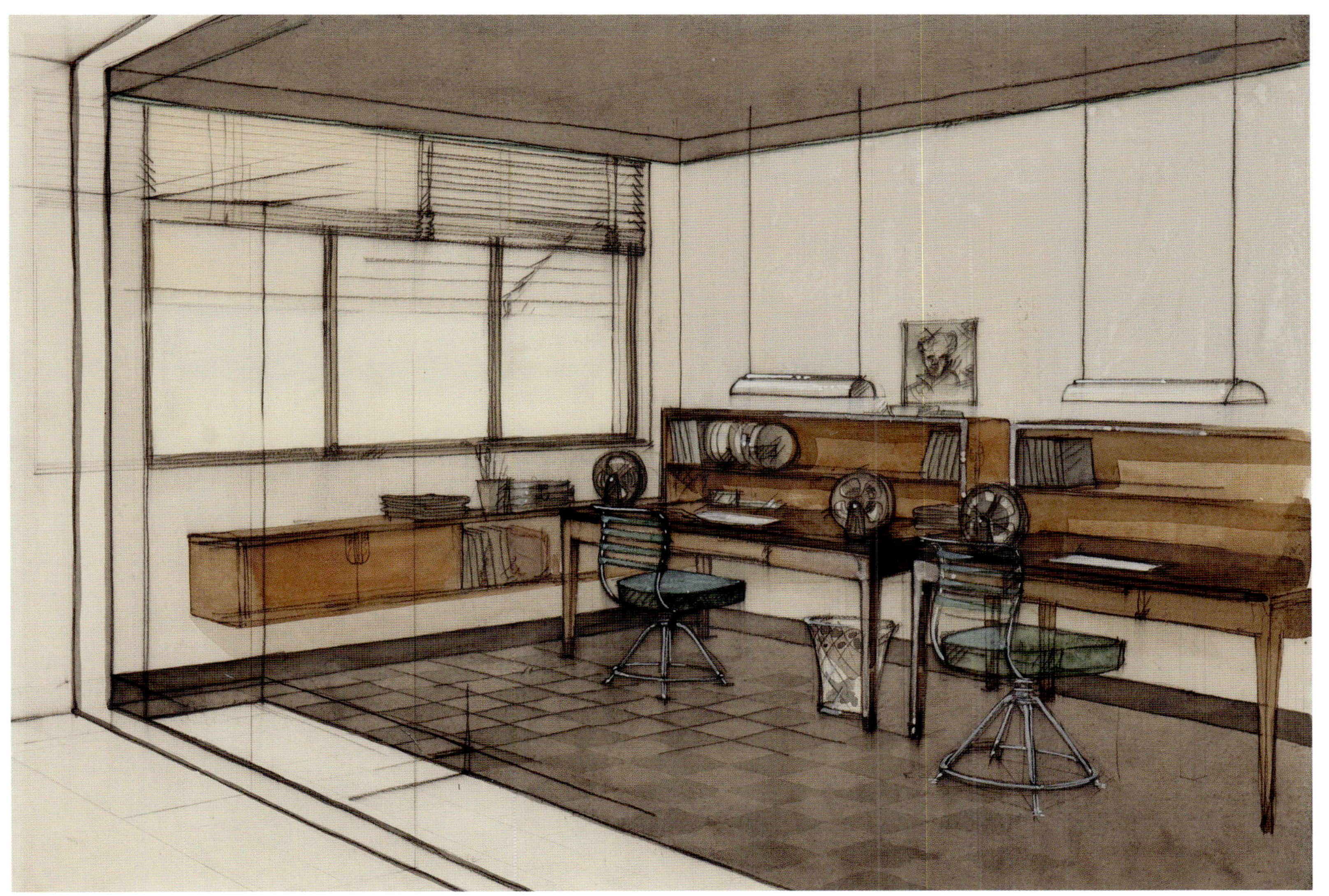

Kem Weber concept illustration of cutting/editorial room, circa 1939. ©UCSB

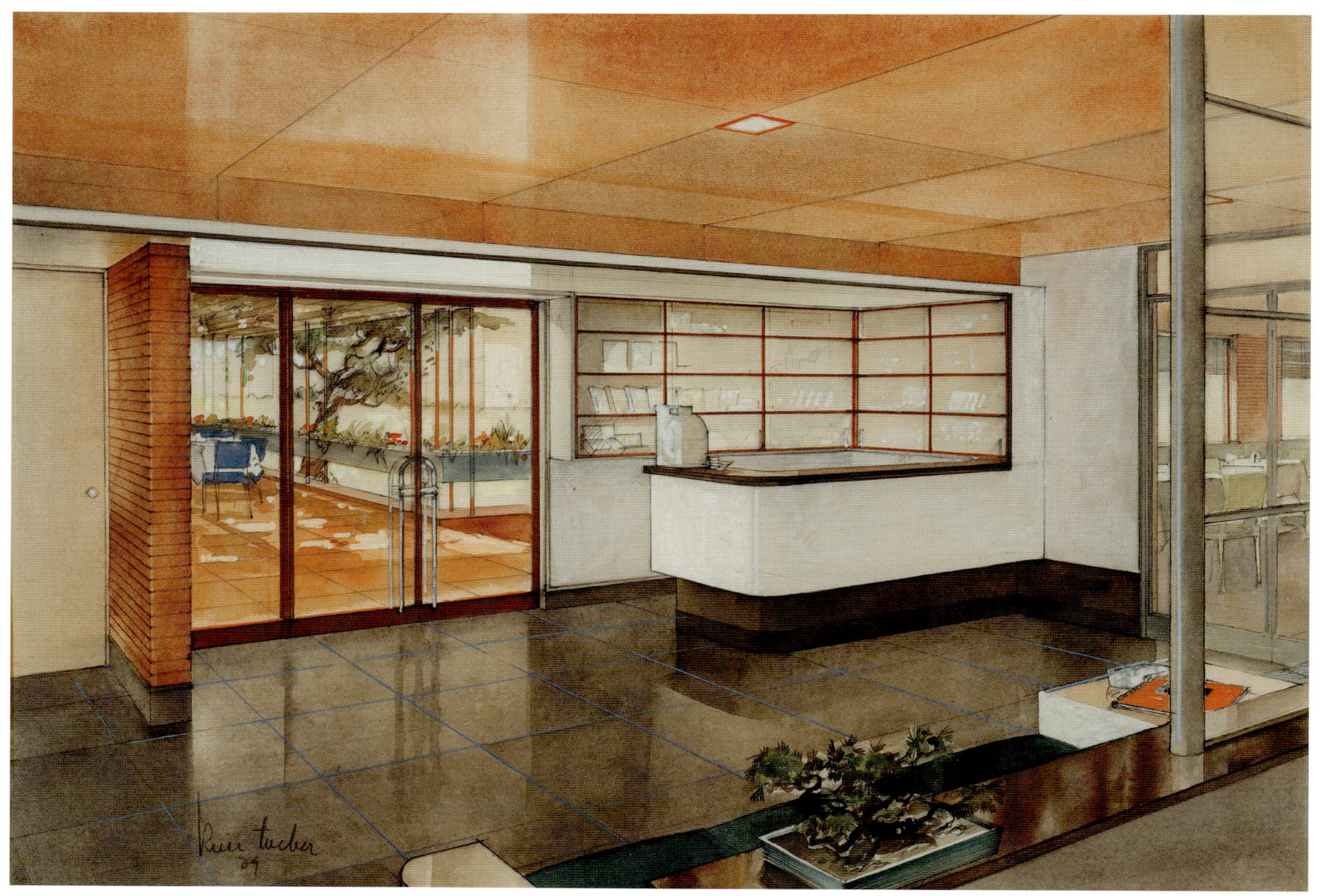

Kem Weber concept illustration for commisary entrance, 1939. ©UCSB

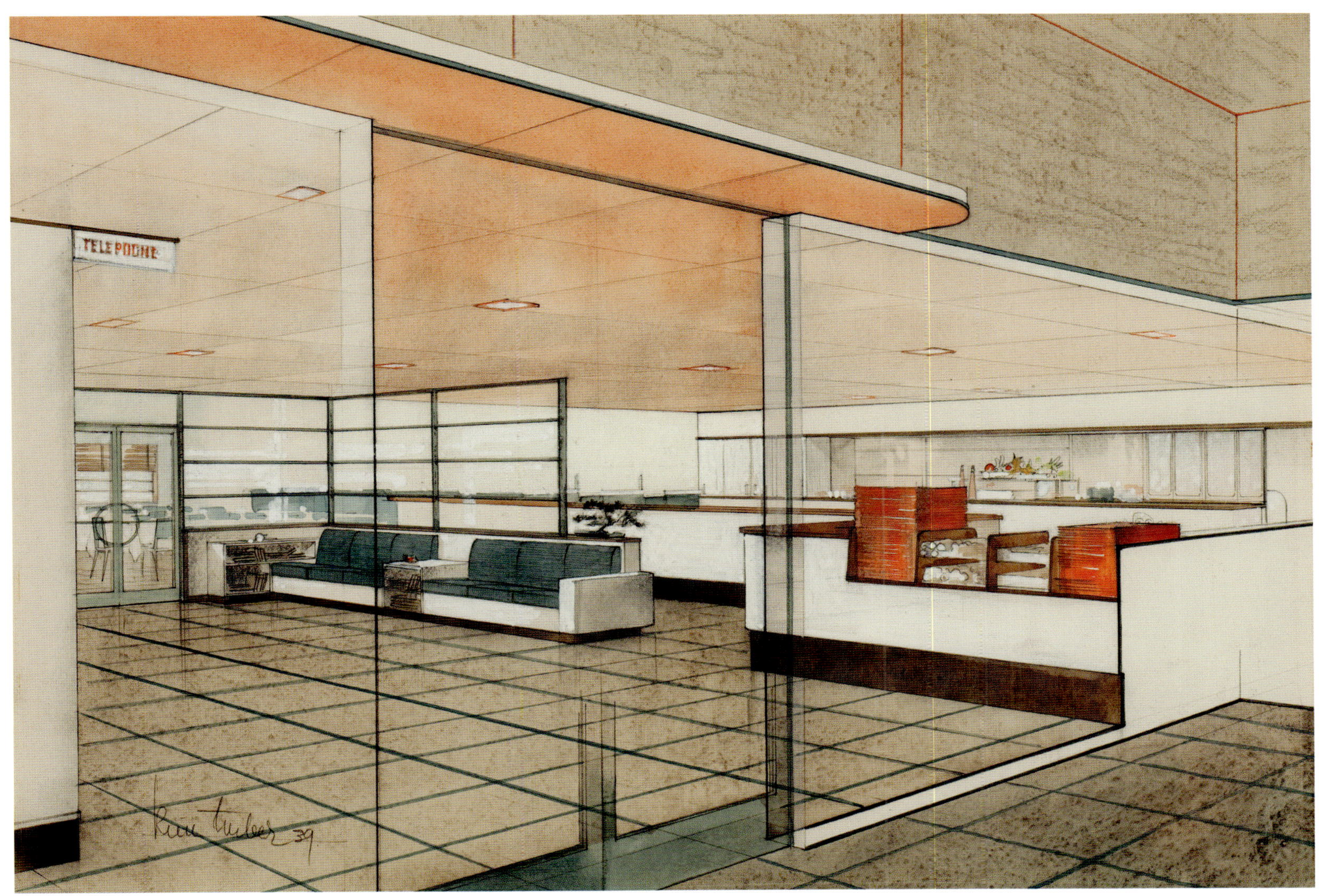

Kem Weber concept illustration for commisary lobby, 1939. ©UCSB

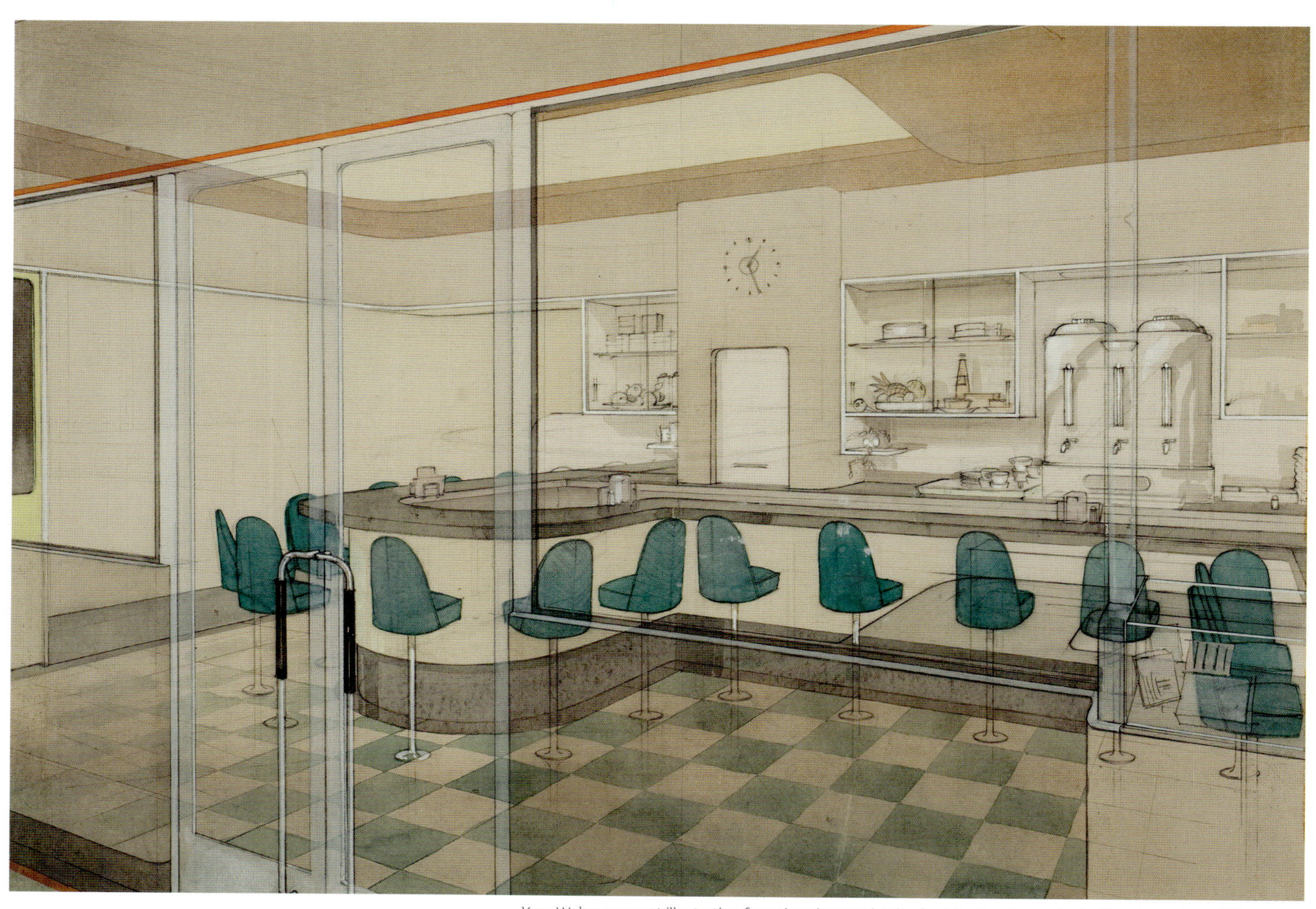

Kem Weber concept illustration for animation production building lunch counter/coffee shop, circa 1939. ©UCSB

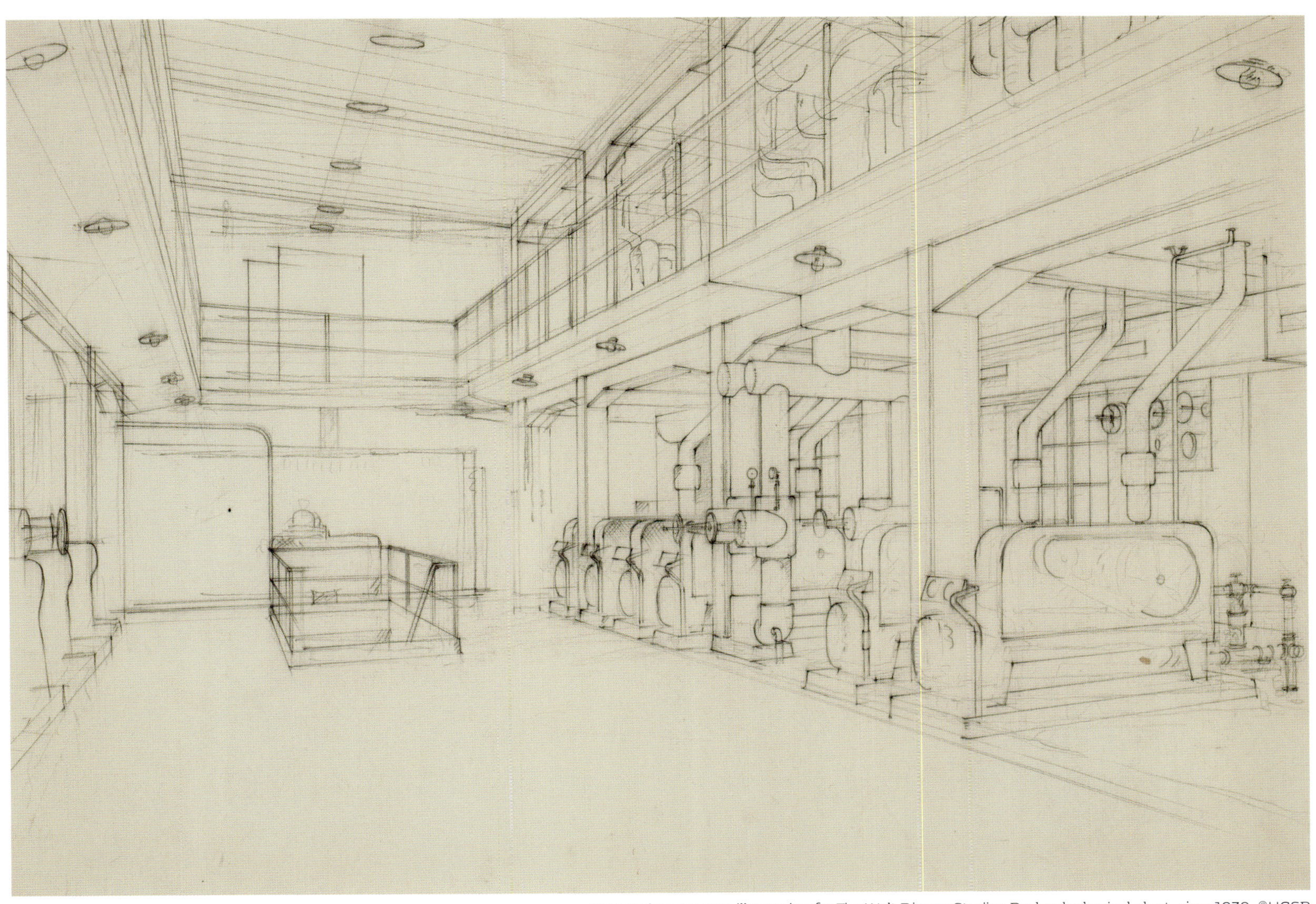

Kem Weber concept illustration for The Walt Disney Studios Burbank physical plant, circa 1939. ©UCSB

ENDNOTES

CHAPTER 2

[1]Fullerton Heritage, "Art Deco: Zigzag Moderne & Streamline (Art) Moderne."
[2]"Kem Weber and the rise of modern design in Southern California," Editorial Staff, *The Magazine of Antiques*, May 4, 2009.
[3]Peter Loughrey interview by David A. Bossert, January 4, 2018.
[4]*Kem Weber: Designer and Architect*, by Christoper Long, pg. 4, Yale Books.
[5]*Kem Weber: The Moderne in Southern California 1920-1941*, Biographical notes, pg. 37.
[6]*Kem Weber: Designer and Architect*, by Christoper Long, pg. 4, Yale Books.
[7]*Kem Weber: The Moderne in Southern California 1920—1941*, Biographical notes, pg. 38.
[8]Weber's note quoted in *Kem Weber: The Moderne in Southern California 1920- 1941*, Biographical notes, pg. 38.
[9]Peter Loughrey interview by David A. Bossert, January 4, 2018.
[10]Peter Loughrey interview by David A. Bossert, January 4, 2018.
[11]A Handbook of California Design,1930-1965: Craftspeople, Designers, Manufacturers, Kem Weber, pg. 286.
[12]A Handbook of California Design,1930-1965: Craftspeople, Designers, Manufacturers, Kem Weber, pg. 286.
[13]*Kem Weber: The Moderne in Southern California 1920-1941*, Biographical notes, pg. 41, 1931.
[14]Paula Sigman-Lowery interview by David A. Bossert, March 23, 2018.
[15]Fullerton Heritage, "Art Deco: Zigzag Moderne & Streamline (Art) Moderne."
[16]Peter Loughrey interview by David A. Bossert, January 4, 2018.
[17]"Kem Weber Tells What He's After in Modern Furniture," *Grand Rapids Herald*, July 3, 1936.
[18]"Classicism in Design Salaams to Progress," by Kem Weber, *Los Angeles Times*, April 20, 1936.
[19]"Classicism in Design Salaams to Progress," by Kem Weber, *Los Angeles Times*, April 20, 1936.

CHAPTER 3

[20]Peter Loughrey interview by David A. Bossert, January 4, 2018.
[21]Paula Sigman-Lowery interview by David A. Bossert, March 23, 2018.
[22]*Kem Weber: Designer and Architect*, by Christopher Long, Yale University Press, pg. 191.
[23]*Walt Disney: The Triumph of the American Imagination*, by Neil Gabler, Knopf, pg. 288.
[24]*Kem Weber: Designer and Architect*, by Christopher Long, Yale University Press, pg. 191.
[25]Walt Disney Studios," *California Arts & Architecture*, January 1941.
[26]Don Hahn interview by David A. Bossert, author, November 6, 2017.
[27]Ben Sharpsteen interview by Richard Hubler, October 29, 1968, pg. 4, WDA.
[28]*Building a Company*, by Bob Thomas, pg. 133.
[29]"Elaborate Studio in Burbank to Be Built by Walt Disney," *Los Angeles Times*, August 6, 1938.
[30]From notes by Tom Sito given to the author for this book, May 26, 2018.
[31]*Walt Disney: The Triumph of the American Imagination*, by Neal Gabler, Knopf, pg. 324.
[32]*Walt Disney: The Triumph of the American Imagination*, by Neal Gabler, Knopf, pg. 324.
[33]Paula Sigman Lowery interview by David A. Bossert, March 23, 2018.

CHAPTER 4

[34]John Musker interview by David A. Bossert, May 17, 2018.
[35]John Musker interview by David A. Bossert, May 17, 2018.
[36]John Musker interview by David A. Bossert, May 17, 2018.
[37]Brenda Chapman interview by David A. Bossert, November 17, 2017.
[38]Brenda Chapman interview by David A. Bossert, November 17, 2017.
[39]Brenda Chapman interview by David A. Bossert, November 17, 2017.
[40]Brenda Chapman interview by David A. Bossert, November 17, 2017.
[41]Chris Hibler interview by David A. Bossert, May 24, 2018.
[42]Chris Hibler interview by David A. Bossert, May 24, 2018.

CHAPTER 5

[43]Jorgen Klubien interview by David A. Bossert, March 20, 2018.
[44]Jorgen Klubien interview by David A. Bossert, March 20, 2018.
[45]Jorgen Klubien interview by David A. Bossert, March 20, 2018.
[46]Jorgen Klubien interview by David A. Bossert, March 20, 2018.
[47]Jorgen Klubien interview by David A. Bossert, March 20, 2018.
[48]Los Angeles Modern Auctions, May 22, 2016, Los Angeles, California.

CHAPTER 6

[49]Letter to Lawrence Kocher, managing editor of *Architectural Record*, 1935.
[50]"Kem Weber: The Mid-Century Designer Who Paved the Way for IKEA," by Ben Marks and Lisa Hix, *Collectors Weekly*, April 4, 2011.
[51]*The Jazz Age: American Style in the 1920s*; Coffin and Harrison, Yale Books, pg. 295
[52]Peter Loughrey interview by David A. Bossert, January 4, 2018.
[53]A letter from Weber to Lawrence Kocher, April 6, 1935, UCSB Archives.
[54]Letter to Lawrence Kocher, managing editor of *Architectural Record*, 1935.
[55]"Demand Increasing for 'Budget Pieces,'" by Kem Weber, *Los Angeles Times*, October 5, 1936.
[56]*Kem Weber: Designer and Architect*, by Christopher Long, pg. 139, Yale University Press.
[57]Letter to Lawrence Kocher, managing editor of *Architectural Record*, 1935.
[58]Letter to Lawrence Kocher, managing editor of *Architectural Record*, 1935.
[59]Author interview with Brenda Chapman, May 4, 2018.
[60]Sotheby's Auction, The Collecting Eye of Seymour Stein, Lot 248, December 11, 2003, New York.
[61]Sotheby's Auction, Important 20th Century Design, Lot 94, June 12, 2013, New York.
[62]Los Angeles Modern Auctions, Lot 125, October 22, 2017.
[63]Based on author interviews with former employees with knowledge of studio operations and inventory. Numbers are only approximations.

CHAPTER 7

[64]Karen Keller interview by David A. Bossert, February 4, 2018
[65]Karen Keller interview by David A. Bossert, February 4, 2018

CHAPTER 8

[66]Andreas Deja interview by David A. Bossert, November 22, 2017.
[67]John Musker interview by David A. Bossert, May 17, 2018.
[68]Don Hahn interview by David A. Bossert, November 6, 2017.
[69]Walt Disney Productions Purchase order to Petersen Show Case & Fixture Co., Inc. September 13, 1939.
[70]Ken Duncan interview by David A. Bossert, November 1, 2017.
[71]Ken Duncan interview by David A. Bossert, November 1, 2017.
[72]John Musker interview by David A. Bossert, May 17, 2018.
[73]John Musker interview by David A. Bossert, May 17, 2018.
[74]John Musker interview by David A. Bossert, May 17, 2018.
[75]John Musker interview by David A. Bossert, May 17, 2018.

CHAPTER 9

[76]Tony Anselmo interview by David A. Bossert, May 4, 2018.
[77]Los Angeles Modern Auctions, Lot 174, May 22, 2016.
[78]Tony Anselmo interview by David A. Bossert, May 4, 2018
[79]Tony Anselmo interview by David A. Bossert, May 4, 2018.

CHAPTER 10

[80]James Coleman interview by David A. Bossert, March 26, 2018.
[81]James Coleman interview by David A. Bossert, March 26, 2018.
[82]James Coleman interview by David A. Bossert, March 26, 2018.
[83]James Coleman interview by David A. Bossert, March 26, 2018.
[84]James Coleman interview by David A. Bossert, March 26, 2018.
[85]James Coleman interview by David A. Bossert, March 26, 2018.

EPILOGUE

[86]Heritage Auctions, December 9-10, 2017, Animation Art Auction, Beverly Hills, Lot #95012, price includes buyer's premium.

CONSTRUCTION NOTES

[87]Hood Distribution; wood products and lumber distribution Irnatural http://www.hooddistribution.com/plywood-core-types/
[88]Master carpenter and cabinet maker Kim Saunders interview by David A. Bossert (June 29, 2018).

"Whatever you do, do it well."

-Walt Disney

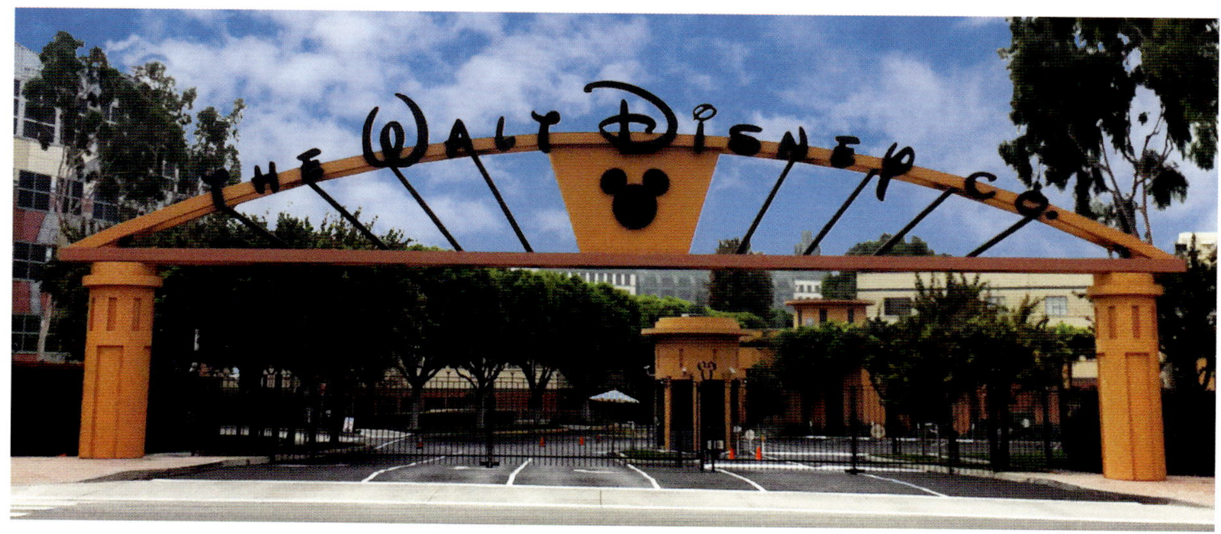

Main entrance to The Walt Disney Studios in Burbank, California, 2018. Photo ©Dave Bossert